WHAT IN THE WORLD
# ARE YOUR
# KIDS
DOING ONLINE?

# WHAT IN THE WORLD
# ARE YOUR
# KIDS
# DOING ONLINE?

HOW TO UNDERSTAND THE
ELECTRONIC WORLD YOUR
CHILDREN LIVE IN

BARBARA MELTON, M.ED., LPC, AND
SUSAN SHANKLE, MSW, LISW-CP

BROADWAY BOOKS
NEW YORK

BROADWAY

PUBLISHED BY BROADWAY BOOKS

Copyright © 2007 by Barbara Melton and Sue Shankle

Published in the United States by Broadway Books, an imprint of
The Doubleday Broadway Publishing Group, a division of
Random House, Inc. New York.
www.broadwaybooks.com

BROADWAY BOOKS and its logo, a letter B bisected on the diagonal, are
trademarks of Random House, Inc.

Book design by Chris Welch

Library of Congress Cataloging-in-Publication Data

Melton, Barbara.
What in the world are your kids doing online? : how to understand the
electronic world your children live in / Barbara Melton, Susan Shankle. —
1st ed.
p.   cm.
Includes bibliographical references and index.
(alk. paper)
1. Internet and children.   2. Internet and teenagers.   3. Internet—Safety
measures.   4. Parenting.   I. Shankle, Susan.   II. Title.
HQ784.I58M45 2006
004.69—dc22
2007001355

ISBN 978-0-7679-2663-8

PRINTED IN THE UNITED STATES OF AMERICA

1   3   5   7   9   10   8   6   4   2

First Edition

TO BOB SULLIVAN, TECHNOLOGY CORRESPONDENT AT MSNBC—

WITHOUT HIS VISION AND FORESIGHT,

THIS BOOK WOULD NOT EXIST.

AND TO THE MANY FINE PARENTS OUT THERE:

KEEP UP THE GOOD WORK!

# CONTENTS

## PART III
. . . . . . . . . . .

## parenting challenges

# WHAT IN THE WORLD
# ARE YOUR
# KIDS
# DOING ONLINE?

# WELCOME TO CYBERWORLD

Back in the 1960s, when Sue was ten years old, she found out how deceptive mass media could be. She heard on the radio an offer for some records that the company offered to send "free." Excited about her prospective treasure trove, Sue ordered half a dozen of her favorite 45s—only to find out that it was the *shipping* that was free, not the records. The records had arrived COD and now Sue owed several dollars that she didn't have.

A few years later, when Barb was twelve, *she* found out how easily mass media could draw you into a potentially dangerous situation. She and a girlfriend called up a radio station when her folks weren't home. Giggling, they told the DJ, "We're two cute girls, and we'd like to hear from some cute guys, so here's our phone number." The message went out over the air, and the phone started ringing off the hook. Luckily, no guys ever connected the phone number to an address, and none actually came to Barb's house. But the phone rang off and on for two weeks straight.

Both of these childish mishaps seem funny in retrospect—

and they certainly seem old-fashioned. If Sue were a kid making the same mistake today, she might have given out her folks' credit card number to a phony Web site ("We won't charge you—for ID purposes only"), putting her family at risk for fraud and identity theft. If Barb had posted identifying information on the Internet, she might have been subject to weeks of online harassment and possibly even greater dangers. At least Barb's ringing phone drew her folks' attention—what might have happened to a twelve-year-old with her own Internet account, afraid to confess her terrible blunder to her parents?

Well, actually, we know very well what might happen, because Sue recently counseled a twelve-year-old who used to frequent chat rooms also in hopes of meeting cute boys. The girl—we'll call her April—knew enough not to give out her contact information online, but she didn't realize that people could use the information she'd given in her profile to locate her. April enjoyed "anonymously" pretending that she was a much older teen—until one night when three guys showed up on her doorstep, looking for the sexually adventurous young woman they had "met" online.

Luckily, April's parents were home and could explain that their daughter was only twelve—but it was quite a shock to everyone concerned. The guys really weren't interested in robbing the cradle; the parents had no idea their daughter was experimenting with an online sexual identity—and April had never realized that anyone might take her sexual offers seriously. This good kid would never have put on makeup and her older sister's miniskirt and hung out at bars—but she thought it was okay to talk about doing those things online. In her mind, she was just having fun—she didn't realize she was extending an invitation.

What's our point? Kids will be kids, and in all eras, they do foolish and risky things—it's pretty much in their job description. Only now, in Cyberworld, little mistakes can have enormous consequences—consequences you may not even know about until it's too late. (April's parents, for example, were *very* glad they happened to be home that night!)

Almost by definition, you're going to be less comfortable in Cyberworld than your children are and less aware of its many possibilities—and yet, in this electronic world that *you* never grew up in, your job is to keep your child safe. How do you do it?

By now, you've heard all about the perils of Internet predators—and in Chapter 1, we'll tell you everything you need to know about protecting your child from them. But the threats to your child's health and well-being go far beyond those well-publicized dangers. For example, every minute your kid sits in front of the computer is a minute he or she is not moving, not breathing fresh air, not getting the benefits of full-spectrum sunlight. Figuring out how kids can have a healthy computer experience while still protecting their physical health can be quite a challenge.

And then there are the social, emotional, and developmental challenges. Cyberworld is a world of instant gratification—you can watch your favorite TV show whenever you want and on your own terms, instead of waiting for it to be on and negotiating with other family members over a common TV set; you can do research when and how you feel like it instead of waiting for the library to open and following library rules; you can basically get what you want without having to go through other people. How do you teach your children that sometimes in life, you have to wait your turn and work things out when so much of Cyberworld contradicts that notion? How do you make it clear that children need to develop empathy and compassion when the electronic world allows them to meet and discard people at the drop of a hat? How can children learn to pay full attention or to use their own imaginations when Cyberworld offers to keep them fully entertained 24/7?

As counselors who have become nationally recognized experts in electronic parenting issues and who've worked with a wide range of kids, parents, and fellow professionals, we can assure you that the Internet offers your children a host of new challenges, dangers, and opportunities that you may never have suspected:

**Cyber-bullying.** E-mail, Web sites, cell-phone cameras, and Web cams have created new arenas for harassment that are becoming increasingly common. What if the school's "Mean Girl" takes cell-phone photos of your daughter undressing in gym class and then posts the pictures on her Web site or forwards them via e-mail to all her classmates? Suppose the school bully starts a rumor that your son is gay and encourages his friends to bombard him with harassing e-mails? Your own child might be involved in cyber-bullying simply by forwarding or receiving messages, or by visiting a classmate's Web site.

**Teenage Blogs.** Youth culture has already created an alternate universe, giving your teenager the impression that every *other* kid in the world has a gorgeous body, unlimited spending money, and complete sexual freedom. A new layer of unreality comes from teen blogs that seem to portray the actual lives of ordinary young people but are often steeped in fantasy, distortion, and wish fulfillment. We tend to believe things that we read and, even more, things we can see for ourselves. How do you help your child develop a healthy skepticism that doesn't turn into an unhealthy cynicism?

**Online Socializing.** Children of all ages can be drawn into a whole alternate life on the Internet, communicating with "friends" or even "dates" whom they've never met. Some children become overly isolated in what often turns into a vicious cycle: as kids become less comfortable in social situations, they grow ever more dependent on electronic relationships, and their secret life may come to seem more real than reality. Even for social children, it may be hard to develop genuine intimacy and empathy when you meet your friends on Web sites, hang out with your dates in chat rooms, communicate primarily by text messaging and e-mail, and generally spend more time with someone online than in person. How do children learn, in this virtual world, that their actions really do affect others?

**The Promise of Instant Gratification.** Working through disagreements is an important developmental task for children and teenagers—but it may be more difficult for your children to learn this key life skill if most of their friendships are conducted via e-mail, text messaging, and cell phones. Likewise, if kids feel that everything they need to know can be found with a search engine, they may settle for easy answers without ever really thinking for themselves. Perhaps most important, the online world of entertainment, distraction, and sensory overload can weaken your kids' ability to become fully absorbed in an idea, experience, or work of art.

## Cyber Warning Signs

As a concerned parent, you've probably read about warning signs a hundred times before: you've already been told to look closely at any dramatic change in your kids' activities, sleep patterns, eating habits, grades, or mood. Any of these behaviors might indicate a problem with drugs, school life, friends, a dating partner—or some aspect of Cyberworld. But watch out as well for these cyber-specific warning signs:

• **more time on the computer**—a diminished interest in social activities, including more time spent online than with their friends (even if they tell you they are IMing or e-mailing their friends)

• **isolation**—going into their room to spend time alone, and *not* pursuing activities that they usually enjoy (reading, making things, listening to music)

• **fatigue**—perhaps resulting from insufficient sleep or disrupted sleep patterns as your child is overly stimulated by electronic media

• **a hyper-focus on e-mail**—rushing frequently and obsessively to check it. And if you yourself exhibit this behavior while you're at home, you might ask *yourself* what's up! Why is e-mail interfering with your ability to relax and focus on your family?

• **furtiveness**—beyond a normal concern with privacy, your child seems excessively interested in hiding his or her cyber-activities from you

• **acting guilty or shameful**—which may indicate cyber-activities of which they are ashamed or of which they know you'll disapprove

• **a new lack of closeness**—with family, friends, boyfriend, or girlfriend, possibly indicating that they're being drawn deeper into Cyberworld

• **desensitization**—not responding to painful events with shock, empathy, or other appropriate emotions, which may indicate a sensory overload of electronic information and a growing sense of un-reality

 • **mysterious activity**—receiving phone calls, mail, or packages from people you don't know

## Keeping Cyberworld in Perspective

As with so many aspects of parenting, there's a good news–bad news aspect to Cyberworld. The bad news is, you'll never be able to keep up with it. By the time you've memorized the latest codes your kids are using for text-messaging (C-P, HH01/2K, NALOPKT),* they'll have developed new ones. (Even older teens feel envious of younger teens and preteens, who know the *very* latest!) By the time you've figured out how to check the history of which Web sites your kids have visited, they'll have figured out how to erase that history. And so on. Even outside of Cyberworld, kids who want pornography, drugs, and other contraband can pretty much always get it—that's just a fact of teenage life. In Cyberworld—given the In-ternet cafés on every corner, the ready availability of cell phones, the growing capabilities of virtually every piece of electronic equipment—you'll never be able to plug all the holes. If you're worried about protecting your kids, that can seem like very bad news indeed.

But the good news is, you can still be a strong, effective par-ent, if you know what to look for. You don't have to be a jailer—in fact, that's about as far from being a good parent as

*Sleepy, Ha-ha, only half kidding; Not a lot of people know this.

it's possible to get. But you do need to become aware of what Cyberworld looks like to your kids and to understand the pressures, challenges, and dangers it poses. Just as you can't isolate your children from ever talking to strangers, you can't keep them out of Cyberworld—at least, not without doing them more harm than good. And just as you can teach your kids how to evaluate which strangers to avoid and how to ask for help when they're in trouble, you can model for them how to evaluate the dangers of Cyberworld and support them through the challenges of this electronic world, setting limits that are appropriate for their age, maturity level, and personality.

Your first step is to become aware of the issues—an awareness that we'll help you develop in this book. The next step is the tried and true one you've already heard about: to build a trusting but skeptical relationship with your children in which they feel safe coming to you for help, know what you expect of them, and want to live up to your standards. Sue tells parents to try a sentence that her own father used with her: *If you ever aren't sure how to behave, imagine that I'm standing right there beside you—and then do whatever you think I'd be happy to see you do.*

Of course, a troubled, frightened, or angry child may make mistakes out of the intense desire to do things his or her own way. And a happy, trusting, loving child may also make mistakes, in a purely innocent misunderstanding. Kids are kids: They're supposed to do stupid things—and what better time than when you're still around to protect them? That's why you need to develop limits that your kids can agree to and even embrace, understanding that your rules are there to protect and support them.

In this book, we're asking you to accept two basic assumptions:

1. You may never be as comfortable in Cyberworld as your kids probably are;
2. You can understand this world well enough to set healthy limits and establish productive communication with your children.

As an added bonus, you may discover that Cyberworld offers lots of exciting opportunities for your child—including your special-needs, gifted, or special-interest child. And you may also find out that your learning more about Cyberworld actually brings you and your children closer together.

So welcome to Cyberworld! It's a fascinating and exciting place, if sometimes a challenging one. But you can take comfort in knowing that you'll feel a lot more at home there after you've read this book.

## CHAPTER 1

# PROTECTING YOUR CHILD IN CYBERWORLD

nternet predators. Cyber-kidnappers. Online child molesters. You've probably heard thousands of warnings about these dangers and wondered how seriously you need to take them. Just how safe is the Internet for your child?

We'd like to set your mind at ease. While your kids face some danger from Internet predators, it's relatively small and fairly easy to manage—and in this chapter, we'll tell you how. We'll also help you protect your child from online gambling and from what some experts have come to call Internet addiction—becoming too focused on or obsessed with the electronic world. And we'll help you set some ground rules, enabling you and your family to relate to Cyberworld in healthy and productive ways.

But we'd also like to stress the positive aspects of Cyberworld, the wonderful ways in which it can enrich and enlarge your child's life. Parry Aftab, an attorney who works with the cyber-safety group, www.wiredsafety.org, points out that one of the greatest risks children face from the Internet is being denied access to it. Although she is well aware of the dangers of abduction, unsupervised chat rooms, and unlimited access to pornography, Aftab nonetheless believes that if children don't learn how to use the Internet and feel comfortable navigating it, they'll be seriously handicapped for life in our increasingly electronic world.

We agree with her wholeheartedly. Cyberworld can be deceptive, disturbing, and downright dangerous. But it can also be a thrilling, exhilarating place, offering your children extraordinary opportunities for learning, socializing, and expanding their horizons.

So let's start with some basic ground rules. Some of these rules apply to virtually any parenting situation; others are cyber-specific. All of them are intended to make you and your family feel happier, calmer, and clearer about your relationship to Cyberworld.

## GROUND RULE 1: Remember that cyber-access is a privilege, not a right

Your child doesn't *have* to have a private e-mail account, a cell phone, or access to the Internet beyond what's absolutely necessary for schoolwork. You get to monitor his or her cyber-activity as you see fit, and you get to give or withhold all or part of these cyber-privileges.

Of course, that's not the message you'd get from the cell phone ads. But they're trying to sell you cell phones—we're trying to help you parent!

## GROUND RULE 2: Pick your battles—don't sweat the small stuff or overreact

Easier said than done, but it's crucial nonetheless. Part of the problem is that your kids are growing up in Cyberworld, while you got there after you were already grown. You won't be able to draw on your own childhood experience as you make judgments for them, which may make you anxious, uncertain, or simply frustrated.

You have a right to all of those feelings. But your child's life—not to mention *your* life—will be much easier if you don't turn every difference of opinion into a battle royal. Accept that there will be some aspects of Cyberworld that you simply hate and that your children love. Figure out what issues matter most to you and concentrate on them.

## GROUND RULE 3: Know what you can and can't enforce— because in Cyberworld, so much can't be enforced

Frequently throughout this book, you're going to hear us suggest putting your kids on the honor system. There's a very good reason for that: much of the time, it's the only system you've got. Face it, if your children want to view Internet porn, have private e-mail accounts, or visit a chat room, they're going to find a way to do it. Sooner or later, they'll figure out that they can undertake any of these activities pretty easily at a cyber-café, the house of a friend, or possibly even at the public library (though libraries are now federally mandated to have certain blocking and filtering programs). This easy availability doesn't mean you shouldn't make rules—but just as with cigarettes, alcohol, and drugs, you'll have to accept what you can actually enforce and what you'll have to trust your kid to do or not do.

In that spirit, we urge you to modify or adapt our suggestions throughout this book based on what your children are already doing. If your seventeen-year-old has been using e-mail for years, now is probably not the time to announce that you'll be periodically monitoring his or her account, as we suggest in Chapter 3. Unless there are signs of trouble, it's actually kind of insulting to start a new oversight program at this late date, though if your eight-year-old is just now learning to log on, you can take a more active role. Either way, though, there's only so much you can supervise—then you'll have to rely on trust.

## GROUND RULE 4: Consider the possibility your child can be trusted—and let your child know what the consequences are when you stop trusting

As you'll see throughout this book, we advocate periodically checking in on all aspects of your children's cyber-activity. Knock on their door during homework time to make sure they're not surfing the Net while they're supposed to be studying. Take an occasional random look at their e-mail accounts to see whom they're writing to and what they're saying. Check their computer's history to see how many chat rooms they've visited lately.

You're doing all this in the spirit of, "I want to know what's going on with you, so I can help if there's a problem." You can back off or come closer as the situation warrants, but it's good for your children to know both that you trust them and that you're not simply leaving them to negotiate Cyberworld on their own. Let them know that "trust" includes occasional monitoring and check-ins, and that the consequence of their forfeiting your trust will be much more extensive supervision. Make sure, though, that they also know they can come to you if they get into trouble, and help them frame their difficulties in a positive light: "This is a real learning experience for both of us and I'm so glad you had the good judgment to come to me."

## GROUND RULE 5: Keep the lines of communication open

As with most parenting situations, that's your best defense, first, last, and always. To get your kids talking about cyber-specific problems, you may want to watch a movie with them about other kids' experience with TMing, e-mail, or the Internet. (See Resources and the box on page 17 for some ideas.) Asking your children what they thought of the film can help them open up about their own experience, even if they never come right out and admit they've been talking about themselves. You'll also find throughout this book a number of suggestions for getting your kids talking about their cyber-experience.

Remember, part of being a kid—and especially a teenager—is to develop one's own sense of oneself, a process that often involves rebelling against even the most well-meaning parents. Your job—and we know it's a tough one—is to work both sides of the street: keeping your kids safe while allowing them to be independent. You need to know what they can handle and what they can't—or at least to make educated guesses about it. Your first step is to start learning what they're up against—and the best way to do *that* is to listen to them.

## GROUND RULE 6: One electronic device at a time

One of the most frantic aspects of our cyber-culture is the way multitasking has invaded even our play time. Think about the difference between watching TV or a DVD with your kids, and having the television on while the whole family TMs, answers e-mail, or chats on the phone. The first is a social experience; the second turns your home into a TV-ridden mini-office.

As Americans work more and more hours with every passing year, we can't help worrying that our society is turning out automatons set at only two speeds: *produce* and *consume*. And as electronic communication becomes ever more invasive, even the time set aside for consumption turns into a type of productivity, with bosses, clients, and colleagues encroaching upon our leisure hours. Bad enough that we adults are prey to this type of super-productivity, must we also inflict it upon our children?

Don't forget: watching TV or a DVD with your kids gives you a golden opportunity to learn more about them, their friends, and their culture, especially if they've picked the show. Asking them what they thought about that snobby girl who broke a date or that jock who was tempted to take steroids can be just the invitation your child was waiting for to open up about his or her own concerns and questions. At the very least, you may learn more about your child's values, assumptions, fears, and desires. Plus, you can just enjoy each other's company!

All those opportunities go out the window, though, if your kid is busily IMing or TMing during the show, or if every five minutes one of you takes a phone call. Consider making it a family rule that when the TV is on, the computer is off, and vice versa. And think about having a "no-phone zone" that includes dinner and maybe an hour or two before or after, when the only people to talk to are the ones actually in the house. Cooking, setting the table, and doing the dishes are all wonderful activities that can be shared with your kids—you'll be surprised what kids will tell you when they're not "officially" spending time with you!

## Movies to Start You Talking

One of the best ways to start a conversation about Cyberworld is to watch a movie with your kids and then talk about what you thought of it. We've listed several in Resources. Here are a few of our favorites:

• **Odd Girl Out,** directed by Tom McLoughlin, 2004, Lifetime, www.lmn.tv. An excellent portrayal of cyber-bullying based on Rachel Simmons's book of the same name. This movie is particularly useful for showing how girls who don't want to bully get caught up in pressure from the "head bully." This is a great movie to view with your child so that you can ask if anything even remotely similar is happening at his or her school.

• **Every Mother's Worst Fear,** directed by Bill L. Norton, 1998, Lifetime, www.lmn.tv. Naïve teen gets kidnapped by man she meets online. This movie shows all the ways that teenagers hide their Internet use from parents. While we think it's more alarmist than realistic, the parts about how teens relate to the Internet are well done. One thing that is well portrayed is the grooming process, in which the predator plays on the teenager's feelings of being misunderstood by her parents to draw her closer to him.

• **A Moment of Truth Movie: A Secret Between Friends,** directed by James A. Contner, 1996, Lifetime, www.lmn.tv. This movie is about two teenage girls, one bulimic and one anorexic; it shows all the classic eating-disorder signs to watch for. Since eating disorders are becoming almost common in school settings, this is a great movie to view with your child to show your interest in his or her world and your willingness to talk about it. Although the Internet per se isn't a major issue in the film, you can use this movie as an occasion to ask your child about pro-ana Web sites—sites that glorify anorexia and other eating disorders. (See Chapter 4.)

## Listen to the Quiet: Some Cyber-Free Experiences to Share with Your Child

Help your child develop his or her full range of responses by providing at least one cyber-free experience each week, ideally one that offers some silent, meditative space in which new thoughts and feelings can quietly emerge. Children need that open-ended downtime to develop their inner resources, especially when their daily lives are often so scheduled and frantic. Some fruitful quiet times for your child to enjoy with you, with friends, or solo might include

- → nature walks
- → city walks
- → browsing a museum
- → a boat ride or a sail
- → fishing
- → a bike ride—without the Ipod!
- → a cross-country run—ditto!
- → a visit to a church, synagogue, mosque, or Buddhist temple—to express your religion or simply to appreciate the deep, meditative silence

## Modeling the Message

Are you modeling good cyber-behavior for your cyber-kid? Are *you* always online when you could be relaxing, or taking cell-phone calls in the midst of a family dinner? Kids do as we do, not as we say, so if you're concerned about the effect Cyberworld is having on your youngster, ask yourself what kind of example you're setting. Show your children that it is indeed possible to turn down the volume on the answering machine, shut off the cell phone, and close out the e-mail in order to focus on family members, meditate, or relax. And then find concrete, specific ways that your kids can join you—preparing or cleaning up after dinner; at dinner itself; as part of family game night or family movie night; for a walk or a shopping trip or another activity that leaves plenty of room for talking and listening. You may be amazed at what a difference it will make!

**TIP** Make sure your child has an ergonomically correct setup. Use a chair that promotes good posture, supporting the spine and giving the feet a good, solid base. Wrist support is also an important consideration. Wristwand is a small baton that your child can use for stretching exercises that may help prevent carpal tunnel syndrome and tendonitis. (See www.wristwand.com for more information.) Position the monitor so that your child is looking at it directly, rather than at an angle. See Chapter 8 for more suggestions on promoting computer health and safety.

## Protecting Your Kids in Cyberworld

Most of this book will be devoted to helping your child negotiate Cyberworld, which includes making the most of its many promises. We'll be looking at the pros and cons of text messaging, e-mail, and the Internet, and we'll show you how Cyberworld can affect your child's development, socialization, health, schoolwork, friends, family life, and experiences with dating.

But before you even consider the positive aspects of Cyberworld, you need to protect your child against three of its primary dangers: predators, gambling sites, and Internet addiction. There aren't any up sides to these features of Cyberworld; they're pretty much all negative. So let's see what you can do to keep your child safe.

### Where Should the Computer Be?

When Internet connections first began to appear in private homes, parents were often advised to put any computer with online access in a central location, so they could see if their children were viewing porn, chatting with potential predators, or engaged in any other potentially harmful activity.

With the increased popularity of wireless connections (technology that allows Internet access without any actual wires or cables) and with the growing affordability of laptops, many kids can pretty much carry their Internet hookup with them. At this point, in our opinion, computer location doesn't really matter very much as far as your child's safety is concerned. Here's what we think does matter:

**1. Don't leave your child alone at the computer for extended periods of time.** No matter where you put the computer, your child shouldn't feel isolated with it, any more than he or she should be left alone for hours in front of the television. If your child wants a quiet, private place to do homework or write e-mails, fine—but pop your head into the bedroom or rec room every thirty to sixty minutes, just to say hello. Look over your child's shoulder occasionally; ask to see what he or she has been viewing. That's what you'd be doing with TV—and it's what you should do with computers, too. If your child is six years old or younger, we recommend that you be in the room the whole time he or she is using the computer—you just never know what might pop up on that screen, especially if you have a wireless hookup or an Internet connection.

**2. Get good filters.** You can block pretty much any Web site or connection that you don't want your child to access—and you should. Read more about your options in Chapter 4. You should also remember that your child has a whole world of cyber-cafés, friends' homes, and other "outside" computers at his or her disposal. So like every other aspect of parenting, it's ultimately a matter of values, communication, and trust.

**3. If you have to, monitor your child electronically.** The options in electronic spyware have multiplied exponentially in recent years. You can get anything from a list of Web sites to a moment-by-moment replay of every minute your child spends on screen (again, this applies only to home computers and laptops that your family owns). We don't advise extensive electronic monitoring for all children— and most children won't need any. But if you're concerned about what your kids are doing online, check out the latest devices described in Chapter 4.

**4. Keep the lines of communication open.** Ask your children what they did online today. Who sent them e-mails? What new Web sites did they find? Did they learn something new about how to track down an elusive fact or a cool product? Listen to their tone of voice when they answer. If your parental antennae go up, keep them talk-ing—and keep listening. In the end, talking and listening will help you protect your child better than any other technique we know.

## Internet Predators

You'll be happy to know that the chances of your child being snatched or stalked by an online predator are very small in-deed. Since this is fairly new territory, no one has exact statis-tics about how many children have been abducted through the use of the Internet. But when you look at statistics on abduc-tions of children in general—although these statistics vary widely depending on who's keeping them—you can see that any way you count them, the chances of your child being taken by a stranger are relatively low.

For example, the FBI says that each year about 300 U.S. children are abducted by strangers, while the U.S. Depart-ment of Justice puts the figure for "non-family abductions" at 114,600 attempted, and 3,200 to 4,600 successful. The Justice Department finds that the risk of abduction by a stranger is lowest for preschoolers, increasing through elementary school and peaking at age fifteen, with teenage girls the most vulner-able. Most abductions involve luring children to a vehicle rather than taking them by force.

So of course, predators are out there. But if your child knows some basic rules, and if you keep the lines of communication open, you'll generally be on pretty safe ground.

Here are the rules we think you and your family should fol-low to keep everybody safe.

1. *Your child should not give out his or her name, address, phone number, or school information to anyone.* If your child thinks there's a good reason to share this information, he or she should check with you.

2. *Children under the age of twelve should not participate in chat rooms.* If your child is geographically isolated, frequently hospitalized, or otherwise limited with regard to regular social contact, you can make an exception—in which case you should spend some time pretending to be in a chat room with your child and modeling appropriate behavior. (See Chapter 4 for more detail on chat rooms.) Children shouldn't disclose any kind of personal information, including the names of school sports teams, landmarks near their homes or schools, or places they like to visit.

3. *Children aged twelve and over can have limited access to chat rooms, provided that they've proven themselves to be trustworthy and agree to alert you and sign off if the subject matter becomes questionable.* Again, for more about chat rooms, see Chapter 4.

4. *Unsolicited pornography should be reported to you right away.* Your children should come to you if they receive pornography—especially child pornography—in an e-mail or if they accidentally access a Web site or get a pop-up with such images in it. Help them understand that pop-ups and porn sites often carry major viruses that could quickly crash your computer and that household members could get into serious legal trouble if child pornography sites are accessed on your computer. (For more information, see Chapter 11.) They should also come to you if they receive disturbing or sexually explicit communications in e-mails or chat rooms. If you're concerned about

anything your child has received from a stranger, you should report it immediately to your local or state law enforcement agency or to your local FBI office. If you or your child has received information that might help to identify missing or exploited children, we urge you to also make a report to the National Center for Missing and Exploited Children at their Web site www.CyberTipline.com or to call them at their 24-hour hotline, 1–800–THE–LOST (1–800–643–5678).

5. *Talk with your child periodically about the issue of Internet predators.* As you'll see throughout this book, keeping the lines of communication open with your child is the best approach to pretty much every issue. Here are some questions you might ask your child to start a conversation about Internet predators:

- **Do you know anyone who has ever been solicited for sex on the Net? What did he or she do? What would you do?** Your child may not have an answer to this question, but your goal is less to hear a specific response and more to create a comfortable atmosphere in which your child is willing to come to you if there ever is a problem. By asking this question, you're helping your child start to think about this subject and make plans for what to do if anything does happen. You're also making it clear that it's okay for your child to talk to you about this topic without fear of punishment or shame.

- **What are some things you can do to keep yourself safe?** You may be surprised at the answers your kids come up with! Give your children positive reinforcement ("What a terrific idea!") and continue to create a comfort zone in which your children feel able to continue the conversation. You can also encourage your children to talk about this issue to each other or to their friends.

- **What can I do to help keep you safe?** Again, you may be surprised! Make a list of their suggestions, post it on the refrigerator, and then follow through as requested. If there's some reason you can't take one of their suggestions, explain why and work with your child to come up with a substitute. Every so often, check out the list again with your child and see if it needs to be revised.

- **Suppose you knew for a fact that someone was stalking you. What would you do differently while you were on line? Would you change anything in your blog?** If your children have a presence on the Web—a blog, Web site, or profile on a social networking site like MySpace—let them know that you plan to check it out, if you haven't already. Give them twenty-four hours notice to change anything they'd like—your goal is to open communication, not to entrap your kids—but do let them know that after this initial warning, you may well be making surprise visits. However, if you think your child is involved in something dangerous or problematic, check out his or her blog immediately, perhaps in your child's presence. You can certainly follow such a visit by saying, "I'm going to need some time to think about how to handle this," but if at all possible, your child should get the message that you are not "spying" but exercising legitimate parental supervision and that you plan to involve him or her in the solution to any problems you uncover. However you handle the situations, you should point out that you're not violating your child's privacy by viewing his or her blog or any other online material—

the whole point of the Web is that it's a public medium where *anyone* can find this information.

You can also be on the lookout for anything odd your child receives by mail. Predators have been known to send gifts or even airline tickets to entice your child to become more involved with them. Most importantly, be aware of any changes in your child's behavior, attitude, or spirits. If you sense that something is wrong, give your child lots of chances to talk to you about it. And keep the Internet and Cyberworld on your list of active topics about which you periodically question your child, along with school and friends. Staying aware of your child and being available to him or her is the best way to hold off any problem before it gets under way.

## Gambling Sites

Teen gambling is growing steadily—in part because of its easy availability online. Some children become compulsive gamblers. Others simply lose more money than they can afford. At the very least, gambling sites keep many teenagers preoccupied with a solitary activity that isolates them from their peers.

Although we have no problem with gambling in general, we do think that gambling poses special challenges for children and teenagers, who often have far less impulse control than adults and who are also more susceptible to becoming addicted to a wide variety of repetitive behaviors. Online gambling is particularly problematic because of how solitary it is and how quickly a child can find him- or herself losing unexpectedly large amounts of money—a problem compounded by the unreal nature of on-line gambling. Gambling is hard enough to self-regulate for adults who are taking physical bills out of their pocket in a casino; it's really difficult for teenagers using their emergency-only credit cards online to realize how much they're spending when they're caught up in the heat of the game. And since both gambling and being online have compulsive aspects (see below), we think it's a poor idea to bring these two activities together.

Whether or not you object to gambling, we think it's important for you to know whether your child is doing it, especially online, where it's technically illegal, especially for teenagers, and where it's possible to lose so much money so quickly. So if you have the sense that your child is engaged in online gambling, we suggest confronting him or her with your concerns. If you continue to worry, let your child know that you'll be monitoring his or her credit card or checking account, to see if unexplained sums of money are going out or coming in. (Simply monitoring your child's use of a home computer won't prevent him or her from gambling at a cyber-café or a friend's house.) And of course, your child should know that if you feel that he or she isn't handling money responsibly, you always have the option of taking away the credit card or closing the checking account.

If your children seem to be interested in gambling and you have no moral or personal objection to it, let us suggest a safer and healthier alternative to the online variety: Encourage your child to start a weekly poker game at your house or at the house of a friend. At the beginning of the evening, each child puts in five dollars. At the end of the evening, whoever has the most chips wins the pot. That way, no one loses more than he or she can afford, the children are engaged in a social activity, and all the parents are aware of what's going on. Perhaps most important, they're learning how to regulate their own behavior: gambling isn't a go-wild, no-holds-barred experience, but a game

that's played in a social context, with rules, limits, and consequences.

If even five dollars a person seems like too much, or if you
don't like the idea of children taking each other's money, perhaps
you or another parent can offer the winner a prize: two tickets to
a movie, a gift certificate for dessert at a nearby restaurant, or
some other fun but inexpensive gift. Certainly, you'll want to
make sure that none of the other children's parents object, but
friends of ours have sponsored poker nights for their kids and, in
our experience, it's a friendly, appropriate, and extremely entertaining way for teens and preteens to spend an evening.

## If You Need Professional Help . . .

If you need to find professional help for your child—either a therapist, a specialist in learning disorders, or a counselor for the whole
family—ask your physician, your child's teachers, and your friends
for recommendations. After you've gotten some names to call, go
online to your state home page (www.[yourstatename].gov) and
find the licensing boards for social workers, psychologists, licensed
professional counselors, and psychiatrists, and check for any sanc-
tions or ethical violations.

Often people get recommendations from insurance companies
and then go with the first professional who calls them back. We suggest talking to at least five or six counselors over the phone and visiting two or three. Of course, if you really click with someone over the
phone, go with your gut—but you might miss your best match that
way. We think it's worth visiting a couple of people—ideally, with your
child—to see who's the best fit for you, your child, and perhaps your
entire family. Good luck, and if you get stuck at any point along the
way, e-mail us at ShankleMelton@msn.com. We'll be glad to help..

# Internet Addiction

Technically, there's no such thing as an addiction to the Internet, although there is some talk of including Internet Addiction Disorder in the next edition of the *Diagnostic and Statistical Manual of Mental Disorders*, the definitive listing of all mental health problems. We ourselves aren't so enthusiastic about calling the Internet addictive because there's such a significant difference between compulsive *behaviors*, such as remaining online, and addictive *substances*, which almost always produce physical withdrawal symptoms when you give them up.

Having said that, we do agree that there's a compulsive quality to the Web, e-mail, and other cyber-activities, much as there is to television. Some studies link this quality to the flickering, hypnotic light behind the electronic screen, while research on electronic games suggests that the compulsivity may be related to levels of dopamine, a brain chemical that spikes with stimulation and falls with boredom and lethargy, and that may also be related to compulsive gambling.

We're not so interested in defining an Internet addiction, though, as we are in helping you to notice if Cyberworld is beginning to occupy too much space in your child's schedule, psyche, or emotional life. Check out this list of warning signs, and if there's cause for concern, take action as we suggest below:

1. Does your child neglect household chores to spend time on the computer?
2. Have your child's grades suffered due to computer use?
3. Does your child seem anxious or furtive when he or she is using the computer and you're in the room?

4. When your family plans an activity, does your child prefer to be on the computer?

5. Does your child seem isolated from others?

6. Are you uncertain about who your child is communicating with online? Does your child answer simply "my friends" when you ask whom he or she is in touch with?

7. Have you recently noticed behavior that is not characteristic of your child?

8. Does your child prefer to use the computer rather than play outside with friends?

9. Would you rather keep the peace than talk with your child about recent changes that have come to your attention?

10. Has your child received any unexplained packages?

If you answered yes to one or more questions, maybe it's time for a conversation with your child. Think about planning some unstructured time—a game, a trip to the mall, a movie—that would give you a chance to bring up some cyber-issues.

If you answered yes to three or more questions, you may have cause for concern. Check with the other adults in your child's life—teachers, relatives, friends' parents—to see if they've noticed any of the same issues. Think about working with your child to set some new cyber-limits.

If you answered yes to five or more questions, the situation may be more serious than you realized. Consider seeking professional help while improving communication with your child.

**If you answered yes to Question 10, take immediate action. Find out with whom your child is communicating and what's being said. Consider taking steps to limit your child's electronic communication.**

PART I

# CYBERWORLD
## FROM YOUR
# CHILD'S
## PERSPECTIVE

Kids need limits. Setting boundaries for your children, helping them learn to follow rules, teaching them to respect propriety, helping them develop empathy, and protecting their safety are among your most important tasks as a parent. But the very nature of electronic media is to offer a world that is seemingly without limits, free of the petty constraints of actual bodies and actual stuff. Instead of going into a music store and looking at actual tapes or disks, your child pushes a few buttons and downloads any song in the world. Instead of making a phone call and speaking to an actual person, your child enters a chat room and has virtually unlimited access to strangers that he or she may never meet face-to-face. Instead of going to a library and pulling a few books off the shelf, your child calls up a search engine and flips endlessly from Web site to Web site.

Indeed, Cyberworld offers extraordinary possibilities for children who want to learn, think, connect, and grow. But it can also be an extremely confusing—and frequently a dangerous—place, where the relationship between taking an action and obtaining a result is not at all clear. What's the difference between shooting a gun in a video game and shooting one in real life? What's the difference between writing an essay and cutting-and-pasting one into your program? What's the difference between your real-life friend, whom you can hurt or comfort or bond with, and the anonymous, not-quite-real people in the online chat room?

On the plus side, Cyberworld offers your child unprecedented opportunities to explore new horizons. Information, images, pen pals in foreign countries, special-interest groups, and ongoing emotional connections are all available through the Internet, e-mail, and text messaging. But on the minus side, Cyberworld often presents an anonymous culture in which there seem to be no consequences for any action, thought, or intention. You push a button, and something happens—but what that means to you or any other human being is not at all clear. If you don't like what you wrote, you simply click and it disappears from the screen. If you don't like what you see, you can make that disappear as well. And if you don't like the kids in a certain chat room, you simply stop going there—and because you've never met them, maybe it feels as though they, too, have simply vanished? The insubstantiality can be extremely confusing even to adults. To children, who don't yet know what their bodies are capable of and who haven't yet figured out how their actions affect others, Cyberworld can be profoundly disorienting.

And yet, you can't ignore it. Your child is growing up in Cyberworld, like it or not. You can limit his or her time online, you can refuse to buy your child a cell phone, but the fact remains: your child is living in Cyberworld.

So in Part I, we'll show you how Cyberworld looks from a child's perspective, helping you identify the major issues facing your kids. We'll talk you through text messaging, instant messaging, e-mail, and Web sites, helping you to see how each of these electronic resources poses new opportunities—and new dangers—for your child.

## CHAPTER 2

# CELL PHONES AND TEXT MESSAGING

l&k 4m3 @8
K, but il b ;-)~
:-x...
143

(for a translation, see the end of this chapter—or go to
www.teenangels.org and use their acronym translator)

I f you read the above sequence of text messages between
your child and a friend, would you have any idea what they
were talking about? Text messaging (TMing) gives kids a
chance to be in constant contact with one another and to speak
a whole new language that parents (and even many older kids)
can't understand. What kid in the world could resist that? And
when parents see their children, happy, quiet, not fighting with
one another, busily TMing their friends, how does *that* look like
a parenting challenge?

Alas, it is. Text messaging opens up a whole new world for
your children—and therein lies the problem. While it's been
true for several decades that young people had a language of

their own, at least it was a language that adults could *hear*—
or at least *see*. Sue and her friends learned finger spelling from
the encyclopedia, provoking their fourth-grade teacher to tell
them, "No talking—with hands or otherwise!" But with kids
TMing silent messages back and forth at all hours and in all lo-
cations, you're completely shut out.

### Getting Up to Speed:
### Cell Phones and Text Messaging

Text messaging is a capacity that comes automatically with most
cell phones, though Firefly does offer a phone intended for younger
children that can be used only to make calls. With all other phones,
you can send a text message by choosing that function from a menu
on the phone, then using the keypad to type the numbers or letters
you want to send.

To understand how this works, look at the keypad of any phone.
Notice how, for example, the number 2 and the letters A, B, C are all
on the second button. To text a message, you'd press that key once
to indicate the letter A, which would then appear on your phone's
screen. If A was what you wanted, you'd hit the select or enter button and move on. But if you wanted to type B, you'd push that first
key twice and watch the letter on the screen progress from A to B before hitting select or enter. If you wanted to type C, you'd have to
press the button three times, and if you wanted to type 2, you'd have
to press it four times. As long as you stay on the same button, you'll
keep cycling through the choices—only when you press select can
you move on to a new letter.

As you can see, it could take several presses to type even a simple
message. That's why TMers need those abbreviated codes: CUL8R
has only 5 characters and requires 20 button-presses; "see you later"

has 11 characters and two spaces and would require 39 presses. Over time, it adds up!

Many cell phones do include a group of pre-entered text messages called Quick Notes. These include the most common TMs that people send, spelled correctly, with no shorthand. But if you want to send a unique message, or to include an address, phone number, or contact information, you'll have to type out every character.

Experienced texters make their thumbs fly, and they can type out messages with surprising speed. But clearly, the form doesn't lend itself to thought or subtlety—it's designed to be quick, direct, and informative.

Receiving a text message is even simpler: your phone beeps—either its regular ringtone or a special signal, depending on how your phone works and on what plan you've chosen—and when you check it, you see the message on the screen.

You can buy a cell phone plan without TM, in which case you'll pay for every single message your child sends or receives. Or you can include a certain number of TMs in the plan, in which case you'll be charged for any extra. With a Disney phone, you can actually limit the number of minutes and messages your child has access to: when he or she reaches the limit, the phone simply stops working. Most other plans don't have that option: after the limit, you're charged extra.

Disney and Firefly offer a number of other parent-friendly limits. For example, with a Disney phone, you can block children from making calls at certain times of day. With Firefly, you approve up to twenty numbers and the phone won't make or accept calls to or from anywhere else. Both companies let you block calls to and/or from certain numbers. Disney phones even come with global positioning system (GPS) technology that allows you to locate the child's phone—helpful if your child loses the phone or if you want to locate your phone-carrying child.

Disney introduced its latest plan as we were preparing the final manuscript of this book, so by the time you're reading these pages, even more options may be available from Disney, Firefly, or other companies looking to get in on the action. To find out more, you might do an Internet search for "children's cell phone plans" or "family cell phone plans."

We have some other concerns about text messaging as well. What about the kids who are TMing each other constantly— even during study hall, school events, and classes? Passing notes to each other in class is one thing; at least those kids are still aware of the world around them and can be caught relatively easily by an alert teacher. But TMing offers entry into an alternate cyber-universe that, like television, tends to dominate your attention from the moment you access it. And children communicating with one another in this fashion can be far more difficult for a teacher or other authority to spot—when they're not letting their phones ring in open defiance of classroom protocol.

In addition, the process of text messaging sends a disturbing message of its own, encouraging children to focus not on where they are but on somewhere else, to cling to a familiar communication with their friends in a way that can insulate them from new experiences and accustom them to a continual level of distraction. Instead of being fully present and aware, children who are constantly TMing always have one foot out the door, always ready to turn from their actual experience to the distraction of a coded message.

Moreover, the very nature of TMing—communicating in

short, rapid bursts rather than in longer, more complicated sentences—has the potential to narrow children's communication skills and diminish their emotional life. Two teenagers gabbing on the phone may not seem to be engaging in the most profound of conversations, but even if they're just gossiping about classmates or reviewing the plays in last night's game, they've got time to explore a thought, pause for breath, try out the way different ideas sound. They have a chance to hear each other's tone of voice, to "read between the lines," to hear the pauses as well as the words. TMing narrows communication to short, functional bursts—and your child's communication skills and emotional life may suffer accordingly.

Of course, there are some positive aspects to TMing as well. When it's not possible or practical to make a phone call, you and your kid can TM about a meeting place or an emergency plan, or your child can alert his or her friends to a last-minute change in plans. You can send your child a quick "I love you" or "Good luck on that test" in situations where you might not want to call. Some kids may find the privacy and secrecy of TM empowering, savoring their near-adult sense of control over their own communication and friendship networks. And there's always that fine-motor-skill practice—have you *seen* how quickly kids' fingers can fly over those little keys?

So we're not saying you should rush to call your cell phone provider, instructing them to disable your kid's access to TM (though you may someday decide that option is right for you). We are suggesting that you take a long, hard look at this increasingly significant medium, figure out how it's affecting your child, and decide what you'd like to do about it. Let's start by imagining life with—and without—the omnipresence of TM.

## To Text or Not to Text?: A Tale of Two Teens

Consider two middle-school boys, Trent, who loves to text, and Sean, whose cell-phone plan has no TM function and limited minutes. Trent uses his cell phone at the drop of a hat, while Sean has been told to use his only for quick scheduling arrangements and, of course, emergencies.

Both boys are meeting some friends for a movie and pizza at the local mall. Both sets of parents had plans of their own and dropped the boys off early, so each boy has about an hour to kill before his friends show up to meet him.

Sean is happy to have the extra time. He's a huge comic book fan, so he makes his way over to Comics Unlimited, noticing how unusually quiet the mall is this Saturday. As he passes through the nearly empty food court, he wonders what's going on. Is everyone home watching the big game on TV? Or maybe the heat wave has caused people to leave town for the weekend? Wow, is that what they mean by global warming? Or maybe it's just that this mall is losing business to the one across town. The thought makes Sean sad—what will the store owners do if all their customers desert them?

When Sean reaches Comics Unlimited, he wanders dreamily through the store, dipping into the series he's familiar with and exploring a few new ones. Each new comic tantalizes him with its promise of an alternate universe, but Sean has to keep reminding himself to keep track of the time or he'll only get to a few magazines, and he wants to check out the whole store. He can only afford two comics this week, so which shall it be: Spiderman, DMZ, or the Walking Dead? Or maybe he should take a chance on a totally new character, some series he's never read before? Sean makes his choice five minutes before he has

to leave to meet his friends: one old favorite and one new series that a friend has recommended.

Sean joins his friends at the movie, which they all love. The
film is so gripping, in fact, that Sean almost forgets where he
is. As the boys share a pizza after the show, they argue passion-
ately about what the hero should have done when the robo-
killer came after him—use his secret weapon, find a clever trick,
or try to run? Then they start ragging on each other about an
incident that happened in school last week. Sean is a little uncomfortable when the insults get too pointed, but he does kind
of enjoy this kind of joking around.

As the evening ends, Sean realizes that he still doesn't know
when tomorrow night's party is going to start. The other boys
don't know, either, but they agree to call another friend about
it when they get home.

So that was Sean's text-free day—browsing, daydreaming,
watching a movie, and hanging out with friends. What happens
to that same outing when we throw in a cell phone and some
TMing?

TMer Trent likes comics, too, but it takes him a little longer
to get to the store because he gets a message on his way there:
his friend Brent wants to know *sup?* [Translation: What's up?]
and if he saw *South Park* last night.

*ya so kewl*, Trent texts back as he ambles along, using the
TM slang for "yes" and the TM spelling for "cool."

*ya*, Brent texts back. The message also goes to a third friend,
Kent, so the three boys spend ten minutes or so texting about
the *South Park* episode:

*what @ kenny?* [Translation: What about Kenny?]
*U R right he is 2 much* [Translation: You're right. He's too much.]

*i like crtmn* [Translation: I like Cartman.]
*crtmn is kewl* [Translation: Cartman is cool.]

After a while, the conversation peters out (CUL8TR—"See you later," Brent TMs), and Trent realizes that he's reached the comic-book store. Just like Sean, Trent starts browsing through the various selections—he, too, can only afford a couple—but he's interrupted by a ring from his cell phone. It's Pete, calling to find out what time the party starts tomorrow night. Pete's in a car, though, so Trent can't hear him very well, and then the call gets cut off.

Trent starts browsing again, but then he gets yet another TM from Brent, who also wants to know when the party starts. Trent isn't sure, so both boys TM Kent, who calls another friend and then texts them back. By the time everybody understands that the party is at 8 p.m., Trent has to leave the store. He hastily pays for two issues of his favorite comic and heads for the movie theater.

Trent likes the movie, too, but his cell phone goes off in the middle of it. It's Pete again, still wondering about the party. Two women sitting in the row in front of him turn around and say *"Shhhhhh!"* so Trent doesn't talk, but he does send Pete a TM, telling him that the party's at eight. Then he puts his phone on vibrate, which is a good thing, because soon Kent calls, and then Brent. Kent wants to know if he can have a ride to the party tomorrow. Brent just remembered something else he wanted to say about *South Park*. Trent TMs them both.

Then the movie gets really good, so Trent ignores the phone, but he can't help noticing the vibrations and registering the fact that he's gotten two more calls. As he and his friends head over to the pizza place, he checks his messages. A guy on his soccer teams wants a ride to practice next week. A classmate wants to know if he can borrow Trent's social studies book. While he and his friends eat pizza, Trent returns the calls, talking to one boy and TMing the other. The other kids roll their eyes: this is par for the course with Trent.

So that was Trent's day—the same visit to the comic-book store, the same movie, the same pizza and hang-out time with friends. But what a difference! Focused on his cell phone, Trent misses the chance to speculate about why the mall was empty—a seemingly simple problem that actually offers Sean the opportunity to think about his community, wonder about his world, and sharpen his problem-solving skills. Unlike Sean, Trent never becomes fully absorbed in either the comic-book world or the movie, losing the opportunity to immerse himself in fantasy that is often a key part of a child's development. Whereas Sean is expanding his capacity to concentrate, dream, and engage with stories, Trent is spending his time stuck in fairly limited and repetitive conversations about familiar events and logistics. And after the movie, as Sean bonds with his friends and thinks more deeply about the film he's just seen, Trent is engaged in more superficial relationships, not fully present either to the friends he's with or to the ones he's texting and phoning. None of the tasks Trent is TM'ed or called about—the party, the ride to practice, the lost textbook— couldn't have waited until he got home and none requires an entire day to resolve. But somehow Trent's time at the mall has been eaten up with petty obligations and limited encounters, while Sean, engaged in precisely the same activities, has had a much richer and more developmentally rewarding experience.

Now, let's not go overboard. It's not as though Trent's entire development will be compromised because of one day at the mall. And Sean's not exactly doing rocket science. But in fact, that *is* our point. It's just those dreamy, casual, open-ended kinds of times that help kids grow into thoughtful, creative, and observant people, able to think, wonder, imagine, and connect. Trivial though Sean's day may seem, he's actually engaged several different kinds of skills: problem-solving, speculation, concentration, evaluation. He's practiced budgeting his time in the comics store, while the pizza session gives him the chance to form his values about the kinds of interpersonal contact he likes and doesn't like (some joking around is fun; too many insults are not). He's learned something about his world, his friends, and himself—not a bad day's work for a growing boy!

What has Trent learned from *his* day? Well, he's become a more efficient multitasker—but as you'll see below, that's not necessarily the best approach to either learning or productivity. He's practiced filling every spare moment with conversation and distraction, rather than allowing himself the down time of wandering solo or browsing through the comics store. He's so involved with reacting to external stimuli—phone calls, TMs—that he never gets the chance to set his own goal (checking out the new comics) and then measure the time he has to accomplish it. His behavior reinforces the notion that no one friend is all that important, because Trent always has two or three conversations going on simultaneously and is never really present for any of them. And he's piled distraction upon distraction—even an exciting action movie isn't enough to occupy his full attention when the ever-present cell phone vibrates and lights up.

Like Sean and his friends discussing their movie, Trent and his friends do communicate about a TV show they've all seen. But because they're having that conversation by TM instead of "voice to voice," they never get into anything very complicated, emotional, or intense. That same conversation held under other circumstances could be a treasure-trove of developmental opportunities: forming opinions, testing them out, learning from others with different ideas, finding out what to do when you and your friend don't agree, not to mention developing values and aesthetics. Again, it may sound trivial, but arguing over, say, whether it's funny or gross or just plain dumb that Kenny always used to die in every *South Park* episode gives children a chance to learn and grow in a hundred different ways. When that conversation is artificially narrowed by the constraints of TM, children learn not to think so deeply or feel so strongly. Interactions remain brief, formulaic, and superficial.

Of course, none of that matters if kids have other opportunities for deeper and more meaningful encounters. But in our increasingly overscheduled Cyberworld, TM and cell phones may be keeping our children from valuable chances to learn about themselves, one another, and the world we share.

## Texting and Learning: A Tough Combination

Kids aren't just texting at home or at the mall: many of them have their cell phones on while they're at school. Barb recently spoke with a group of apparently well-behaved middle-class children who bragged to her about how one of them had a cell phone with an obscene rap ringtone that suddenly rang during class. Hidden in someone's backpack, the phone wasn't visible, and the teacher had no way of figuring out where the brief but disruptive sound had come from.

"That teacher was so totally lame," one of the boys told Barb. "She had *no* idea what to do." They contrasted her with another teacher whose class they never would have disrupted. "We'd *never* get away with something like that in Ms. Jones's class," the boy said. "We wouldn't even think of trying."

Even more disturbing was the children's general agreement that many of them texted each other answers to test questions— in that case, keeping their phones on vibrate—and their assurances to Barb that neither their teachers nor their parents knew. While Barb was inclined to discount some of this as middle-school bragging, she also observed the children talking about this with one another. "You totally screwed me up with that last answer," one boy said to his friend. "I'm lucky I didn't fail."

Cheating and disrupting class are two obvious ways that texting and learning don't mix. Here are some other ways that cell phones and TMs might interfere with your children's learning or otherwise affect their school experience:

**Poor spelling and grammar.** It's hard enough for children to learn proper spelling and usage without the daily, constant re-inforcement of doing it wrong. TM conversions—U for "you," R for "are," and so on—make logical sense but don't fit the rules of standard English, which are already pretty difficult! Every good speller will tell you that good spelling has to become second nature—the words just have to "feel right," to the point where really good spellers often know how to spell words they've never even heard of. For kids who spend more time TMing than at any other form of written communication, "U" can't help but seem more natural than "you."

Of course, we do have spell-check. But there are still *some* occasions on which we need to know how a word should be written! And of course, if your spelling is too far off, even your spell-check program may not understand what you're trying to say. So if your child has a learning disability, speaks English as a second language, or just isn't good at spelling, he or she is going to have a much harder time thanks to all that bad-spelling practice. (For more on how to help your learning-disabled child cope with Cyberworld, see Chapter 6.)

**Impaired attention span and ability to focus.** The relationship between TM, cell phones, and kids' attention spans is one of those areas that's too new to have been tested, but pretty much any experienced teacher will tell you: children are showing a steady and continuous decline in concentration spans, while increasing numbers of students are being diagnosed with various types of attention-deficit disorders—an extraordinary 381 percent increase between 1989 and 2000, according to a recent study of hospitalized children. Whether the culprit is a high-sugar diet, electronic overstimulation, or a multitasking culture, we're concerned—and we think you should be, too.

Again, we're not saying that a daily hour or two of TMing will impair your child's abilities in any immediately significant way. Kids are resilient, and unless your child is learning-disabled, he or she can probably handle a certain amount of distraction. (Again, we'll talk more about special-needs kids in Chapter 6.) But a child who, like Trent, is constantly bombarded with ringtones and TM beeps learns to value distractions while avoiding that deep, focused immersion out of which great ideas, intense relationships, and profound self-knowledge may come.

**Reduced memory and productivity.** Study after study agrees: when your mind is trying to do two things at once, it can't do either very well. So multitasking makes you less likely to remember the information involved in either task.

Thus, in a recent article in *Time* magazine, significantly entitled "The Multitasking Generation," Jordan Grafman warned of the dangers of multitasking. Grafman should know: he's head of the cognitive neuroscience section at the National Institute of Neurological Disorders and Stroke (NIDS), and he's predicted that children who grow up doing their homework while IMing, playing online games, and watching TV "aren't going to do well in the long run." Reporter Claudia Wallis comments, "Decades of research (not to mention common sense) indicate that the quality of one's output and depth of thought deteriorate as one attends to ever more tasks."

In the same article, Stanford University professor of communication Donald Roberts also warns that the cell-phone generation evinces "almost a discomfort with not being stimulated—a kind of 'I can't stand the silence.' " Wallis goes on to cite other professors at top universities whose students don't seem to be able to sit still in class without checking e-mail, setting up electronic chats, or doing online research. "People are going to lectures by some of the greatest minds, and they are doing their mail," says Sherry Turkle, who teaches the social studies of science and technology at MIT. If even top-level college students are having trouble shaking the multitask habit, imagine how great the obstacles must be for your child.

**Increased anxiety.** Think about the last time you went for a few hours without checking your messages. Did you start to get a little antsy? Or what about when you did check them? Perhaps you noticed some anxiety about who might want something from you or whether you'd get bad news?

If so, you're not alone. Lots of people report increased anxiety around TM, phone messages, and e-mail, which can leave you feeling as though you're never alone, never off-duty, and never safe from intrusion. If you're the type who feels guilty for not doing enough, every message becomes a possible rebuke. If you worry that your friends may be mad at you, every ringtone makes you wonder who's angry *now*. Children, too, are prone to these anxieties. And if your child is going through an especially stressed, vulnerable, or awkward stage, TM-related anxiety may well make it worse. (For more on anxiety and e-mail, see Chapters 2 and 5.)

**Cyber-bullying.** E-mail offers so much more fertile a field for cyber-bullying than TMing that we'll look at this topic more completely in Chapter 3. Still, cell phones and TM can offer some wicked possibilities, especially if the cell phone is equipped with a camera. What if some guy takes pictures of your son in the boy's room and then TMs them to all his classmates? What if your daughter is bombarded by anonymous TMs telling her she's fat, ugly, and a slut? A depressed, vulnerable, or lonely child can be assaulted through text messaging in a more private and intimate way than could ever happen by regular phone or that old-fashioned note in the locker. With electronic bullying, the meanness can follow you home.

**Emotional availability and empathy.** One of our favorite books is *Harriet the Spy*, the classic children's story of a sensitive, quirky girl who copes with life by constantly analyzing others and then recording those thoughts in her ever-present diary. When a teacher objects to Harriet's distracted quality and confiscates the diary, Harriet falls apart. Without her notebook, she can no longer distance herself through her sharp observations. Eventually, though, the lack of the notebook forces her to develop another kind of inner strength, and she learns to empathize rather than judge.

Looked at from the perspective of Cyberworld, Harriet was

an early TMer, even if she kept her messages to herself. Like many of today's cyberkids, Harriet distanced herself from every situation by commenting on it rather than experiencing it. Her diary—an otherwise admirable outpouring of her curious, insightful nature—became a shield between Harriet and her emotional responses, so that every encounter turned into subject matter. We're totally in favor of thinking, analyzing, observing, and commenting—as therapists, we could hardly be otherwise! But there's a time to stand back and comment and a time to simply allow your experience to unfold. Too much TMing might keep children from really opening up to their own experience.

Recently, Sue spent the weekend with a group of friends at a mountain home they had all rented together for a "girls' getaway." One of the friends spent the entire weekend TMing her children. Sue was struck by how distant the woman's communication was, both with her children—whom she never phoned—and her friends, who never had her full attention. She felt the woman had the illusion of connection without experiencing any real connection. Too many children, Sue feared, clung to their cell phones and that same illusion.

**Overvaluing urgency and productivity.** As Trent's text-ridden day made clear, cell phones and TM produce an overwhelming sense of urgency. Something about that ringing phone or beeping message says, *"Listen to me! I'm the most important!"* Even if we only pause to check who's calling, we've given ourselves and our companions a clear signal about what really matters: not the book we're reading, the show we're watching, the walk we're taking, or the conversation we're having—but The Call or The Message.

This is bad enough when it hurts a friend's feelings or keeps encounters at a superficial level. But what about the way it keeps us from fully enjoying our leisure time, from savoring our experiences of art and nature, and maybe even from opening up to our religion? How can that cell phone or TM trump our commitment to being fully present in a theater, an open field, or a place of worship? We seem to be teaching our children that they need to be always "on call," always responsive to others' demands, even when they're supposed to be enjoying their "time off" or absorbed in an important experience. That may be one of the most destructive text messages of all.

## The Joys of Text: How TMing Can Benefit Your Child

Now that we've looked at the minus column, it's time to focus on the plusses. Here are some things we like about text messaging:

**It's good for emergencies and last-minute changes.** As any parent knows, having two, three, or even four backup plans is often a matter of necessity. Sometimes your biggest emergency is figuring out which entrance of the mall to meet at; other times you have more serious problems to deal with. Both of us have spent time counseling survivors in post-Katrina Louisiana, where we heard story after story of how the TM function helped families find each other when phone service just wasn't working. We later learned that there's a very good reason for the discrepancy: phones of any type need a constant signal to transmit, while text messages require only a millisecond to send or receive. As a result, the Red Cross recommends that emergency workers rely on text messaging as a backup when they deploy people to disaster zones.

**TIP** Since TMs are short bursts of communication, they can get through when cell phone signals cannot. Even if you discourage TMing under most circumstances, you might want to instruct your children in how to send emergency text messages.

Of course, Katrina-scale emergencies are few and far between, and you may decide that such extreme protection is less important to your child than insulating him or her from the more ordinary effects of daily text messaging. But if you need a backup to your cell phone contact, TMing may well be your best solution.

**It's good for quick, encouraging messages, reminders, and expressions of affection.** "Have a nice day, honey. I love you!" "Big test today—you can do it!" "Don't forget—it's Dad's birthday." "Did you remember your history book?" Any of these quickie TMs can give your kids a little boost without the intrusiveness of a full-scale phone call. Especially as your kids get older, TMing them may be a great way of communicating while still leaving them some space.

TMing can also give your kids a nice measure of control over their communication, offering them the chance to ask a parent a quick question. One day, Barb was counseling a young woman who made a joke. "Surely you jest," Barb replied playfully. The teenager didn't know what "jest" meant, and when Barb defined it for her, she was a bit skeptical. So she TM'ed her dad to see if he'd define the word in the same way. Neither of us thought she'd have called her father—that made the question

way too big a deal—but a quick little TM was just enough contact to keep her teenage heart feeling both connected and independent. For some kids, TMing can be a great face-saving
way of staying in touch without quite admitting that's what
they're doing.

Then, too, you can TM your kids with reminders that allow
them to preserve their privacy and spare them from possible
embarrassment: "Remember to let Mom know you'll be late"
or "You have a doctor's appointment today, so meet me out
front at 3 p.m." Calling your kid on a cell phone means everyone knows that Mommy or Daddy had something to say; leaving a discreet TM gives your kid a bit more privacy, not to
mention preserving silence in the classroom!

**TMing can keep your messages short and sweet.** Sometimes,
as parents, we have a tendency to do too much. We tell our
kids more than they need to know or belabor our feelings beyond the point where our children—especially as they reach
the teen years—are comfortable. Text messaging is good discipline for us, too, because it means we have to find succinct and
direct ways of getting our point across. Sometimes less is
more—and for those times, TM can be the perfect medium for
our message.

## Rx for TM: A Step-by-Step Plan

So now that you've got a better sense of how TM may be affecting your child's world, what's your next move? Here are
our recommendations for helping your kids use text messaging
in a responsible way that keeps them present, focused, and on
task:

## Step 1: Talk It Through

Make sure your children understand why you care so much about the role TMing plays in their lives. Remember, they're living in a world where everyone they know—parents, kids, even their teachers—takes TMing for granted, and probably your kids have never even thought of TMing or cell phones as a category for concern. Their friends' parents may restrict them to one hour of TV a day; they may know classmates who aren't allowed to eat sugar, meat, or dairy—but *everybody* has a cell phone, right?

Since you may be the only parents in your child's world to make an issue of TMing, we advise you to "start low and go slow." For example:

> *You know, honey, I'm kind of concerned about the way people use TMing these days.* [Keep it impersonal—you're concerned about TMing, not about them.] *It seems to me we often end up ignoring the people around us in order to take a call or read a message. I know when my cell goes off, I have a really hard time not getting it out to see who's calling, even if it's only on vibrate.* [Involve yourself in the problem—you live in Cyberworld, too!] *But I also hate it when I'm with someone and they just ignore me to jump to the phone. How do you feel when that happens?* [Build empathy by helping them see for themselves how TMing can be rude and dismissive as well as distracting. Keep the conversation going and stay open to your child's thoughts and feelings.]

If your child is very invested in TMing and constant cell phone use, you may need to negotiate:

**YOUR DAUGHTER:** Gee, Mom. You're telling me you don't want me TMing except in an emergency, but last week, at the mall, it *was* an emergency! Cindy was so *upset* about her fight with Lisa—she just *had* to talk to someone about it, and I'm her *best friend*. What was I supposed to do, tell her I wouldn't look at her TMs just because I was out with you and Grandma at the mall?

**YOU:** I'm glad you're concerned about your friend—that's great, and Cindy is lucky to have a friend like you. But I think it's important to *be* with whoever you're with. When you're with Cindy, you need to be *with* Cindy—but when you're with Grandma and me, I need you to be with us. If you absolutely have to talk to Cindy, I would rather you excuse yourself for a short time, call her back on your cell phone, and limit the call to five minutes. That way, you're really talking to her—and then you can focus on us again.

### Step 2: Set Your Limits

If your kids are onboard with your feelings about TMing—if they, too, find it annoying to be constantly interrupted or to spend time with friends who are—then you may be able to stop right there at Step 1. In fact, if you possibly can, we suggest starting with the honor system: explain to your kids what you expect of them, and let them agree to live up to it.

The honor system may work even if you and your children don't see eye to eye. If you think cell phones should be saved for emergencies and your daughter thinks they're tailor-made for three-hour fashion critiques, she's entitled to her opinion—and you may still be able to trust her to stay off the phone. Her opinion—your rules—no problem.

But if your kids want a different cell-and-text policy than you think is wise, and if you don't trust them to simply follow your wishes, then you may have to set some more restrictive limits. Ideally, you'll involve your child in figuring this out, because the more your child participates in setting a limit, the more invested he or she will be in sticking to it. So ask your kid what *he* thinks will work or what *she's* willing to live with. You may be surprised at how cooperative your child becomes.

Meanwhile, here are some possible limits for you to consider. Pick the ones that will work best for you, your children, and your situation, being aware that everyone involved—including you—may need to compromise.

**Use basic cell phones only, no phones with Internet access or cameras.** Adding Internet access to a kid's cell phone is simply unnecessary—he or she can wait to check e-mail at home! And having the Web capability 24/7 really ramps up the distractability factor. Cell-phone cameras are another extra that kids don't need—there are just too many temptations to take and transmit pictures inappropriately. For taking pictures, they should use a camera, so that everyone can see that's what they're doing.

**Ask your phone company for detailed billing.** You can usually get a listing of every single call—who it was to, when it was made, how long it lasted—and you can also find out how many TMs are being sent or received each month. If your children know that you can follow their doings in such detail, they may be more inclined to follow your rules.

**Send them some places without their phones.** Again, if you trust your children to stick to the honor system, no problem. But if you think a working cell phone is just too great a temptation, you may not want them to have phones at school, especially if you think they're using phones to pass answers around during test time. Even for straight-A students, cell phones in school can be distracting. (As we were preparing this book, news came out of a ringtone so high that only dogs and children could hear it—no adults—which sounded like the latest in techno-teacher-torture!) Even if your child is excelling at school, he or she may be tempted to fit in or succumb to peer pressure by helping others cheat. Make sure your children know that if cheaters are caught, the person supplying answers gets into just as much trouble as the person receiving them. And schools have started coding kids' transcripts to show if they've cheated—information that could hurt their chances of getting into college later. You may also want to insist that your kids leave the phones home during family outings and on some or all excursions with friends, to help them focus on the people they're with.

## Ringtone Rigamarole

If your kids have their own cell phones, they've probably already learned how to assign different ringtones to people on their contact list, so that a tune that signifies doom might signal an incoming call from Mom or Dad, while, say, the *Twilight Zone* theme might signify that your UFO-obsessed pal is calling. This can be a good or a bad thing: Barb has observed kids hearing a certain ringtone tell their friends "I'm not getting that—it's just Rudy!" or "Shhhh! That's my parents! They think I'm in the library!"

Of course, many cell phones have caller ID, so your children don't necessarily need ringtones to screen calls. But we do think you might help your children learn to be tactful about how they screen.

Your children's other friends don't necessarily need to know that they're not taking Rudy's calls—and then your kids needn't worry that word of their choice will get back to Rudy!

**Make a pledge to go "phone-free" together.** Why not try a trip to the mall with your daughter or a walk around the park with your son while *both* of your cell phones are turned off? At the very least, it will give you and your children a shared reference point when you've all figured out the family's cyber-rules.

**Put them on a budget.** Buy a plan with a fixed number of TMs and monthly minutes or buy a prepaid plan that requires payment as you go. Then help your children to budget their time: show your kids, for example, that 30 messages a month breaks down to about 1 message per day, whereas 50 messages a month means they can send/receive about 12 each week. Remember, even adults run over budget now and then, so try to steer a middle course between shelling out a fortune and punishing your kid for making a few honest mistakes.

## Step 3: Establish the Consequences

You've started with the honor system, but what if it's not working? Again, talk it through: ask your child how he or she feels about how things are going. Maybe your kid will ask you for help or give you some insight into why he or she is having trouble. Admit your fears and concerns ("I worry that you're texting during study hall instead of working," "I'm concerned that you're texting one friend while you're talking live with another, which to me seems like a hurtful way to behave, though I know you don't mean to be hurtful"). Try not to ascribe bad motives to your kid ("I know you don't mean to be rude—but I think that's the effect of that behavior"). And please try to share your concerns in terms of what *you* feel, not in terms of what your child is doing. Instead of "You're being rude," try, "I don't like that kind of behavior and I don't feel comfortable with you doing it."

If talking isn't enough, start with limited consequences and work your way up. Maybe you'll want to further limit your child's TM allotment or cell-phone minutes. Maybe you'll need to take away the phone, temporarily or permanently. Lay out for your child what the possible consequences might be: "This time, I'm letting you off with a warning—that's your freebie. If you take and send TMs while you're out with me or Grandma again, I'll limit your minutes and your messages for at least three months. If it happens a third time, I'll consider holding on to your phone, except when I need you to have it for family scheduling."

Another common problem is kids using their phones to TM after they go to bed. You think they're resting, but they're busily—and silently—keeping in touch with their friends! If this is a concern, charge the cell phone overnight in *your* room.

Sometimes "consequences" can be a code word for punishment, but if your child is trying hard and the system still isn't working, please model tolerance and compassion. There's no shame in going back to the drawing board and trying another system:

> I thought you'd be able to have a phone with you at all times, but I'm beginning to think that's just too much

temptation. I know there are lots of things I can't resist, and maybe it's that way with you and the phone—you just can't keep from using it if it's in your bag. Let's try this: You'll get your phone only on weekends. If that works out, we might reconsider letting you have it during the week again.

On the other hand, what if *you* need to be able to phone and/or text your child—to arrange after-school pickups, for example, or simply because you become anxious without that kind of access? Then you'll need to figure out another type of consequence, one that doesn't punish *you*. Maybe every extra minute on the phone bill is worth an hour of work around the house or every breach of your agreement means a special trip is canceled. Just be sure that, whenever possible, you're both involving your child in setting up the system and letting him or her know the consequences *before* any mistakes have been made. Both measures will help ensure your child's cooperation.

You should also make sure your kids understand that every time they press send to make a call, their phone charges a minute for that time. So repeated redials count, even when there is no answer!

It can be challenging to help your child learn a new relationship to text messaging, especially when so many of his or her friends are busily TMing. We think it's worth it, though, to limit this communication as part of helping your children relate more fully and thoughtfully to the world around them. Save the TMs for emergencies and brief messages—and free your child's attention for better things.

**Translation of Text Message**

| | |
|---|---|
| l&k 4m3 @8 | Look for me at 8. |
| K, but il b ;-)~ | OK, but I'll be drunk. |
| :-x... | I'll keep my mouth shut. |
| 143 | I love you. |

## CHAPTER 3

# E-MAIL

Recently, Barb was called in to supervise a counselor dealing with a high school girl—let's call her Tammy—who had gotten into a fight with another student, whom we'll call Michelle. When the counselor called the two girls into his office for mediation, Michelle was tearful, defiant, and self-righteous. "Tammy was yelling at me," Michelle told the counselor. "I couldn't take it anymore."

The counselor looked over at Tammy, a shy, withdrawn student whose face was half-hidden by her wispy blond hair. He found it hard to believe that Tammy had even spoken above a whisper, let alone yelled.

"She *did*," Michelle repeated. "She's *always* yelling."

"I never yell," Tammy said softly.

"When you e-mail," Michelle insisted. "You're always yelling at me when you e-mail."

Finally, the story came out. Tammy had recently modified her e-mail program to appear in a brilliant royal blue, with bold-face type—and she used capital letters. In Michelle's perception—and according to standard Netiquette—capital letters symbolized yelling. Tammy had chosen her new presentation because she thought it looked cool. But to Michelle, the simplest phrases—"WHERE WERE YOU LAST NIGHT?" or "I CAN'T SEE YOU TOMORROW"—had become angry accusations and rejections.

Once the counselor sorted out the problem, he was able to resolve the quarrel, and Tammy agreed to modify her e-mail program to a kinder, gentler presentation. But the story stands as an example of the new communications challenges posed by Cyberworld.

## Getting Up to Speed: E-mail vs. Instant Messaging

• **E-mail**—aka electronic mail, or ee—is just like regular mail except instead of being sent physically, with paper and envelopes, it's transmitted electronically, from one computer screen to the next. When you send an e-mail, it goes through the World Wide Web—an international electronic system that connects computers around the world—on a four-step path:

1. your computer screen
2. a Web site run by your e-mail provider
3. a Web site run by the recipient's e-mail provider
4. your recipient's computer screen.

Sometimes people download their e-mail from a Web site onto their computers; sometimes they read it right on the Web. Either way, though, there's inevitably a time lag—anywhere from a few seconds to several hours—as the message makes its way through these four steps.

• **Instant Messaging (IM)** also relies on the World Wide Web, but it allows you to talk with someone in something close to real time. You start by choosing one or more IM buddies. IM will automatically notify you and your buddies whenever any of you is online. If you want to communicate with a buddy, type a message on your computer keyboard into your IM program, and that message appears instantly on your buddy's computer screen. You can IM one person at a time, or several—either way, the idea is to get a (written) conversation going:

**SARA:** Did you see what Lucy wore today?
**JANIE:** What?
**SARA:** This really cute skirt.
**JANIE:** Was it short?
**SARA:** Long. With ruffles.

As you can see, IMs, like TMs, tend to be quick and to the point. (They are also rich in jargon and symbols—see the Acronyms list on page 355 in the Resource section for more detail.) Unlike e-mail, which can be used to send links to other Web sites, electronic images, video clips, and attached documents, IM can only be used to send on-screen messages.

Both e-mail and IM require passwords, but some computers are set up so that these passwords are provided automatically as soon as the e-mail or IM program is accessed. In other cases, the user needs to enter a password each time he or she accesses the account. You can assign different passwords to each of your children, giving you the capacity to restrict an individual's access to e-mail, IM, or both. For more detail on those options, see Chapter 4.

Since IM is so similar to TM, this chapter will focus on e-mail. Many of the points we make about e-mail, though, may apply to IM as well.

Like most adults we know, we've become totally dependent on e-mail for our personal and professional lives. We certainly couldn't live without e-mail, so we're not surprised that kids

can't either. And we think it's terrific that children are learning
to communicate in writing. Sure, the grammar, punctuation,
and spelling may be atrocious—but there's something wonder-
fully therapeutic about putting your thoughts and feelings into
written language, and it's nice that kids of both sexes are learning to stay in touch that way.

At the same time, e-mail does present a unique set of parenting challenges. First, as we just saw, e-mail is rife with potential for miscommunication. Even adults get into trouble by
sending hasty replies, cc'ing groups of people on what should
be private issues, forwarding e-mails that the sender never intended anyone else to see, and misreading statements that
could be taken in more than one way. Learning how to use
e-mail is easy; learning how to master it, isn't—but that's a gap
that both children and adults often misjudge.

Then there are all the emotional issues that e-mail brings
up. What happens when you conduct an argument through
e-mail at various hours of the day, rather than face-to-face in real
time? Does the time lag give both parties a chance to make
cool, well-reasoned replies or simply prolong and intensify a
quarrel? Does e-mail take on a life of its own, creating a constant need for communication, reassurance, response? If you
can get an e-mail from a friend, teacher, or sworn enemy at any
hour of the day or night, then when are you no longer "open
for business"? As you can see, e-mailing creates unique problems and opportunities that your child may need help with.

Of course, there's always the concern about extra e-mail addresses, the online ones you don't know about that your kid
has set up at Yahoo! or Hotmail while at a local cyber-café or the
public library. Whom might your children be e-mailing at these
untraceable accounts, and who might be sending e-mails to

them? E-mail allows your child to communicate directly with virtually anyone in the world who has access to a computer— but what happens when you aren't there to supervise? (Your child can also easily access these secret accounts on your home computer, too. See Chapter 4 for filters and spyware you can use to prevent your child from accessing "forbidden" sites and for monitoring his or her activity on your home computers.)

Finally, there's the increasingly common phenomenon of cyber-bullying: using e-mail, Web sites, text messaging, and other electronic communication to harass young people in new ways. Bullying is nothing new—but at least the old kind was unlikely to follow you home. Now your child can wake up at 3 a.m. to find disturbing new messages, images, and links in his or her in-box. Or perhaps your own child is tempted to engage in cyber-bullying, possibly under pressure from teammates or friends.

How can you help guide your children through this challenging aspect of Cyberworld? As always, the first step is to get them talking. After all, your children may be spending two or three hours a day e-mailing. That's a huge part of their lives, and you need to know how it's working for them. So start asking them about their experiences in a genuinely curious, non-judgmental way. We recommend having these conversations as casually as possible, ideally while the two of you are doing something else together, like shopping for shoes or raking the lawn. Ask—and then listen. Although your children may act bored and annoyed with the conversation, underneath, they may be eager to talk. This is your opportunity to learn more about their world.

## Real-Time Questions to Spark Cyber-Talk

**1.** Has anybody ever sent you a sexually explicit e-mail?

**2.** What would you do if you got an e-mail from a kid who said some other kid likes you?

**3.** What would you do if someone you like sent you an e-mail asking to meet you in the bleachers after the game? *(See if your kid knows that the e-mail might not really be from the person he or she likes.)*

**4.** What would you do if an e-mail came with a Web site linked to it?

**5.** What would you do if a friend sent you a picture of another kid in school in the locker room, naked?

**6.** What if you got a mass e-mail saying that someone at school had a gun?

**7.** What if you got an e-mail saying Marc is gay or Julie is a lesbo?

**8.** What would you do if got a picture of yourself in an e-mail with your head attached to a different body? What would you do if you got a picture like that of one of your classmates?

**9.** What would you do if someone offered you diet medicine by e-mail? What if it was "natural, herbal" medicine?

**10.** What would you do if someone sent you an e-mail saying mean things about someone? What would you do if someone forwarded you an e-mail like that?

**11.** What would you do if you got an e-mail saying something mean or weird about a teacher?

**12.** What would you do if you got a notice saying that AOL will send thirty cents to every person that you send a certain ad to? Would you send the ad?

**13.** What if you got an e-mail saying you could have a hundred dollars free credit for online gambling?

**14.** What if you got an e-mail telling you how to make weapons? You might also invite your kids to play the what-if game. Have them make up a question, and then answer it together.

## Netiquette and Good Communication: Mastering the E-mail Basics

Now that the discussion has begun, you and your child can get back to basics: overcoming some of the most common obstacles to good electronic communication. If your child is old enough to push the send button, he or she is old enough to consider these concerns—especially if you're there to help.

# Four Simple Rules for Good EE-communication

### 1. Don't use all caps unless you want people to think you're shouting

Such a simple thing—and yet look how it disrupted the budding friendship between Tammy and Michelle! We must confess, when we get an all-caps message, we, too, have come to feel "shouted at," even though we know that the sender may simply have been using a program set on all caps, thought that all caps were easier to read, or perhaps didn't even notice that the cap lock was on. Your child needs to know that in basic Netiquette, caps will be read as shouting, so save them for good news, expressions of enthusiasm, and perhaps the occasional emphatic point.

By the way, all caps is also more difficult to read—it's harder to scan words visually when all the letters are the same height, which is why newspapers and magazines hardly ever use an all caps format, even in a headline. So if your child has any trouble reading, and particularly if he or she has a learning disorder that involves difficulties with reading, that's another reason to avoid the barrage of capital letters. If necessary, show your kids how to copy the e-mail they receive into a more readable format—that also goes for eliminating confusing colors and distracting graphics. Every e-mail program is different, but it's usually fairly easy to hit the forward button and then modify the text right there in the e-mail program or else to use the copy-and-paste function to copy the e-mail into a regular document to be edited.

### 2. Be aware that humor, irony, sarcasm, and other nuances may not come across by e-mail

Again, this is something that we adults struggle with, too. We read an e-mail and take it at face value, when the sender was only being playful. Or we hear a scolding sarcasm where the sender was asking a genuine question.

To help your child understand this point, try the exercise below. Share the following list of common expressions with your child. Together, see how many different ways you can say each of the phrases on the list—for example, with anger, accusation, humor, surprise, pleasure, confusion, sarcasm, or concern. Try to make each phrase convey at least three different meanings, just by your tone of voice, variations in emphasis, facial expressions, and gestures:

Oh, I'm sure!
What do you mean by that?
Where were you last night?
Have you ever heard of anything like that?
I don't get it.

Now ask your child to imagine what kinds of misunderstandings might arise if these or similar phrases show up in an e-mail, bearing in mind that many people don't use italics, capital letters, or punctuation when they're sending e-mail. Thus, for example, a reader and/or sender might confuse the following implications:

*What* do you mean by that?—"I'm frustrated, I don't know what you're telling me."

What *do* you mean by that?—"Just checking, did you want Option A or Option B?"

What do you *mean* by that?—"I'm hurt that you could even think such a thing."

What do you mean by *that?!!!!*—"Okay, now I'm really angry!"

Then, with your child, role play some different ways that miscommunication might happen. You can use some of the following e-mail conversations as examples:

**JOE:** WHERE WERE YOU LAST NIGHT?

**TINA:** Why are you so bent out of shape? I TOLD you I couldn't study with you!

**JOE:** CHILL, DUDE. JUST WONDERED WHERE U WERE.


**MALCOLM:** What do you think of that new teacher.

**PAT:** Oh, she's cool.

**MALCOLM:** Really? I think she's LAME.

**PAT:** Me, too. And you don't have to yell at me!

**MALCOLM:** I wasn't yelling! And you said she was COOL!

**PAT:** I was being sarcastic.

**J O N I :** I just don't get why anyone still likes Spiderman. Guess I must be the dumbest person in the world.

**L E E :** No, you're not. You're really smart.

**J O N I :** I know I'm smart! I was making a joke. Do you think I'm dumb?

As you probably know from your own experience, even the most articulate speaker or the most literate writer can get into trouble by confusing e-mail with actual conversation. Learning-disabled children—especially those with Asperger's and other types of autism—may have special difficulties separating literal meanings from colloquial expressions, hyperbole, or sarcastic comments. (For more about how to help your learning-disabled child with e-mail, see Chapter 6.) Help your children sort out these issues in both the e-mails they receive and the ones they send.

### 3. Be careful of responding to an e-mail with inappropriate urgency, anger, or panic

We've all done it. That little "you've got mail" logo flashes or we hear a beep or we push the send/receive button and watch the e-mails roll in. And then we can't wait to answer them. All that small type isn't always so easy to read, but hey, wait a minute, why is our colleague so high-handedly dismissing our agenda for next week's meeting? We'll show *him!* There—a quick e-mail to express our annoyance, and we're on to the next. Oops, our boss wants to know why we weren't at the sales conference on Monday. Of course, it's 10 p.m., and he's probably gone home for the day, but we can't live with the idea that he thinks so badly of us—reading the e-mail makes us feel as though he's right there, accusing us—and so we dash off a quick excuse that turns into a three-paragraph apology. We can't rest until it's sent, then we feel as though the problem has been solved. Now, what's this? Oh, our best friend wants to have lunch on Thursday—great idea! *Yes!* we reply, without even checking our date book. Whew! E-mail done for the night, we head off to bed.

The next day, we read all the e-mails far more slowly, and our stomach starts to sink. That colleague wasn't being dismissive, we realize—he was just asking a few thoughtful questions. Now we've probably insulted him. Our boss wasn't upset, just making sure we were okay—in fact, he sent that e-mail to everyone who wasn't at the meeting. Now that three-paragraph response seems like overcompensating—and to make matters worse, our humble plea for forgiveness went to all the other absentees as well. How embarrassing! Hey, wait a minute, isn't there another sales conference scheduled for this Thursday? Now we'll have to cancel lunch with our friend—that's the third time this month we've made that mistake.

Your child may not be operating at such a frantic pace, but this is the type of quick, panicky, or angry response that e-mail often inspires: we respond to e-mail as though we've been spoken to and blurt out a hasty reply that we later regret. Help keep your child from making these kinds of mistakes: encourage him or her to leave lots of time between reading an e-mail and replying to it, especially an e-mail that generates a lot of emotion. If possible, your child should avoid expressing or even responding to anger via e-mail; most emotional issues are best dealt with in person. Model some "time-buying" e-mails for your child and talk about when they might come in handy:

> I hear you, and I'm sorry you're upset. Let's talk more when we
> see each other.
> Got your e-mail. Need to think. Talk later?
> Great invitation! Not sure about my schedule—I'll tell you tomorrow.
> I'm not totally sure what you're saying. Can we talk in person?

**TIP** Set up your e-mail program so that you have to push the send button twice—first to get a completed letter into the outbox; then to get it *out* of the outbox and into cyberspace. The extra step gives your child two chances to think about whether the letter is really ready to go. Just go to the Tools section in your e-mail program, then to Options, then to Mail, and deselect the box that says "send message immediately." You can also encourage an impulsive child to compose e-mail in the draft of their e-mail folder or offline; leave it for a few minutes or even overnight before sending it on.

You might also explain to your child that hasty responses can sometimes distort our thinking, causing us to commit prematurely to incorrect interpretations. For example, suppose Petey gets the following e-mail from his friend Dave:

> Hey, Petey, don't worry about the game—even GOOD players
> screw up like that sometimes!

Reading this, Petey feels hurt, angry, and betrayed. Dave is supposed to be his friend—yet he's mocking Petey in the cruelest possible way, pointing out that Petey isn't really a very good player and reminding him that he screwed up. So Petey dashes off a quick reply:

> HOW WOULD YOU KNOW WHAT A GOOD PLAYER IS? YOU HAVEN'T HAD A HIT ALL SEASON!!!!

He even uses all caps, so Dave will see how angry he is.

Then, later that night, Petey rereads Dave's e-mail. Now he starts to hear it the way Dave might have said it, in Dave's teasing drawl. What if Dave was actually trying to be nice? Dave would never come right out and *say* that Petey was a good player—that would be way too sentimental. Teasing is Dave's way of communicating support: "Hey, Petey, don't worry— you're a good player, and, like all good players, you screwed up. No big deal." So maybe, instead of acting like a jerk, Dave was actually being a good friend.

If Petey had waited to respond to the e-mail, he might have had time to come around to this second opinion. Then he could feel grateful to Dave, or, if he still didn't understand what Dave meant, try to find out more. He might also decide to just let the whole thing go. But once he's responded quickly, with an angry e-mail, he's committed to his initial interpretation. He's given himself a stake in staying angry until Dave apologizes—while Dave, who actually *has* been insulted by Petey, may now see himself as the victim of an unprovoked attack. Suddenly, there's a fight where there didn't need to be one—a fight that could easily have been avoided if the whole exchange had happened in person and the boys had worked it out on the spot.

See if you and your child can think of other examples of how a hasty reply might lock you into a problematic response, whereas giving yourselves a cooling-off period might open up the space to see things differently. Help your child understand the virtues of staying flexible, calm, and open-minded.

## 4. Remember that e-mail is really easy to pass on, and anything you write may come back to haunt you

Ah, e-mail! It *seems* so private—but it can become public at a moment's notice. Make this idea more real to your child by showing him or her some e-mails like the following:

> I hate Jared. He's just lame!
>
> Last night, I kissed Vince for the first time. It was awful! His tongue was like a big, wet fish!
>
> You'll never believe what Maria told me yesterday! It was this thing about her mother—it's SO sad, I felt like crying when she told me! Her mother used to drink too much and now she has to go to meetings every week so she won't drink anymore. Isn't that terrible?

None of these e-mails is inappropriate as part of a private conversation. In fact, it's healthy for kids to share their feelings about friends, sex, and parents. But ask your child to imagine any of the following scenarios:

1. The recipient forwards these e-mails to Jared, Vince, Maria ("I think you should know what your so-called friend is saying about you").
2. The recipient sends the e-mails to some of the other kids at school ("Poor Maria—we all need to be extra nice to her—here, you can read what Lauren wrote me about it").

3. The recipient sends these e-mails to her *other* best friend, swearing her to secrecy—and then that best friend sends them to *her* other best friend, swearing *her* to secrecy—and then . . . ?
4. The recipient's parents check out the e-mail.
5. Your child and the recipient have a fight and stop being friends.

Help your child distinguish between two issues: the trustworthiness of the recipient and the ease with which e-mails can get passed around. Gossip is bad enough—"Lauren told me this thing about Maria's mother"—but with e-mail, the cold, hard evidence is right there. One push of a button, and potentially everyone in your school can read what you wrote.

You might also share with your child stories of how e-mails you sent came back to haunt you, or ask your child to give you examples of how gossip—by either voice or e-mail—has hurt other kids at school. Gossip, bonding, and loyalty are hot topics for children, especially girls, who tend to form intense friendships—and, often, to have intense fights. As you help your child think about how she or he wants to handle these issues, remember to take e-mail into account.

# 133T 5|*34(|<: |*16-1@+1|\|4 +|-|3 lz

## [Translation: Leet Speak: Pig-Latin for the Eyes]

Back in the 1980s—when the Internet was still in its *very* early days—hackers who didn't want their Web sites, newsgroups, and other online activities to be picked up in a keyword search began using the clever device of substituting some numbers for the letters they sort of resembled. In this primitive code, 4 became A, 3 became E, and so on, so that the word "hacker," for example, would have been spelled "h4ck3r." At that point, only a few advanced computer jocks knew this special jargon and even they used it only rarely.

Then, in 1994, id Software added Internet connectivity to the popular PC games Doom and Doom 2. Suddenly, computer gamers were battling each other online, trash talking their opponents by e-mail and bragging about their "elite" status. From the simple boast, "1 4m 3133t! ("I am elite") came, eventually, the notion of "133t speak," or "leet speak," the language of the computer elite. Although for a while leet speak seemed on the verge of becoming a dead language, the popular Web comic *Megatokyo* made it popular again, leading to a number of innovations that made the language more complicated and even harder to read. Now you have a choice: light 133t, medium 1337, hard |_337, or ultra |_33-|-.

Leet speak also includes a wide variety of slang words, such as jO ("Yo!"), wOOt ("Woot!" a version of "Yay!"), or |4m3r ("lamer," someone who is, well, lame). So even if parents can crack the "leet" alphabet, they may still find themselves defeated by the vocabulary. Using leet speak may seem time-consuming, but once you've mastered the lighter forms, it actually goes very quickly, though hard and ultra leet speak can indeed be challenging. Still, for kids who want to keep their messages secret, the extra effort may seem worth it.

Do you have to go out and master a whole new language? Happily, the answer is *no*. Even if your kids are fluent in leet speak, we don't recommend you trying to keep up—by the time you learn the lingo, you can be sure it will have changed. Instead, go to http://www.brenz .net/1337Maker.asp, a handy little Web site that actually translates text into and out of leet speak. You can use it to decipher your kids' e-mails if you're really concerned about what they're saying, or, for extra parent points, translate something *into* leet speak and then e-mail it to your children. If they don't know about the Web site, they may actually think you know leet speak—and even if they do know about the site, they'll realize that you can crack their code anytime you want. In fact, kids themselves are often taking the easy way out: going straight to the translator to encode and decode their messages rather than learning leet speak themselves.

Leet speak isn't the only type of cyber-code your child may be using. Acronyms—abbreviations using the initial letter of every word in a phrase—are also very popular, including LOL for "laugh out loud," TMI for "too much information," and BTW for "by the way." Kids may also use emoticons, a sequence of ordinary printable characters intended to represent a human facial expression and convey an emotion, such as ☺ to represent a smile or ;) to indicate a wink (turn the image on its side and it sort of looks like a face with one eye closed). We've listed several common acronyms and emoticons in the Glossary, and you can also translate acronyms at www.teenangels.org—just look for the acronym translator at the bottom of the Web page. Many children use some combination of all three codes, or invent their own.

Of course, in theory, it's fine for kids to have a special language of their own—remember how cool it was when you discovered pig latin? Ow-nay ee-way an-cay ell-tay eat-nay ecrets-say! On the other hand, if you're concerned about what your kids are up to, you need to be able to check them out. We don't want to be alarmist, but we would like to share with you a couple of samples of actual kid-written messages that parents have had translated on the leet speak Web site. Though these messages appeared in one of the lighter forms, we've translated them into ultra leet, just so you can see how the more difficult code works:

1 4m r34||y worr13d 4bou7 J3nny. 5h3 7h1nk5 5h3 m16h7 b3 pr36n4n7 bu7 15 4fr41d 70 73|| h3r p4r3n75 b3c4u53 7h3y wou|d prob4b|y 53nd h3r 4w4y. 5h3 541d 5h3 700k b1r7h con7ro| p1||5 3v3ry 71m3 5h3 h4d 53x bu7 7h3y mu57 no7 h4v3 work3d. 5h3 found ou7 y3573rd4y 7h47 on3 6uy 5h3 w45 w17h m16h7 h4v3 41d5. 1 c4n'7 b3|13v3 5h3 w45 50 57up1d.

OR

1 4|V| |234||`/ \X/o|2|213[) 4|}o|_|7 J3|\|||\`/. 5|-|3 7|-|1|\||<5 5|-|3 |V|16|-|7 |}3 |*|236|\|4|\|7 |}|_|7 15 4|=|241[) 70 73|| |-|3|2 |*4|23|\|75 |}3(4|_|53 7|-|3`/\X/o|_||[) |*|20|}4|}`/ 53|\|[) |-|3|2 4\X/4`/. 5|-|3 541[) 5|-|3 700|< |}1|27|-| (0|\|7|20| |*1||5 3V3|2`/ 71|V|3 5|-|3 |-|4[) 53>< |}|_|7 7|-|3`/ |V||_|57 |\|07 |-|4V3 \X/o|2|<3[). 5|-|3 |=o|_||\|[) 0|_|7 `/3573|2[)4`/ 7|-|47 0|\|3 6|_|`/ 5|-|3 \X/45 \X/17|-| |V|16|-|7 |-|4V3 41[)5. 1 (4|\|`7 |}3|13V3 5|-|3 \X/45 50 57|_||*1[).

**Translation:** i am really worried about Jenny. she thinks she might be pregnant but is afraid to tell her parents because they would probably send her away. she said she took birth control pills every time she had sex but they must not have worked. she found out yesterday that one guy she was with might have aids. i can't believe she was so stupid.

1 4m 50 51ck of 7h47 5|u7! 5h3 h45 b33n 5cr3w1n6 4round w17h 3v3ryon3'5 boyfr13nd 4nd 1 7h1nk w3 5hou|d 734ch h3r 4 |3550n. |37'5 637 m|k3 70 45k h3r 70 m337 h|m und3r 7h3 b|34ch3r5 4f73r 7h3 64m3 4nd 7h3n 5c4r3 7h3 5h17 ou7 ofh3r.

OR

i a|V| so si(|< o|= t|-|at s1|_|t! s|-|e |-|as |}ee|\| s(|2e\X/i|\|g a|2o|_||\|[) \X/it|-| eVe|2|}o[)`/'s |}o`/|=|2ie|\|[) a|\|[) i t|-|i|\||< \X/e s|-|o|_|1[) tea(|-| |-|e|2 a 1esso|\|. let's get |V|i|<e to as|< |-|e|2 to |V|eet |-|i|V| |_||\|[)e|2 t|-|e |}1ea(|-|e|2s a|=te|2 t|-|e ga|V|e a|\|[) t|-|e|\| s(a|2e t|-|e s|-|it o|_|t o|= |-|e|2.

**Translation:** i am so sick of that slut! she has been screwing around with everyone's boyfriend and i think we should teach her a lesson. let's get mike to ask her to meet him under the bleachers after the game and then scare the shit out of her.

If your kids are using leet speak to talk soccer strategy or complain about their new teacher, let them have their secrets. But if you've got any reason to be concerned, now you know you can crack their code.

## E-mail Fraud

Fraudulent e-mail solicitations for money and other types of help are becoming increasingly common. Recently Sue, for example, got an e-mail purporting to be from an Iraqi official who wanted her help in moving large sums of money out of his home country. Sue wasn't fooled—she even noticed that the "Iraqi" e-mail had an Italian address!—but lots of adults have fallen for these phony pleas, and a child might be even more gullible. Let your children know that they should never reply to e-mails from people they don't know, and they should never provide any personal information about your family, including such seemingly harmless and public information as addresses, parents' first names, places of employment, and kids' schools, let alone credit card numbers, bank accounts, or even bank names. If they get an e-mail that asks for help, financial information, or any personal information, they should let you know. Even replying with a "no way!" might help strangers confirm that they have a live e-mail address, perhaps setting you up for other attempts at identity theft or fraud.

## Secret E-mail Accounts: Do You Know What Your Kid Is Doing Online?

As we suggested in the Introduction, you should give your kids the message that Internet access is a privilege, not a right, and let them know that you'll be looking over their shoulder, even as you respect their privacy. All well and good for the home computer and the e-mail account you know about—but what about the free Yahoo!, Hotmail, or other online account that your child has set up without your knowledge? What about the time he or she spends at the cyber-café downtown or even at the public library, sending and receiving e-mails that you'll never know about?

Again, a little perspective is in order. Kids are going to resist the limits we set—that's their developmental task, and sometimes part of the fun for them is just to see how far they can push boundaries. They may be e-mailing the same admiring comments about *Spiderman 3* on their secret accounts as on their home computers—the thrill is just in *knowing* that you don't know. And even before the Internet, any child with a quarter and a phone number could contact someone without your knowledge, as long as they had access to a pay phone.

On the other hand, even the best kids don't always have the best judgment. And unlike the old-fashioned pay phone, the Internet gives your kids a vastly expanded opportunity to meet strangers, including adult strangers pretending to be children. To be honest, we're less worried about children being snatched by predators—that *is* a danger, of course, but statistically a minor one—and more worried about kids getting into situations that make them uncomfortable or present them with information they're not ready for.

For example, the Web site ICQ ("I seek you") (www.ICQ .com) is known for its sexually explicit chat rooms, to the point where most public libraries restrict access to it on their computers. But when Barb, pretending she was a kid, set up her own free Yahoo! account and gave out that address to adult guys she "met" on ICQ, she discovered she could send and receive e-mails to them at the library on her Yahoo! account. If a real thirteen-year-old girl had done what Barb did, she might have felt overwhelmed, disturbed, or frightened at the vast numbers of adult men suddenly sending her sexually explicit messages. And then, knowing how angry her parents would be about the secret address, she might have felt anxious about going to them for help.

It can be difficult for a parent to grasp just how disturbing these messages may be for a teenage girl or boy, particularly one who hasn't yet had any sexual experience. Explicit messages—especially if they're accompanied by photos—may push the child to visualize acts that he or she isn't really ready to think about. Children may become sexualized too early, seeing themselves as sexual beings before they have the feelings and experience to handle a physical relationship.

Young people may also take such messages far more personally than an adult might. Even experienced adults are often disturbed by sexually explicit comments, but most adults can put such unwelcome overtures into perspective. "Oh, that guy will come on to anyone he thinks might be interested," a woman might tell herself. "I won't take it personally—I'll just avoid him!" Or, "That man is a sick person—what kind of man talks to a woman like that?" Adults understand that they're not necessarily responsible when someone makes an inappropriate remark or treats them in a disturbing way.

But a teenager, who tends to see the whole world in terms of her- or himself, might take the situation more personally. He or she might think, "That person made those remarks *to me.* What did I do to encourage them? What about me seems so sexually available? I must be a very dirty person to have attracted such a dirty invitation." Particularly if the teenager *did* solicit the attention—but didn't expect it to be so sexually explicit—he or she may feel guilty, anxious, or ashamed, believing that the sexual communication reveals something significant about who he or she "really" is. Such feelings might make it even more difficult for a teenager to ask his or her parents for help.

Frankly, we don't think you can keep your kids from getting a secret e-mail account if they want one—we don't think you should even try. Like drugs, alcohol, and other contraband, it's out there, and if your kid wants it enough, he or she will find a way to get it. Your line of defense is not at the point of contact, but in a deeper, more intimate place: in the values and judgment you've instilled in your child and in his or her sense of safety in coming to you when things get tough. Your children should be aware that you know about secret e-mail accounts and that you don't approve of them—and then you've got to rely on their willingness to "just say no."

On the other hand, we do advise you to keep the lines of communication open. Just as you'd talk to your children about drugs, alcohol, and teenage sex, so should you talk to them about illicit online activities. For example:

> I know there are some kids who get extra e-mail accounts, ones their parents don't know about. My concern is that everything is so anonymous online—you really

don't always know whom you're writing to. I hope if anything ever happens that upsets you or causes you concern, that you would come to me. I'm less concerned with punishing you than with making sure you don't get into something that you can't handle.

Remember: kids are often very conflicted about how much independence they really want. They might run out and get a secret account, especially if their friends are doing it, but they may also feel enormously relieved to know that they really aren't alone in handling whatever comes up. Letting them know that *you* know what goes on, and maybe even hinting that you could check up on them if you wanted to, might actually make them feel safer, even if their public position is to roll their eyes, groan, and protest.

---

### If Your Child Feels Anxious About E-mail

If your child is in the midst of an ee-fight or is receiving disturbing e-mails from classmates, help him or her to set some boundaries. Encourage your child to . . .

• . . . **check e-mails only when he or she feels alert and ready to respond.** Reading e-mail when you're tired or stressed can exacerbate angry, anxious, or panicky responses. Save e-mail for when you're feeling well-rested and energetic.

• . . . **scan e-mail quickly and open it selectively.** Although e-mail often lends itself to a kind of compulsive response, you really *don't* have to open all your e-mail all the time. Suggest that your child pick and choose which e-mails he or she is going to read, saving the potentially disturbing ones for a better time.

- **... mobilize support before opening a disturbing e-mail.** Just because e-mail is usually a solitary undertaking doesn't mean your kid has to face his inbox alone. Suggest that he or she have you, another loved one, or a friend standing by—either in person or available at a moment's notice by phone. Having another person hear the disturbing words can be a great way to gain perspective, not to mention advice and comfort!

- **... commit before opening a disturbing e-mail to not answering it.** Suggest that your kids promise themselves to "sleep on it" or at least to walk around the block. Answering an upsetting e-mail in haste is probably the worst ee-mistake you can make: it's very hard to avoid and impossible to undo. Preparing for a more measured response is your child's best defense.

- **... get off the Internet before replying to a disturbing message.** Your kids can download the messages, sure, but then they should get offline so they can't just impulsively respond. This is an especially important suggestion if your child has problems with impulse control. For extra distance, compose answers outside the e-mail program and paste them into e-mails later.

## Cyber-Bullying: When the Bullies Follow Your Kid Home

One of the most disturbing uses of e-mail we know is the growing phenomenon of cyber-bullying. Barb recently worked with a teenage girl—let's call her Carly—whose classmates decided to victimize her. The popular kids organized a little electronic gang who bombarded Carly with TM and e-mail messages: *You're so fat, you're such a bitch, you're such a slut,* and so forth. They started a rumor that she was gay and circulated phony pictures of her and her "lesbian girlfriend." They used a wide range of cell-phone numbers and e-mail addresses, so Carly didn't know who was sending the messages, which gave her the sense of being surrounded by enemies. They even created a slanderous Web site, just to taunt her.

The bullying went on for almost eight weeks before Carly's parents found out. She was a quiet child anyway, so when she became even quieter, her parents didn't flag it as a problem. Only when she started getting stomachaches and insisting that she didn't want to go to school did they catch on. Carly's mother went to the school to complain, but school officials insisted that they had no responsibility for what students did with their own computers and cell phones.

Luckily, Carly's mother didn't give up. She insisted that the school call a parent-teacher meeting to spotlight this kind of cyber-bullying. She and her husband also contacted the parents of the popular girl whom their daughter believed was behind the campaign. The bully's parents denied vehemently that their darling daughter could have behaved in such a fashion. Almost instantly, though, the e-mails stopped.

Bullying is a tough problem—but it can be solved. If you're persistent, determined, and above all, calm, you can turn the situation around, while offering your child the support he or she needs to cope with a truly devastating situation. Don't worry, we'll talk you through it, step by step.

## Coping with Cyber-Bullying: A Step-by-Step Plan

Is your child a victim of cyber-bullying? Here's one crucial piece of advice: first, last, and always, *stay calm*. It can be tremendously upsetting to see your child suffer—and bullying is one of the most painful and undermining situations that we know of. But your child needs you to be the one who's calm, clear, and firmly rooted in reality. Support your child and let her know you're angry or that you're feeling his pain, but try not to go on a rampage or sink into your own version of their despair. As you deal with the school officials and the people who you believe are the bullies' parents, you'll want to act from a calm and grounded sense of strength—not from the rage, hurt, and anguish you may be feeling.

### Step 1: Identify the Problem

Be aware that your child may not feel comfortable telling you about the bullying. He may feel deeply ashamed of the teasing, embarrassed that he didn't know how to handle it himself, or worried that you won't take it seriously. She may also fear that you *will* take the problem seriously and, by interfering, may make it worse.

So how do you know whether your child is being bullied? We know this sounds way too simple, but you should probably just come right out and ask, either directly or more subtly:

→ I've been hearing lots of stories about kids getting cyber-bullied—is that something that goes on at your school?

→ My friend at work has a kid who's being cyber-bullied—she's getting all these creepy e-mails and some of them even have pictures. My friend wants to know how to help her kid—what advice should I give her?

→ I saw a TV special on cyber-bullying, and it got me to wondering: Has anyone been hassling you that way? I promise not to take any action until we've talked it through, but I need to know if anything like that has been going on.

Don't just bring up this topic once—maybe the first time you mention it, your child *isn't* being bullied and doesn't think too much about it. But if you casually raise the topic every three or four months, you have a chance to keep your antennae up. Listen for the tension in your child's voice or notice that a kid who once was happy to chat about this subject is now freezing up and refusing to talk. We hope you never *do* have cause for concern, but by raising the topic, you're keeping the door open and, at the very least, you're learning a lot about the social dynamics at your kid's school. You're also engaged in a kind of preventative medicine: knowing that you know about this issue, and seeing how calm and supportive you can be, your child will be far more ready to come to you at the first sign of trouble, trusting that you will neither dismiss the issue nor fly off the handle.

Of course, if you notice any of the warning signs we've listed in the Introduction, you should be especially persistent about unearthing any possible problems. Personality or behavior changes in your child are important to track, along with any differences in how your child relates to e-mail or the computer. Pay attention to whether your child seems anxious, fearful, or uncomfortable before, after, or during e-mail sessions—and if he or she does, step up your efforts to find out what's going on.

## Step 2: Be Aware That It Can Get Worse

Often both kids and parents take a laissez-faire attitude toward bullying: "There's nothing we can do, but if we ignore it, I'm sure it will go away." Maybe—but maybe not. Bullies who get no response frequently keep escalating their attacks until they do. Or they like the response they do get and look for new ways to up the ante. Cyber-bullying is even more insidious than regular bullying, because it partakes of that "no-consquence" Internet culture of anonymity. Did you know that there was actually once a Web site called www.rumors.com where kids could go to post rumors about their classmates? It's since been shut down, but there are certainly similar ones out there.

Unfortunately, the hurt your child feels from being a cyber-target may not seem quite real to the bullies, who never have to see his face or hear her voice. Or they may actually escalate their bullying, hoping to provoke a response that they *can* see. So if your child's bullying has gone on longer than a few days, you may want to take action.

## Step 3: Get All the Information

Knowledge is power—and never more so than when you are dealing with a bully. Encourage your child to tell you specifically about every incident that happened, in all its detail. These may be painful experiences for your child to relive, but it may also be therapeutic for him or her to share these stories.

Work with your child to prepare as detailed a log as possible of the bullying events. Arrange them in chronological order with supporting detail. Supplement them where you can with physical evidence: printouts of e-mails, tapes from voicemail, detailed phone bills that show the times when text messages arrived. Your goal isn't to put together a court case—that's often not an option—but to show school officials and the bullies' parents the extent and nature of the harassment. For example:

→ 8 p.m., October 6: e-mail calling Rena a "lesbo," copy attached.

→ midnight, October 7: TM arrived on her phone with a fake picture of Rena and her "girlfriend," naked together.

→ 3 a.m., October 10: 50 identical e-mails arrive from unidentified Web sites, with comments like, "You're a bitch," "You're so fat and ugly," "You're a slut." (See attached.)

By the way, if that log seems a bit exaggerated to you, think again. This is a pretty accurate picture of the kind of bullying that goes on all across America, and we'd be willing to bet that sometime in the last five years, at least one similar incident has happened at your child's school. A recent study found that one in six pre-teenagers and one in three teenagers have been targeted by cyber-bullying—so if your child hasn't been victimized in this way, he or she probably knows someone who has. Both of us have been involved in cases where cyber-bullying drove kids to seek new school placements or sent them to the hospital with nervous exhaustion. Depression and anxiety are common for the victims of cyber-bullying as well. Kids can be cruel, and cyber-cruelty, with its anonymous, invasive, and somehow intimate quality, can be very painful indeed.

## Step 4: Work with Your Child to Decide What to Do

Again, when your child is telling you about being bullied, try to listen calmly. It's crucial to express support for your child's feelings, and certainly it's fine to let your kid know that you're angry, hurt, or outraged, too. But don't let your feelings swamp your child's responses. Remember, this is your child's problem, not yours. Help your child to feel that he or she is in charge of solving this problem, and that it's your child's feelings, not yours, that matter most. Be available and supportive—but as far as possible, let your child take the lead in deciding what to do. This can actually be a good opportunity to let your child practice decision-making, which after all is a key part of growing up.

Of course, there may come a point where you simply have to take charge. Your child may insist that you do nothing, but if your kid is being harassed in the ways we've described, doing nothing is simply not an option. You're the parent; it's your call. You can at least begin the process by letting your child tell you what she thinks and offering to formulate a plan together. Review the options with your child: talking directly to the bullies; having your child report the incident to school authorities; having you speak to the parents or to the school. Figure out a step-by-step approach: if this doesn't work, then we'll do that; if that doesn't work, we'll go on to Plan C. Determine how you'll know whether a step worked or not and decide how long you'll give each step before moving on to the next one. Being bullied is a profoundly disempowering experience, so help your child regain a sense of empowerment by figuring out a fight-back strategy *with* him, not *for* him.

Even if at some point you overrule your child's wishes—she

wants you to do nothing; you insist on acting—remember that your child is still the main person affected by what's happening, so let her feelings hold center stage. If you explode in rage or dissolve in tears, your child may feel responsible for making things harder for *you*. He may also have a harder time trusting that you'll act in a productive, helpful way. More likely than not, your child's greatest fear is that punishing the bullies will make things even worse, so you need to model calm, not revenge, retaliation, or a punitive attitude.

## Step 5: Approach the Bullies' Parents

This is a tricky one. Often, the parents of bullies are in total denial about what their children are doing. In one recent case of Barb's, the mother of a cheerleader, herself a former cheerleader, was even acting as a kind of ringleader, getting the girls on the squad to gang up against the weakest member. Even parents who don't go that far may not realize how serious bullying can be and may not want to face the fact that their children are responsible for it.

So put yourself in their place—we know you're steaming, but take a deep breath—and think about how you'd want and need to hear the unpleasant news that *your* child was behaving so badly. As always, in conflict-ridden situations, try to frame it in terms of yourself, not the other person, and use facts, not feelings. Here are two possible ways of raising the issue: Which do you think will get better results?

> My daughter Rena has been having a terrible time at school lately—and it's all your daughter's fault! She's been bullying my child, and it's got to stop! We get e-mails

at all hours of the day and night, horrible pictures taken by those new cell phones, and now they've even started a blog called DumponRena.com. What kind of parents would *raise* a child like that?

My daughter Rena has been having some trouble lately, and I thought you ought to know about it. She's been getting some disturbing e-mails and doctored photos from various anonymous e-mail addresses, and now it seems there's a blog that's all about her. I'm not saying your daughter was involved—I haven't yet started the process of tracing those anonymous e-mail accounts, so I don't yet know who's behind this. But I'm worried for your daughter if she's in with the crowd that's doing this, and I wanted you to hear about it from me before any lawyers or police or school officials got involved. I don't want your daughter's name to be smudged—but once this all becomes public, I won't have control over the process. So I'm coming to you, the way I'd want you to come to me.

As you can see, the second option is by far the more effective. Parents of possible bullies are far more likely to say, "Tell me more," because you've offered them a way to save face *and* to protect their son or daughter. They may keep insisting that their kids are innocent—and your job, hard as it may be, is to reply calmly that you're not accusing anyone, you just wanted them to know.

Meanwhile, you've made it clear that anonymous e-mails and blogs can be traced, and this is true even if the bullying was organized from a cyber-café or a library. In pretty much every case, records can link the bullies to cyber-harassment, just as phone logs can identify TMers—and the bully's parents are now on notice that you'll perform these traces if you think it's necessary.

Beyond the purely legal issues, though, you may have spurred these parents to find out more and even to discipline their child, whether from fear of consequences, a genuine moral concern, or both. They may never admit to you or your child what has really happened, but that doesn't mean they haven't taken action.

---

### Bullying: It's (Mostly) Against the Law

Many states have anti-bullying laws, and some of those laws include language that prohibits cyber-bullying. If you're lucky enough to live in one of those states, you can invoke these laws. For more information, go to the very useful Web site www.bullypolice.org. There you can find out if your state has a law against bullying and even read what it says. You can also find resources on what to do if your child is being bullied, as well as some suggestions on how to mobilize your school and community to fight back against bullying.

Whether or not your state has an anti-bullying law, though, your best bet is to try to work through your school. Courts have a hard time distinguishing between "bullying" and "free speech," and they're often reluctant to curtail a student's right to set up a Web site or send an e-mail. We've worked with parents of cyber-bully targets who wanted to sue the bullies' parents, but that's hard, too: to win a suit, you need to establish that the parents knew about their child's bullying or propensity to bully—and who's going to testify to that?

So our best advice is to go through your school. First, contact the abuse department of your phone company (if your child is getting

TMs) or your Internet service provider (ISP) (if your child is getting e-mails), and they'll trace the source of the cyber-bullying. Then let the bullies' parents know that you want the bullying to stop or else you'll have no choice but to provide those records to your school principal.

Ideally, your school has an anti-bullying policy that applies to students whether they're on- or off-campus. If your school has no anti-bullying policy, you might work with the PTA or with a group of concerned parents to establish one—in fact, we urge you to work for such a policy even if your child isn't currently being bullied. With or without a school policy, though, bullies' parents will probably be reluctant to have you share evidence of their child's actions with school officials.

## Step 6: Involve the School

This is a tricky area, because many school officials will insist that they're helpless when it comes to preventing a bully's attack. Without hard evidence, they point out, they can't expel or even mildly punish a suspected bully, and there's often a conspiracy of silence among students who are afraid of facing the bully's wrath. Or, as at Carly's school, school officials might protest that they can't control what students do with their own phones and computers.

With all due respect, we don't buy it. Most schools know quite well that bullying takes place, and often the teachers and administrators know exactly who's responsible for it. They may not have evidence that would stand up in court, but they do have ways to make the bullying stop, which is all you really care about.

These days, most schools have anti-bullying programs, although these may be dormant or in name only. The most effective programs proclaim zero tolerance for bullies: two kids following your child in the hall one day shouting insults is just as unacceptable as a three-month schoolwide cyber-campaign. That's just as it should be—bullying hurts at any level, and schools need to take action as soon as it occurs.

But, sadly, they often don't—and that's where you come in. Even if the school can't or won't act, you can still enlist the school community on your child's behalf. That's why Barb advised Carly's mother to go to her PTA meeting and address the parents about bullying. Carly's mom explained that her child was being cyber-bullied and that she was going to involve the police if it didn't stop. She also made it clear that there were plenty of ways to trace cyber-bullying. No parents came forward, and no school administrator took official action. But somehow, the bullying stopped.

We feel strongly that bullying is a community problem, not a personal one. Even if your child isn't being harassed, or if the harassment has stopped, there's still the next generation of kids to think about. See what you can do to help your community show zero tolerance for bullying. At the very least, you can ask your child's school to be more proactive. Schools are always sending home newsletters and other messages to parents, so suggest that your school publish a regular column about bullying: how it's handled at the school, helpful Web sites and handouts, information on how parents can help, and other anti-bullying messages. At least have them send something home at the beginning and middle of the school year.

## If Your Child Is Bullying Someone Else . . .

What if your child is doing the bullying? That's a tough one, but start by facing the situation with compassion and, once again, calm. Your first step is to try to determine exactly what your child has done. Was he the ringleader or did he get roped in by a more powerful classmate? Was she bullying by herself or as part of a clique? Encourage your child to open up as far as possible so that you can understand what actually happened.

Then, try to understand why your child was involved in this hurtful action. Kids who bully usually do it out of a sense of inadequacy and a need for power and control somewhere in their lives. They also get caught up in social structures whose message is "bully or be bullied." If your child was the ringleader, he may have trouble resolving conflicts or solving problems and may feel that bullying another child is his only way to assert his sense of self. If your child got caught up in the excitement, she might need help developing empathy and impulse control. And if your child felt he had no choice—that anyone who didn't go along with the bullying would end up as the next target—you may need to work together on strategies for staying true to your values and enlisting help in difficult situations.

Another possibility is that this style of communication has been modeled for your child by a caregiver or someone else who is important in that child's life. We take the stand that it's never too late to try to correct these behaviors. But it may take a real lifestyle change or even therapy to really effect results.

In all these cases, help your children achieve empathy by modeling compassion and kindness for them. When you are angry, disappointed, or disapproving, let them know in appropriate ways so that they will know how to express their own feelings in appropriate ways. Bullies, like their victims, often have self-esteem problems, so praise your child as often as you can—sincerely, briefly, and specifically—and spend as much quality time together as possible. Letting your children know how valuable and important they are to you will go a long way toward turning things around.

For more specific advice on this issue, we recommend *Odd Girl Out*, by Rachel Simmons, and *Queen Bees and Wannabes: Helping Your Daughter Survive Cliques, Gossip, Boyfriends, and Other Realities of Adolescence*, by Rosalind Wiseman, excellent books about bullying among girls. For more on boys' bullying, check out *Real Boys' Voices* (Penguin, 5th ed., 2001), by William S. Pollack PhD, with Todd Shuster, and *Bullying from Both Sides: Strategic Interventions for Working with Bullies and Victims*, by Walter B. Roberts, Jr. (Sage, 2005). *Cliques*, by Charlene C. Gianetti and Margaret Sagarese, is especially good for parents of middle-school boys and girls. There are also several recent movies on this issue, including *Hoot*, *How to Eat Fried Worms*, and *The Ant Bully*. Watch one of these movies with your kids, especially if you suspect your child is a bully, is being bullied, or may be condoning bullying in his or her school.

## Coming to Terms with E-mail

Keep that conversation going! Help your child process his or her e-mail experience with such conversation starters as the following:

• I heard once about some kids who sent embarrassing pictures around by e-mail. That sounded like a hard thing to deal with. What would you do if you knew something like that was going on?

• You know what I hate? I hate sending e-mails when I'm angry. I'm always upset afterward, when I realize I said stuff I didn't mean—but then it's too late to take it back. Has that ever happened to you?

• The other day, I got an e-mail from my friend Terry, and it really upset me. It was hard reading what she wrote and not being able to talk to her, but I didn't read it until it was too late to call her. Has that ever happened to you? How do you handle it?

• What if you got an e-mail and you weren't sure who it was from. What would you do then?

• My friend Sandy told me that her son got an e-mail that looked like it was from a girl he knew. He thought this girl really liked him, but it was really just these other kids pretending to be that girl. I'd never heard of anything like that before. Have you?

• Something I've noticed about e-mail—once I start writing them, I have a hard time stopping. I just stay on the computer for a long time—then afterward, I wonder where the time went. Does that happen to you, too? What do you do about it?

• Can you help me with a problem I'm having? Someone just forwarded me an e-mail from someone else that had something in it about me. The person who wrote it probably didn't want me to see it, but now I have. What do you think I should do?

• You know, lately I've felt very nervous each time I check my e-mail. I keep feeling like I'll have more work to do or sometimes I worry that someone will be mad at me. Does that ever happen to you? What do *you* do to feel better?

E-mail can be a rich, satisfying way to stay in touch with friends, conduct school business, or share information. So it's well worth the time you invest to help your child develop a healthy, productive, and satisfying relationship with e-mail. And who knows? You may learn something about your own relationship with e-mail along the way!

CHAPTER 4

# WEB SITES, CHAT ROOMS, AND BLOGS

t almost reads like a hypothetical question in a game of Scruples or Truth or Dare: If you could take on a new identity, with no more effort than composing a few sentences that no one you know would ever read—would you do it? Would you take the chance to become a popular, sexy girl or a hot, sought-after guy, with a gorgeous photo and a daily calendar full of glamorous, exciting activities? Or perhaps you'd like to try life as a one-hundred-year-old Buddhist monk, wise and serene, to whom lesser mortals come seeking answers to their most troubling questions. If you could be anyone in the world, would you make yourself younger? Older? More sexually experienced? More popular? Maybe you'd enjoy changing genders for a while. Or would the thrill simply be in the escape, in knowing that you can lead a parallel life with no consequences to you or anyone you care about?

If you felt even a twinge of wistfulness or desire as you read the previous paragraph, then you have some idea of what your child might feel like when confronted with the online world of the Internet. Think of it: an entire universe of possibilities— with absolutely no consequences. You can present yourself as rich, beautiful, sexually experienced, and popular. You can post photographs that look nothing like you. You can play with alternate identities, and, even more thrilling, create entire relationships with strangers based on those identities. If something doesn't work out—if someone's feelings are hurt or if a potential friend is disappointed—so what? You simply block that person's e-mails or maybe start a whole new profile.

## Getting Up to Speed: The World Wide Web

The electronic world can be intimidating, for sure—but it doesn't have to be. When we started counseling children and families with "Internet issues," we were two fairly ignorant technophobes, but we got up to speed pretty fast, and you can, too! The following two books can teach you everything you need to know about using the Internet. They're easy to read, fun to use, and very practical. They won't load you up with technical jargon you don't need, but they will boost your comfort level in using the Internet and keeping up with your cyber-kid!

• *The Internet for Dummies,* 10th ed., by John R. Levine, Margaret Levine Young, and Carol Baroudi
• *The Rough Guide to Internet 12*

No matter what age your children are, they probably enjoy exploring fantasy and alternative identities, whether it's your five-year-old imagining she's a princess or your teenager trying out a weird new hairstyle. Kids of all ages wonder about who they are and how they're perceived, and fantasy, experimentation, and role-playing are all part of the process. But now the Internet offers a whole new world for taking on fantastic and alternative identities—not just the sandbox or the halls of high school, but a whole public online world. False identities and blogs from supposedly "real" people are rife on MySpace and other popular Web sites, including Xanga, Friendster, Facebook, Bebo, and many others. (For example, that one-hundred-year-old monk is really a teenage girl, as reported in a recent news story about MySpace.)

We have each been involved in several cases in which teenage clients explored the online world of fake identities and fake relationships. One of the most troubling was a teenage girl—let's call her Genie—whose high school counselor recently consulted with Barb after Genie told him that she regularly assumed a wide range of adult identities on various dating Web sites. This sixteen-year-old girl wrote and answered ads, posted phony pictures of herself, and began long, involved e-mail exchanges with various men on the site. Most of her fake identities were female, but sometimes she even pretended to be a shy single guy, and once she represented herself as a lonely gay man. "I get two hundred e-mails a day," she bragged.

The counselor was skeptical, and at first, Barb was, too. "Ask her to bring in her laptop and show you," she suggested, thinking that would call the girl's bluff. To everyone's surprise, Genie did indeed bring in her laptop, and if anything, she'd been playing down the extent of her activities. The counselor found e-mails from men who wanted to date her various female and male personae. He found e-mails from guys who were turned on by her "dominatrix" persona and wanted to set up an S&M relationship. He even found e-mails from lonely men who were looking for potential marriage partners and saw one of Genie's characters—an equally lonely twenty-seven-year-old virgin—as a possible mate.

The range of replies to Genie's various alter egos was phenomenal. But most troubling was Genie's response to them: she was amused. At least a dozen men had poured their hearts out to her about how they had been looking for someone like her for a long time and that now they finally had hope. One guy even shared that he had considered suicide in the past due to his profound loneliness. Genie viewed him as "pathetic" and stopped all correspondence with him abruptly.

When the counselor tried to get Genie to see things from the e-mail-writers' perspective, pointing out that these people were seeking a relationship in good faith and would be hurt if they knew the truth, Genie was totally baffled.

"But I've never *met* these people," she kept repeating. "They've never met me. What difference does it make?" To her, this was a game, and she enjoyed the sense of power it gave her. Empathy and compassion seemed irrelevant in this anonymous world.

Significantly, Genie had first gotten interested in simulating online identities by playing The Sims, a computer game that presents players with hypothetical situations. Based on choices that the player makes for various family members, the characters' destinies are altered. For example, you can choose to send someone to school—and then watch them graduate and get a good job. Or, as Genie did, you can have a character fail to feed the family pet, and then watch that pet languish and die. The counselor thought that one of the first steps in Genie's loss of empathy was when she felt no remorse or regret about the death of this creature—why should she? It was only a game; the cat wasn't real, and the men and women who wrote to her online seemed equally unreal. To us, Genie's lack of remorse about the cat's death should have been a red flag to her parents that here was a troubled child. Had her parents been more aware of Genie's online life, they could have caught this problem at a far earlier stage, providing much-needed support for their daughter.

Instead, Genie lost interest in The Sims when she discovered she could create her own online personae to whom actual human beings would reply, a real-life game that seemed far more thrilling than the purely virtual version. (To be fair, we have also seen positive effects from games like The Sims, with kids learning useful things about the responsibilities of a household, getting and keeping a job, pursuing various careers, and even maintaining relationships.)

Genie was a troubled child for many reasons, and her lack of empathy had far deeper sources than anything she was doing online. But certainly, the online culture of anonymity and lack of consequence fed this tendency in her, as opposed to, say, volunteering at a day-care center, nursing home, or animal shelter, which might have opened her up to deeper and more emotional connections. Certainly, too, the number of normal, happy kids who adopt online personae—anything from a slightly more experienced version of themselves to that one-hundred-year-old Buddhist monk—suggests a troubling trend.

In this chapter, we'll explore the world of online Web sites, forums, and blogs, and help you evaluate the positive as well as the negative ways in which they might affect your child. We'll also consider some other major Web site concerns, including consumerism, drugs, sites that glorify eating disorders, and the threat of financial risk and identity theft.

As you read through this roster, you may be thinking, "Oh, no problem. I'll simply block all of the 'danger' sites so my kids can't access them." You might as well try to keep your kids from dialing a particular phone number. With all the computers at school, the library, friends' houses, and Internet cafés, your children can access pretty much any site on the Net if they're really committed to doing so. You can't possibly block their access, even if you do install the appropriate filters—which we recommend; more on that, too, in a minute. Still, your primary parental task isn't to physically prevent your children from accessing particular sites, but to give them the tools they need to cope with Cyberworld's challenges.

So let's get started. Your first step is to find out what your children are already doing.

## How to Know What Your Kids Are Doing Online

**Ask them.** We just can't stress this often enough: cyberworld is your children's world, and if you want to know what's going on in their lives, you need to know what they're doing online. Of course, you need to know if they're involved in anything potentially dangerous or unhealthy, but almost more important, you need to learn what they're thinking, feeling, and wondering about. Did they see a Web site that provoked them to change their opinion about the Mideast crisis or that local controversy over the traffic light? Did they find an online profile of someone who might become a pen pal or even a real-life friend? Have they been getting interested in forums on chess, softball, tarot, photography, Brazilian tree snakes? What about that cool joke they heard in a chat room or that totally lame opinion they read in a blog? If you don't ask, they might not tell you—and then you'll never know about this enormous, rich, and significant part of your child's daily experience. And of course, if they're totally unwilling to talk about what they're doing online or if every instinct in your body shouts "cover-up" when you hear them talk, then, yes, maybe that's a danger sign and you need to follow it up. But follow up on the good stuff, too.

**Notice how they respond when you walk by.** Do your children seem to move more quickly when you're around them and their computers? Might they be hitting a key or clicking on the mouse in order to switch screens? If you have the impression that your kids don't want you to see what they're working on, that may be reason enough to find out more. And if they're moving *less* when you walk by, maybe they're just waiting for you to leave so they can return to their real interests.

**Check out the bottom of the screen.** Most computers have tabs at the bottom of the screen showing how many windows are open and labeling each Web site. Computer-savvy kids know this, of course—but it's still not a bad idea for you to take an occasional quick look over your child's shoulder, just to see what's up.

**Check out the history of sites your kids have visited.** On your browser, just click on the arrow to the right of the box where you type in Web addresses and a list of the most recently viewed Web sites will drop down. You'll only see what your kids (or the computer's other users) have sought directly—no links—but at least you'll have some idea of what your kids have seen. And by clicking on the sundial or clock in your browser's tool bar (it should say History when you scroll over it), you can see what Web sites your child has been accessing for the past several days or weeks. We recommend that you set your computer to reveal thirty days' worth of information: go to Tools, then Internet Options, and then the General folder, where you can choose how many days of history you want your computer to log. And if your kids have cleared their computer's History, address drop-down tab, or Favorites tab, then that's a real red flag. What don't they want you to see?

**Look under Favorites and visit the sites occasionally.** Just as you should watch movies and TV with your kids to get an idea of what they're viewing, you need to visit their Cyberworld as well. This is less about being the Parent Police than about getting to know the kind of person your child is becoming. What are your children interested in? What voices are they hearing each day—the cool, reasoned statements of an encyclopedia article or the urgent, intense calls to action of a political blogger? Are their interests changing? Are they reading at a grade level that surprises you? What does Cyberworld look like from a kid's-eye perspective—from *your* kid's perspective? Check out their Favorites—and then start some conversations.

**Notice if your child is staying up late at night using the computer.** The flickering light from a computer screen stimulates the portion of the brain that keeps us awake, so with every e-mail or late-night Web search, your child may find it progressively harder to sleep. Promote healthy sleep with a computer curfew, and then check for the telltale light under your child's door, or for the telltale towel they've put there to hide the light! (For more on computers and sleep, see Chapter 8.)

## Cyber-Safety Begins at Home

Are you concerned about what your kids are viewing—or saying—online? You can't be there twenty-four hours a day, but you can take some simple steps to keep them safe.

You probably won't be able to keep your kids from accessing sites they're really interested in: determined kids will eventually find an unfiltered computer on which to get where they're going. But at least the parental controls will keep your children from accidentally stumbling upon disturbing violent or sexual images, which is incredibly easy to do—one wrong click or ambiguous search, and you can find yourself on a porn site. Many filters can also be set to keep your children out of some or all chat rooms. And just the fact that you have installed filters—and they know it—lets your children know that you're concerned about what they view and that you take seriously your job as a cyber-parent.

Here are your basic options for monitoring and control.

## Your Antivirus Program: Blocking and Filtering

Blocking and filtering features usually come with your antivirus program. At your command, the filter removes objectionable words used in IM, chat rooms, and e-mail, replacing them with pound signs or other symbols. It also prevents access to sites that contain certain keywords, such as "sex" or "pornography." In response, certain sites have taken to intentionally misspelling certain words, such as "sxe" or "prngraphy" to keep from being filtered out. Some sites also deliberately mimic the addresses of "good" sites, so that www.crazygirls.com, a dating site, may be confused with crazygirls.org, a hard-core sex site.

The blocking component of these programs uses a "bad site" list for wholesale blocking of access to sites on the list. Usually the list can be customized so that you can add or remove sites. However, new unsavory Web sites are created every day, and your kids may find them before you have time to put them on the list—so consider yourself warned. In addition, filters can also block legitimate sites. We know of one fifteen-year-old boy doing a school report on sexual reproduction whose dad had to sit with him throughout the whole research process because his parents had chosen "sex" as a keyword for their filters. If we'd had the opportunity to advise this family, we'd have suggested temporarily turning the filter off. But if you worry that your child will take advantage of such freedom, then by all means, stick around.

## Monitoring and Tracking

Monitoring and tracking software really varies. At a minimum, it tells you which Web sites your child has visited; many programs also allow you to track and/or restrict the types of activities in which your child engages (e-mail, chatting, and the like), as well as to control the times of day your children can access the computer and/or the Internet.

## Keylogging

Keylogging software registers every keystroke that a user types, so that you can record Web sites visited, get transcripts of chat discussions, read e-mail, and even view passwords. This software varies as well: some actually records every screen your child has viewed. This type of comprehensive software basically gives you a full record of your child's online activity, as well as recording offline time spent on the computer, including game-playing. Some of these programs run in stealth mode where they cannot be easily detected; others are more easily noticed as running programs or may slow the computer processing down.

## Limiting Instant Messaging

As we saw in Chapter 3, IM access usually requires a password. If several people use a home computer, you can set up your account so that each has a different password. Then you can arrange it so that you and your older children have access to IM, while your younger children do not.

We recommend not allowing IM to kids under the age of six—they just don't need to be on the computer that much. From six to thirteen, you may want to allow limited access, which gives you the chance to approve each IM buddy. When you trust your kids to have good judgment, you can allow them unlimited IM access, and then monitor them occasionally to see if they're abusing the privilege.

## Online Timers

Some parents limit time on the computer and Internet access time the way they limit TV watching. We think that's a terrific idea, and we'll share with you our detailed age-based recommendations in Chapter 5.

Ideally, you'd rely on the honor system. Just hand your kid an egg timer and tell him or her how many minutes to set it for. Many of the latest programs also have pop-up timers that can give warnings such as "only 5 minutes left on the computer" or "bedtime in 15 minutes." These alert your child to the passing of time but don't necessarily affect the computer itself.

If necessary, you can buy software that limits your children's online minutes: the Internet access will simply switch off at a certain point, and then your kids will have to come to you if they want another chunk of time. These filters don't compromise your own ability to use the computer—you just have to enter your password. Be aware, though, that kids are sometimes very smart about figuring out their folks' passwords—it seems to come with the territory!

---

### Getting Up to Speed: The Internet Service Provider (ISP)

An ISP is a company that provides you access to the Internet. Major ISPs include America Online (AOL), Microsoft Network (MSN), AT&T, and Earthlink. Often, the ISP's name will be in your e-mail address, as a kind of advertisement: jane@aol.com or jose@earthlink.net. However, many people who maintain their own Web sites put the Web site's name in their e-mail address: for example, info@bigcompany .com or john@johnjoneslawyer.com. These Web sites still rely upon an ISP to get them on the Web.

---

## What Your Internet Service Provider Offers

Before you invest in additional software for blocking, filtering, monitoring, or tracking, find out what your current Internet service provider (ISP) already offers. Most major providers, including America Online, Microsoft's MSN, AT&T Worldnet, and Earthlink, offer built-in Internet controls at no additional cost and new features are added every day. As of spring 2007, here's a sampling of what you could get:

**AOL** allows you to select predetermined limits for every user's time spent on e-mail, on the Web, or in chat rooms; or you can create separate customized controls for each of your children. You can't prevent your kids from accessing specific Web sites, but you can limit their ability to IM or use e-mail.

AOL will also filter out sites that use words on a list that you've deemed unacceptable, for example, sexually explicit words. (However, be warned: many Web sites try to frustrate these filters with creative spellings, such as a$$ for "ass.") AOL will also send you e-mail reports of your child's activity upon request. And it offers anti-phishing software to its customers. (For more on phishing, see below.)

**Microsoft MSN** enables you to block specific Web sites and limit access to such features as e-mail, IM, and music. If your child requests access to blocked sites, MSN sends you an e-mail with a link to the site so you can review it and respond. You can also get a weekly report of your child's online activities. However, MSN controls don't filter e-mail or chat or allow you to set time limits. MSN does provide software to filter phishing. (For more on phishing, see below.)

**AT&T Worldnet** offers free, downloadable filtering software; for your first year with AT&T, you have free use of CyberPatrol and its companion software, Kids Cyber Highway (including updates), and after the first year, you can have this software at a discount. The CyberSnoop program is also offered to AT&T customers at a 20 percent discount. For more on CyberPatrol, see below.

**Earthlink** offers free Web blocking and filtering, and it also allows you to limit your child's access to e-mail by creating an approved Cyberfriends list, as well as limiting children's access to chat rooms, bulletin boards, and IM. You can also restrict the hours per day, week, or month that your child can use the Internet.

Regardless of what we've listed here, please don't make the assumption that your service is inadequate. Internet service providers recognize the importance of these services and are viewing this as a very competitive area in getting new subscribers; we are confident that the bar will continue to be raised with regard to the free availability of quality filtering/tracking services.

## Online Monitors

Ideally, you won't need these monitors because you're relying on your filters and on the honor system. We don't recommend extensive monitoring unless you think your children need it based on their personalities or past behavior. But if you feel you need more detailed information on what your kids are doing online, either to monitor potentially unhealthy activity or simply to learn more about what they're doing, you've got lots of options—which will also allow you to restrict access to various parts of Cyberworld.

The software prices we've listed here were current in early 2007, but they seem to be falling quickly: between the time we started this book and the time we finished it, many prices had dropped considerably and more features were being included, a trend that seems to be continuing. So by the time this book comes out, you will almost certainly have even more options. Two pieces of advice:

1. Don't assume you need the best, biggest, and most complete filtering device. If you're absolutely committed to tracking your child's every cyber-move or setting firm computer-based time limits, then go ahead and invest in something high-tech—it won't even be all that expensive. But if all you want is to keep your kids from accidentally stumbling on a porn site and if you're willing to rely on the

honor system for the rest, you can probably get by with your antivirus program and your ISP.

2. If you are in the market for something with more bells and whistles, check out www.consumereports.org before you buy. We've provided you the latest information as of this writing—but Cyberworld changes quickly. This information will give you a terrific start, but it is almost certainly *not* the last word.

## Tracking/Monitoring Software

The programs listed below are all considered to be Internet Safety or Internet Protection Programs. They all generally offer Web site filtering/keyboard blocking features, as well as Web activity reporting and weekly summary reports, telling you which sites were visited on your computer. Most include a time management feature, but this varies as well. Some of the differences between the programs are noted below.

**CyberPatrol 7.6** can block IM, chat, and e-mail on any program, which you may find to be a useful feature; the filters can also be modified as needed. This is also one of the few programs that filters inbound and outbound chat, as well as protecting personal information. It can also limit the amount of time spent online, in chat rooms, or using IM; and it can prevent illegal or copyrighted material from being downloaded. It also operates in stealth mode, so that the computers users have no idea that they're being monitored. This program is a good choice if you want something more than just filtering/blocking but don't particularly want to view every move your child makes (as the keylogging software allows). $39.95 for a onetime download at www.cyberpatrol.com. The company also offers a free fourteen-day trial.

**Safe Eyes** also filters instant messaging and monitors kids' time on the computer or online; the program even allows you to set up different protection levels for each child. You can set it up to notify you through e-mail, text message, or phone call when inappropriate Web sites are visited. It is one of the few available programs that works on Macs, and it can be installed on up to three systems for a $49.95 onetime download at www.safeeyes.com. They also offer a free fifteen-day trial.

**SnoopStick** is a device that fits into your USB port and allows you to secretly monitor what your kids are doing while on the Internet—live and from anywhere in the world. Just plug the SnoopStick into the computer you want to monitor and run the setup program, which takes less than sixty seconds. Then plug the Snoopstick into any computer to see what Web sites your kids are visiting or to view their e-mails and chats. SnoopStick can also block social networking sites such as MySpace. You can even disable Internet access, set time restrictions, or turn the computer off—all by remote, and all in stealth mode. While we don't recommend this kind of long-distance control in most circumstances, it would be useful for children who need very firm limits. Or you can use it for positive communication with your child: if you're out of town, for example, you can still talk your child through a homework assignment as the two of you view a Web site together. SnoopStick can monitor up to three computers for $59.95 (a onetime purchase) at www.snoopstick.com.

**NetNanny** has a really good time-management feature (as do many other programs), which allows you to choose a time limit for each day, as well as allowing or blocking Internet access at particular times. So if your kid can't stay away from e-mail after bedtime, this is a good feature. (Or you can simply confiscate his or her keyboard every night.) NetNanny can also be set to block the transmission of personal information or to keep your children from accessing certain applications you don't want them to use, such as file trading or sharing, IMing, and chatting. It does not filter IM's or chats, but it does filter incoming and outgoing e-mail and provides copies of all IM communication. The software also allows you to make different rules for each user of the computer. One possible downside is that it does not run in stealth mode and may be easily detected—though again, we don't normally recommend secret viewing anyway: it's always better to simply let your child know that you're interested in what he or she is doing. The latest version, 5.5, offers an e-mail notification feature and remote administration, so you can manage it from any Internet connection. We've worked with a number of foster parents caring for high-risk kids who've been using NetNanny for years and really like it. For a $39.99 annual fee, you also get monthly updates through www.netnanny.com. The company offers a free trial.

**CyberSitter 9.0** has all the standard features and runs in stealth mode; it also gives you detailed daily reports of your children's activities by e-mail and allows you to override blocked sites—although filter strengths are not adjustable; you either block a site for all users or you unblock it for all users, so that the filters you put on for your youngest child will apply equally to your oldest. CyberSitter also records both sides of chat conversations from AOL, Yahoo!, and MSN, and allows you to block social networking sites such as MySpace and Facebook.

For $39.95 you can get a onetime download at www.cybersit
ter.com. This company also offers a free trial.

**KidsWatch** also runs in stealth mode and it also has great
time-management features. It can be set to e-mail daily reports
to you, as well as automatically logging your child out of the
computer when it's time for bed. This useful program also allows you to set time limits on Internet surfing, chatting, and
game playing. $39.95 for a onetime download of the Web-
Filtering edition at www.kidswatch.com. Again, a free trial is
available.

## Keylogging Software

The programs listed below all go the extra mile to record every
single keystroke a user makes on the computer. They also all
run in stealth mode, so your kids won't even know they're
there (though again, our advice would usually be to tell them).
All of these programs record both sides of chat conversations,
e-mail communications, passcodes, and every other occasion
that a user hits a key. The usual Web filtering/keyboard blocking features are also automatically included. We have listed a
few special features of each below, but again, prices and features are changing all the time, so check them out for yourself
if you're ready to buy.

**PCTattletale** presents you with a complete visual record of
your child's online experience, taking you from address to address so that you can see for yourself every single site your
child has visited—almost like watching a little TV documen-
tary of your kid's online experience. You'll also get a word-for-
word record of his or her chat-room activity. The advantages
are obvious—you get the full picture. The disadvantage is that

it can be tedious—you're watching one visual image after another—though you can fast-forward, rewind, move to a specific date and time, and even print individual screenshots. This program can be set to send you copies of your child's e-mails in real time so that you'll know what's going on when you're away from home. They even offer a free online video tutorial to help you with all aspects of downloading, installing, and using the product. A number of the parents we work with are very pleased with this software. $49.95 for a onetime download at www.pctattletale.com to as many as two computers. A free trial is also available.

**IAmBigBrother 9.1** provides a helpful feature whereby you can access the computer you are monitoring remotely—a great feature if you're concerned about what your children are doing on the nights you're away from home. Just log on to the I am Big Brother Web site, where a record of all your computer's activity is saved for you on their secure server. They also offer free e-mail tech support. $29.95 for a onetime download at www.iambigbrother.org. No free trial is available, but they do offer a money-back guarantee.

**Spector Pro 5** is comparable. In addition to the common features listed above, this software actually examines online activity and analyzes it to see whether you should be notified immediately. If your child has really been testing the limits and giving you great cause for concern, this is a great feature. Spector Pro 5 is also one of the few programs that offers a Mac version. They also offer free live phone tech support. $99.95 for a onetime download at www.spectorsoft.com.

## Getting Up to Speed: Malware

"Malware" refers to any software designed to cause damage to a computer, server, or network, whether it be a virus, spyware, or something else. Your computer—and the information you have on it—may be at risk whenever you visit certain Web sites, download certain materials from the Internet, or load shareware on your computer. Here's a quick tour of the electronic dangers that might threaten your computer.

• **Virus:** A computer program that, like a real-life virus, spreads itself, making its way through your computer files without your knowledge or consent. The most common way to contract viruses is through e-mail attachments.

• **Worm:** A specific type of virus that reproduces over many computers and makes copies of itself in computer memories.

• **Trojan horse:** A type of virus specifically designed to destroy, modify, or erase data in your hard drive. A Trojan horse can search for passwords, credit card numbers, and other important personal information, and can be used for identity theft.

• **Cookie:** A legitimate tool used by Web sites to track user information. Many Web sites automatically load a bit of text on your computer when you access them, enabling the site to track your habits and then to tailor the ads and special offers you see on that site. For example, when you access Amazon.com, a cookie enables Amazon to suggest books and CDs based on your previous viewing or buying activity. Generally, it's considered acceptable for a company to track your activity on its own Web sites, but it's considered an invasion of privacy when the tracking extends across many different sites. For example, a site that sells furniture might track your viewing habits across sites that sell books, music, and art—and then use your viewing habits to customize ads and special offers that might be more likely to appeal to you.

• **Shareware:** Programs you can download for free, perhaps to help you view video or listen to music. Shareware is deceptive, because it often comes loaded with spyware.

• **Spyware**: A program that you pick up unknowingly from another Web site as you download another type of program, most often shareware. The purpose of spyware is to track information about your computer-based activities and send it on, most often to commercial Web sites that want to track your purchasing habits. Usually—but not always—spyware slows down your system and may keep it from responding at all, especially while you're viewing Web sites or retrieving e-mail. It's designed in such a way that it sometimes causes problems after you've removed it because the changes it has made in your system linger on.

### To avoid problems with Malware:

• Install a good antivirus protection program, such as Norton/Symantec or McAfee. Some Internet service providers also offer antivirus protection, but they're rarely enough—you want something stronger.

• Warn your kids not to download applications or files from unknown sources, and to be careful about trading files.

• Update your virus protection at least weekly, to make sure you're protected against the latest viruses, worms, and Trojan horses. Most antivirus programs can be set to update automatically, and many will notify you as they add new protections against more recent threats.

• Download antivirus updates from reputable sources only. You're safest if you stick with your antivirus program, though if you have Windows, you can go to http://update.microsoft.com/microsoftupdate/ to find out about new threats and possible protections.

• Read the licensing agreements of what you install, and always beware that tucked away in the fine print may be a warning that you are about to install spyware!

• Install and use a firewall, which will further protect your information from hackers (people who enter your computer through the Internet). Windows XP has a free built-in firewall; a good antivirus program usually includes a firewall as well.

• To delete cookies, go to Control Panel, then to Internet Options. Under Temporary Internet Files choose Delete Cookies. Be aware, though, that many Web sites will not offer you access unless you let them install a cookie.

## Talking to Your Child About Online Activity

Whatever you choose for your child—the honor system, a timer, or a monitor—we recommend talking through your decision rather than taking the stealth route. True, a child who knows he or she is being monitored might have a greater incentive for either trying to disable the monitor or finding other computers, but think for a moment about your motives in installing the monitors. Are you trying to catch your children in bad behavior or give them the message that you know how confusing and problematic the online world can be? After all, you wouldn't let them go to a movie without checking out the reviews and the rating, and you wouldn't let them watch a TV show without looking at the TV listing and maybe wandering into the TV room for a few minutes to see what it's all about. So you're using the same parental oversight to track their online activities—not to trip them up, but to keep up with them.

If your kids object to the monitoring, consider steps you might all take to get to the point where you could use the honor system. Explain that you want your children to tell you what they're viewing online, to come to you if they find something disturbing, and to use good judgment when making comments in chat rooms, forums, and blogs. You might say something like this:

> I know this Cyberworld can be exciting, and it seems as though what you do there has no consequences. But it does, and that's why I want to be sure you can handle yourself before I let you fly solo. It's not that I don't trust you—it's that I want to be sure I've done my job preparing you for what you might encounter. Let's see how you do for the next few months. If we don't run into any problems, I'll think about backing off.

We've recently been monitoring all the hoopla on blogs about MySpace and its attempts at increased security. We're all for MySpace cleaning up its act, but we have been alarmed by the number of bloggers bragging that they plan to use devices like SnoopStick to monitor their husbands, wives, girlfriends, or boyfriends—or others they may want to spy upon! Please don't model this behavior for your children; it really sends the wrong message.

**TIP** **To turn off the image toolbar so that your browser won't automatically download visual images, including pornography:**

**1. On the Tools menu, click Internet Options.**

**2. On the Advanced tab, under Multimedia, clear the Enable Image Toolbar check box.**

## Getting Up to Speed: Advergames

Advergames are free online games that your kids learn about from Web sites, print and TV ads, and the packaging of actual products, such as cereal boxes. Having learned about the game, your children are supposed to visit the manufacturer's Web site, where they play for prizes—and where the manufacturer exposes your children to further advertising via branded characters, logos, and other corporate imagery. The company may also pick up valuable marketing information.

According to a recent study by the Kaiser Foundation of seventy-seven major Web sites aimed at children, some 73 percent of the sites contained one or more advergames. The study found that this was a particularly common way of reaching younger children, especially those aged 2 through 11. Children are encouraged to send links to their friends or to challenge them to a game at home, thereby spreading the advertiser's message.

It's our impression that most parents don't even realize that their children are interacting with advertising in this way. Now that you know, we urge you to help your child become aware of the many ways that corporations try to sell their products and build customer loyalty—even in the apparently harmless guise of a free online game.

## Shopping 'til You Drop Online

We'll admit it: we have very mixed feelings about online shopping for kids. On the one hand, we're concerned about the prevalence of consumerism in children's lives, and we object to the way that virtually every online experience is peppered with advertisements, images of products, and opportunities to buy things. Rampant consumerism is hard enough for kids to resist when they have to make a special trip to the mall—how much more seductive is it online, where buying items can be as easy as clicking a button? Even if your children are not over-spending, they're getting a constant message of "buy, buy, buy"—and the impression that everyone else is comfortable with that message.

On the other hand, both of us have shopped happily online for books, specialty furniture, and wedding presents listed in an online registry, not to mention housewares, posters, and a host of other products that are well-priced, easy to pick out, and convenient to order. So how can we quarrel with kids doing the same? Moreover, there are lots of products that are far eas-ier to find online than in actual stores—used books, craft items, old-fashioned toys and train sets. And for children with special interests or special needs, online shopping can be a terrific way of matching interests with availability. Online shopping also enables children to comparison shop more easily and with more autonomy: you don't have to drive them to fifteen differ-ent stores when they can just do some clicking on their own time.

What's our verdict? Encourage your children to understand how shopping works online, help them to become savvy shop-pers, and make sure they understand the limits as well as the benefits of online shopping. In other words, teach your chil-dren the ins and outs of cyber-retail.

## Comparison Shopping

Model for your children how to do online research and how to make intelligent comparisons. Make sure they're factoring in such hidden costs as shipping and handling charges, taxes, and other extras, as well as checking to see whether the items they're comparing really are comparable: a well-made coat is worth more money than a badly made garment, but you can't always tell the difference from the on-screen picture.

Encourage them to be a bit skeptical: if prices on eBay seem too good to be true, maybe that's because they are. Help them learn to ask tough questions so they can figure out why an item might be so incredibly cheap: because no one else wants it? Because there's something wrong with it? Because the manufacturer is starting a new line and dumping the old one? Help children distinguish between "low, low" prices offered by well-known chains or reputable online companies, and those unbelievable bargains by companies whose only address is a PO box in the Cayman Islands. Show your children how to check buyer ratings on such sites as Amazon.com and eBay, and help them figure out what those ratings mean for their purchasing decisions.

## Online Safety

On sites that are protected by Internet security systems, there's a little padlock at the bottom of the screen. Show your child how to look for it and explain that if the padlock isn't there, your children shouldn't use the site. (You probably shouldn't either!)

We also advise getting your children a PayPal account rather than letting them use your credit card. PayPal is an online payment service that you access with a password and can use to shop online. You can go to www.paypal.com to set up an unlimited PayPal account linked to a credit card or checking account, or you can open a limited PayPal account with the option of adding more to it as you go. If you cash out a limited PayPal account, they'll send you a check for your unused balance within about two weeks.

There are lots of advantages to having your children use PayPal rather than a credit card. First, you can preset a limit, which has obvious advantages, especially when your children are young or when they're first learning what a budget is. Second, you can get a detailed statement about what the PayPal money was spent for, which, again, is a plus for beginning shoppers. You should know that if your children figure out how to change their PayPal password, you won't be able to access their history—but then, if you've started them on a limited account, there's only so much money they can spend. And you can certainly let them know that they'll face consequences for changing a password or mishandling your money. Finally, even if you give your older children unlimited access to your credit card via PayPal, it's not quite the same thing as giving them your credit card number itself—you're still retaining a modicum of control. Recently, many credit card companies have begun offering gift cards, which you might consider as yet another alternative. Buying your child a gift card to use online means that he or she gets some practice using a credit card–type arrangement without the temptations of unlimited spending that a credit card seems to promise.

## Online vs. Live Shopping

When you buy something online, you don't really know what it looks like or how it fits. It may be easier to confuse your appearance with the model's: that slinky little dress looks terrific on that tall, slender, size-2 woman but not so great on your own short and curvy size-8 figure. Help your children learn how to evaluate the pictures they're seeing and to imagine themselves wearing the clothes—not looking like the models!

Your kids can make online shopping a social event if they do it with friends, but it's not the same kind of fun as going to the stores together. Besides, your children need both online and in-store shopping skills—how to deal with salespeople, how to try on clothes, how to pick things off the rack—so make sure they get both.

Teenagers are especially likely to want clothes that fit exactly, so make sure your kids understand that they may be less happy with garments bought online, the colors, styles, and details of which may not look the same in person as they do in the picture. Show them how to find out about refund policies, who pays for the shipping, and what kind of packaging is needed to send things back. If you need to return an item bought online, you often face the hassle of arranging for a UPS pickup or a trip to the post office, so encourage your children to figure those possibilities into their evaluation of online shopping convenience.

## Handling Money

Every family has its own values when it comes to allowances, budgets, and kids' spending, so we'll just point out that everybody has to learn money-handling skills. With the best will in the world, your child is going to make mistakes—most adults do, too—so you want to come up with a system where he or she can learn in a protected situation. What happens if your child spends out a PayPal account and then has no "fun money" left for the rest of the month? Is that expensive online antique train set *really* worth all his birthday money? Does she want that pretty horse statue enough to spend *all* her savings on it?

You have the last word, of course, but ideally, you'll work with your children to figure out how they can access their money, when they need your permission to make a purchase, and what happens if they overspend. We're great believers in approaching these issues as a work in progress. Maybe you want your kids to come to you for every purchase, which you'll then make with your own credit card. Or perhaps you want to start them out with a limited PayPal account that they have to budget for the week, the month, or even for the school year. Over time, you may find out that they're ready for more responsibility—or maybe less. There's no shame in saying, "Well, I thought you were ready to handle that responsibility, but I think it may have been too much for you—let's try it again next year."

## Values

We think it's important for your children to have other activities besides shopping, whether online or in person. Of course, you can track how much time your child is spending at the mall or downtown, but having a sense of how much time they're window-shopping or actually shopping online may be a bit more difficult, so keep an eye out. In a society that makes consumption a major form of recreation, children get the message that you are what you buy, and that your personality, goals, ideals, and values can be seen through your purchases. If you find this as dispiriting and unhealthy as we do, then talk about these issues with your child. Give them the clear message that you're more concerned with who they are than what they wear and that there's more to life than a day at the mall. As always, kids will take their cue from what you do, not what you say, so think about your own buying and spending activities. If you've made shopping your primary leisure activity, you can't criticize your kids for doing the same, even if they're buying clothes and shoes while you're purchasing books, art objects, and rare jazz CDs.

## Drugs and Diet Pills

Remember the old days, when you could find ads promising breast enhancement or Charles Atlas bodybuilding in the backs of comic books? When you're a kid, you look at those glorious women and magnificent men, and you don't think, "What a crock!" You think, "Hey, it's printed on a page—it must be true! Besides, they have photographs!"

The Internet plays on that same credulity, except that there are far more ads and way more products. Online shopping is one of the easiest ways to get Xanax, Cialis, Viagra, and other medications. It's also a treasure trove of natural products supposed to promote muscle development, weight loss, attractive skin, sexual potency, and relaxation. Even children who understand that they shouldn't take drugs may think it's okay to buy legal and/or natural medications, not realizing that they're putting their health in danger.

So make sure your children know that "natural" doesn't mean "safe." Tell them about the dangers of taking any type of medication without supervision, especially if they're taking more than one med at a time. No matter what it says on the Web site or promotional e-mail, help your children understand that *all* medications and supplements—natural, herbal, over-the-counter, and prescription—can have powerful effects on their body, mind, and mood, and that it's important to take them only under a professional's care.

Weight-loss products hyped on the Internet are a real mine-field, and we strongly advise warning your kids about them. In some extreme cases, they actually contain parasites. And even such natural weight-loss aids as ephedrine have been shown to have serious health consequences for many people. Help your weight-conscious children resist the temptation to buy any weight-loss aid online: at best, it's probably a waste of money; at worst it could be a serious threat to their health.

If you *do* find your child trying to obtain weight-loss prod-ucts via the Internet, use your discovery as an opportunity to have a heart-to-heart conversation. If you think losing weight would be a good thing for your child, help her do it safely and with your full support. If your child's losing weight makes no sense to you, sit down and try to understand where she's com-ing from—and then figure out what to do about it.

Girls seeking information on weight loss may also end up at one of the many pro-ana Web sites that glorify "the anorectic lifestyle" and give readers tips how to starve themselves with-out their parents finding out: e.g., sew weights into your run-ning shorts, hold fishing weights under your armpits, or insert weights into your orifices to add some extra ounces when you get weighed. Sites like http://angelfire.com/anime6/am_i_thin _yet/ also feature pictures of anorectic girls, praising them as beautiful and thin. So if you suspect your child of having an eating disorder, check out her online history to see if she's vis-iting any of these sites. Even if she's not, you can—either to see what techniques she may be using to hide her disorder or to start a conversation with her about the whole topic.

Of course, your child may simply be checking out a pro-ana site out of curiosity, so don't overreact if you find one or more such sites in your computer's history—maybe she just has a friend who told her to check out the site. Just start the conversation and find out if you need to take further action.

**TIP** To check out rumors, hoaxes, and frauds of all types— including those spread by e-mail—visit www.snopes.com, a Web site dedicated to exposing false ideas. Visit Snopes and see how it works—it's very user-friendly! Then show your children how they can use Snopes to find out whether something is true, including medical information, stories about product safety, and even urban legends.

## Financial Risk and Identity Theft

These days, your kids have probably heard about identity theft, if only because of the clever commercials that various banks have taken to running on TV. It's often hard, though, for children to connect an abstract problem with something they themselves are doing, especially if it seems safe to them.

One of Sue's clients, for example, entered a contest that promised "nothing to buy," adding, "Just give us your credit card number—we won't charge it." When the boy's parents asked about the unexplained charges that began appearing on his emergency-only credit card, he assured them in all honesty that he hadn't bought anything. He genuinely didn't realize that he'd put his family's finances in jeopardy.

Another online danger are the phishing e-mails that might show up in your kids' inbox. Typically, these appear to be from a bank, credit-card company, or PayPal, explaining that they're doing a routine security check and asking you to verify name, address, social security number, checking account number, and credit card information. The language is often urgent, if not threatening—"We've recently become aware of online fraud and need your help in stopping it immediately"—and a child might well feel compelled to help his or her family by providing the requested information as soon as possible. Sometimes legitimate companies send out actual inquiries, making a judgment call even more difficult.

Recently, a number of phishing e-mails have purported to be from religious people offering to will their fortunes to the recipient "to continue God's work." Whatever their form, phishing e-mails are bad news: a January 2007 report conducted by security services provider MessageLabs indicates that phishing has become even more dangerous to a computer system than viruses and Trojan horses. As we explained earlier, MSN, PayPal, and eBay have mechanisms for reporting phishing e-mails, while MSN and AOL offer phishing blockers for their customers to download. The latest about security regarding these e-mails can be found at www.onguardonline.gov.

Basically, as with online and real-life predators, you want to make your child aware of possible dangers without leading him or her to feel inordinately unsafe. Have a calm, clear conversation about the kinds of online fraud that he or she might encounter and come up with some simple rules about never providing certain types of information online, including information that relates to checking accounts, credit cards, and social security.

**TIP** Sometimes when you try to close a pop-up ad by clicking on the X, it may actually take you to that site! One clue is when

**your cursor turns into a little hand rather than remaining an arrow when you poise it over the** X.

## MySpace: Whose Space?

Social networking Web sites like MySpace, Friendster, Xanga, Bebo, and Facebook are becoming increasingly popular arenas for people of all ages to create an online presence, make friends, date, and socialize. Although each of these free sites works in a slightly different way, the basic model is the same: you post a profile, usually accompanied by a photo, that gives basic information about who you are—age, name, where you live, what your hobbies are, and other special interests such as favorite movies, TV shows, books, and even heroes. You're encouraged to download your favorite songs so that visitors can get a sense of your likes and dislikes. People often list the school they currently attend or ones they used to attend.

You don't post an e-mail address on a MySpace profile—people can reach you through the site—but you often end up giving out your e-mail address to people whom you meet online with whom you want to correspond privately. A person's full name never appears on the site, yet if you do a search for someone by name, you will come up with his or her site if a real name was used to set up the profile.

You can attach a blog to your profile, so that visitors can learn even more about you (for more about blogs, see the section below). And you have the option of attaching a wide variety of photos, anything from your trip to Yellowstone Park to semi-erotic pictures of you washing your car or lounging on the beach. Most of these sites ban nude or obscene pictures, but suggestive and titillating photos do get through.

These sites also have chat rooms, which we'll discuss below, and dating services, which we'll talk about in Chapter 11. Their fundamental principle, though, is the notion of "friends." In theory, if you're a kid whose three best friends are also on the site, you'd list them as your friends, so that they—and they alone—would have special access to your information. The sites seem to offer restricted access—only your friends can communicate with you privately. But in fact, as soon as you post a profile, you are flooded with requests from people who want to be your friend—and in some cases, not even people. When Barb posted her sample profile on MySpace, she had more than 64 million potential "friends" within twenty-four hours. As of this writing, a few months later, her network access is more than 160 million—including local bands, current movies, car companies, and the like. There's a group on My-Space that talks about Volvos (Volvos for Life), for example, and every major commercial movie that comes out now has a MySpace profile—commercials on TV even direct you to them. More than thirty-nine thousand groups on MySpace deal with pets and animals. There are also lots of actual people, many of whom boast thousands or even millions of human "friends." People actually have contests to amass the most "friends" on these social networking sites. In theory, you can re-strict friends access to particular people whom you've specifi-cally granted that privilege. However, your friends' friends may also have access to you.

So right away, we see a number of potential problems with these sites. We admit it: we just don't like them. We're all for kids making friends online, especially when they're seeking out people who may be hard to find in daily life—children who share their special interests, cultural background, or special needs. But we think that's best done on special-interest forums, blogs, and specialized Web sites—online communities in the best sense of the word. These mega-sites are a different story—so let's take a closer look at why we're so critical of them.

### They Offer the Illusion of Privacy—While Making Your Child's Life Public

By doing no more than posting a routine profile, Barb made her name and basic information the property of some 160 million entities, from people to car companies. That's a staggering thought—and one that's beyond the comprehension of most children, who simply don't realize how public the Internet is. Barb spoke with one middle-school kid who recently discovered that his parents had been reading his MySpace blog. "That was private!" he said indignantly. "They had no right to violate my privacy that way." The boy had absolutely no idea that a blog—posted on the Internet—is by definition a public forum. To him, it was a journal he was sharing with a few chosen friends, not a publication that all the world could see. Kids just don't get those distinctions—they're hard enough for adults to get in this new cyber-era—and sites like MySpace only further blur that crucial public-private distinction.

In theory, you have to be fourteen to get a MySpace profile, but the site works on the honor system. Talk to pretty much any middle-school kid and you'll hear about twelve-year-olds and even younger children who have posted their profiles, simply by giving the wrong age, though if it's brought to the site's attention that a member is under age, it will delete the profile. (Friendster's age requirement is sixteen; Xanga and Bebo are

open to kids of thirteen; and the rules for Facebook are changing.) Kids get on a site with their friends, thinking it's like a
cool clubhouse with a secret password, and indeed, some parts
of it *are* private: if you e-mail another site member through the
site, only you two (and the site administrator) have access to
that mail. Blogs, though, are open to the public; even to those
who aren't site members. And profiles are visible to anyone
who logs on, including you.

That's a lot to keep straight—and kids don't. The possible
problems are almost too numerous to list: predators, of course,
but more routinely, school gossip; invasive (even if not actively
dangerous) communications from older teens and adults; and
potential fallout from future colleges and employers, who
could end up reading stories of sex, drugs, and other illegal
behavior—true or not—and make admissions or employment
decisions accordingly.

If you'd like to illustrate for your child just how easy it is for
a stranger to find out information online, do a Google search of
your child's name. (You might want to try this alone first so
you can absorb this information in private!) Help your child
see how anyone can access all sorts of personal information,
just with a few keystrokes. If your child is on MySpace or one
of the other mega-sites, demonstrate how easily you can obtain
information just by logging on to that site and doing a search
for your child's name or by searching for the name of a friend
who has a MySpace presence. Click on your child's profile and
blog, then do the same for your child's friends—perhaps you'll
find something about your child there as well. Many kids don't
put their whole or real names on their MySpace profiles, but
you can search for a MySpace presence by e-mail address or by
viewing profiles of kids who attend the same school as your

child, so you might recognize your child's nickname and photo in their friends' listings.

### They Offer the Illusion of Intimacy—While Delivering Mainly Superficial Relationships

How can anyone have a million friends? Even a hundred would be more than most people can keep up with! These sites have spurred in both children and adults a new tendency to tally their number of friends and compete accordingly—the most popular kid may have 8 million friends; the second-most popular, only 7.5 million!

But a friend isn't someone you list on a MySpace account. A friend is someone you trust, confide in, share a history with. A friend is someone you count on in times of trouble, with whom you rush to share your most joyful moments. A friend makes you feel less alone in the world—that's why friends are so valuable and also why friendships take so much work. In fact, among childhood's key tasks is learning friendship skills, including resolving conflicts, setting boundaries, and building intimacy.

None of these skills have anything to do with the vast majority of "friends" on MySpace. True, MySpace takes up an enormous amount of time as kids post new information, update their blogs, and e-mail their growing roster of friends. But the very nature of the activity keeps most of the relationships trivial. How could they be otherwise? What your children learn from this frantic round of Internet socializing is not how to create and nurture the relationships that will sustain them throughout their lives, but rather how to spend hours maintaining an increasingly broader and more superficial network of limited contacts.

Certainly, it's seductive. Kids report an almost addictive response to their MySpace log-ons, eager to see who's e-mailed them today or to note how many more "friends" they now have. And when everybody else in your group is doing it, staying off MySpace can make you feel left out. But in the end, much of MySpace is like make-work—going through the motions of friendship without the depth, conflict, intimacy, or genuine trust.

*Nation* columnist Patricia Williams makes another excellent point about MySpace profiles. In a clever column entitled "The 600 Faces of Eve," she chronicles her experiences joining MySpace and Facebook in order to relate better to her current crop of Internet-obsessed college students. What she discovers is how structured the sites' "personal interest" statements are and how strictly organized along consumer lines. She wonders about right-wing media magnate Rupert Murdoch's ownership of MySpace and points out how much personal data is now available to marketers and government officials alike: information about drug use, sexual activity, gun ownership, and income, as well as whether you like Hello Kitty or what type of car you want to drive. And she suggests that within these structured, consumerist questionnaires, young people may be losing their ability to define their own selves, needs, and desires, even as they also forfeit their sense of connection to others: "This is not about substantive engagement, but numbers. It's ruled by . . . the misplaced faith that an actuarial table is any kind of community—beloved, political, or 'other' wise."[1]

**TIP** To delete a MySpace account, just go to www.Myspace.com and click on FAQ at the bottom of the screen; scroll down to "your account" and click on "how do I delete my account?" which gives you step-by-step instructions. We suggest

**discussing this measure with your child before taking action—but both you and your child need to know that you have the power to do this.**

## They Promote Fantasy Identities in an Anonymous Culture of "No Consequences"

Teenagers are supposed to try out different identities; that's part of their job description. But sites like MySpace and Xanga offer children the perception of a safe place to try out identities with very little sense of the consequences, to themselves or others. Hence the multiple faces of Genie, the teenaged girl who used her fake online identities to attract men whom she never intended to meet. (See Chapter 3.) Hence, too, the many teenagers and adults who adopt alternate online personae, changing their sex, age, background, personality, and establishing anonymous relationships on that basis. The anonymity of Cyberworld may seem to promise a sense of safety, but it can also encourage your children to objectify other people rather than to identify with them. To be fair, these social networking sites warn people not to lie about their age or their identities, but the practice is rampant.

For lonely, awkward children, this kind of cyber-culture can be the gateway to an increasingly unhealthy reliance on fantasy life. There's a kind of addictive quality to this world where you can control who you are and how others see you, so that a lonely child spends more and more time online. If your child seems lonely and unhappy, keep a close eye on his online activity. Help your child find ways to build from online relationships to real ones, perhaps by encouraging her to develop in-depth e-mail relationships with people whom she may eventually meet; or to use the Internet as a way of locating real-life groups, classes, and other activities where she can meet congenial people. (For more on using the Internet for special-interest kids, see Chapter 7.)

Sometimes, of course, the use of fantasy can allow children the chance to develop confidence and prepare them for more reality-based relationships. If your son or daughter is writing dreamy e-mails to an anonymous pen pal that he or she has never met, that kind of fantasy relationship may indeed be a useful step on the path to real-life dating, relating, and falling in love. (For more about online relationships and dating, see Chapter 11.)

The problem, as we see it, lies not in the fantasy, but in the deception. If you know you're a thirteen-year-old boy who lives in Tucson and goes to middle school, but your correspon-dent thinks you're a motorcycle-riding college senior who is taking an extended road trip, then you know something she doesn't. If you can get away with the deception, you may feel a bit superior, maybe even contemptuous, to have fooled her in this way. Certainly she would feel foolish, hurt, and maybe even humiliated if she knew the truth. Instead of mastering empathy, compassion, and trust, your teen is learning callous-ness, contempt, and deception.

The teen years are insecure ones, to say the least, and a teen-ager may well feel that any advantage acquired in the service of self-confidence is justified. "So that cute college student won't talk to me as myself, but she will if I'm a motorcycle jock? Fine, then I'll tell her I'm a motorcycle jock—and even that won't put me on her level! She'll still have the power to reject me and make me feel small—so anything I do to make her admire me, even lying, is only fair."

Sadly, these kinds of fake identities only reinforce the idea that your own identity isn't good enough. If the only way you can make friends, let alone date, is to pretend to an age, look, and life history that you don't really have, you're only reminding yourself of your own inadequacies. It's a poisonous message, especially for teens, who are already staggering under the burden of trying to find out who they are and what they're capable of. We urge you to talk with your children about this issue and put them on the honor system: no fake identities, no lying, no deception. They should never tell the whole truth to a stranger online—but they shouldn't lie, either.

What about the kids who take on fake identities as a form of creativity and play? Suppose your child pretends to be a one hundred year old monk, for example, or a mad scientist, or some other character that seems to offer the gateway into another aspect of the child's own self. In such cases, the emphasis is less on fooling people and more on exploration; less on relationships and more on identity. Is that an acceptable use of fantasy?

In our opinion, it's fine for children to take on these characters—but they need to do it in the name of fiction. Let them write fiction and post it online, or create plays with a local drama group, or even create a blog with an obviously fake photograph and identity. So long as this "other character" is clearly fictional, no one is being fooled, hurt, or treated with contempt—and your child still has the space he needs to explore. She's learning about the difference between truth and fiction, and about how to create fictions while respecting real people. If he or she becomes a novelist, playwright, journalist, or any other type of writer, this distinction will prove to be crucial. It's pretty important for regular human beings, too.

## Truth or Consequences

If you're looking for a quick, clear way to tell your child what's okay and not okay online, you might simply say, "You can do whatever you like on sites that I've approved, as long as you're being safe and not being mean."

Safety involves not giving out personal information to someone you've never met and not putting personal information in places where anyone can read it.

Not being mean involves not lying, deceiving, or offering relationships that aren't really available. Explain that by posting fantasy information, your child is in effect putting other kids down by telling them lies—treating them as though they're not good enough to be given the truth. You don't have to tell the whole truth online—in fact, you definitely shouldn't—but you also don't have to go out of your way to fool people. That's just mean, and your children need to understand that you don't want them to behave that way.

**TIP** If you'd like to help your child see how deceptive MySpace and other social-networking profiles can be, look up some profiles of people he or she knows and talk about how the profile differs from your child's own view of the person. Then encourage your child to imagine that other people on the site are likewise distorting or at least enhancing their online personae.

## The Pros and Cons of Chat Rooms

A chat room is a virtual room that makes it possible for people from anywhere in the world to communicate in real time. It's like a written conference call: instead of talking to your fellow chatters, you're typing in your contributions. Or you just sit in the room and listen without contributing anything, an action known with some scorn online as lurking. (People who practice lurking are referred to with equal scorn as lurkers.)

Most chat rooms require you to set up a profile about yourself so that anyone in the room can find out some basic information about you just by right-clicking on your name. But of course, anything on your profile could be a total fantasy, so lots of people enter chat rooms pretending to be different ages or even different genders.

MySpace and the other mega-sites all have chat rooms or forums. Because of the "friendly" quality of MySpace and the others, and because of the illusion of privacy they offer, people in MySpace chat rooms—teenagers and young people particularly—may be more likely to open up and be truthful, thinking that they're talking to people of like age and experience. As we've just seen, this is not necessarily the case, and you need to impress upon your child the need for caution. (Again, we recommend simply steering your child away from MySpace and toward more specific special-interest sites.)

Nevertheless, there are lots of wonderful aspects to chat rooms. Think of it: at any hour of the day or night, from anywhere in the world, you can engage in a conversation with people of like minds and similar interests! That's pretty amazing, especially if you're a lonely, isolated kid with special interests, but also if you're a happy, social kid who just likes talking about, say, Brazilian tree frogs, or who just wants the chance to talk to people who don't already know you as "the athlete," "the drama queen," or "the popular one."

On the other hand, as we've already seen, the Internet is an anonymous, no-consequence culture, and chat rooms often partake of that quality. There's a lot of deception, of course, and you can't always tell what you'll find. Sue, a dedicated gardener, has been struck by the number of grownups-only Yahoo! gardening chat rooms whose conversations are actually dominated by flirtatious teenagers. If the kids were talking about the proper time to set bulbs, she wouldn't care—but of course, gardening is the last thing on their minds!

Chat rooms also pose various safety issues. There are open chat rooms that anyone can get into, as well as private chat rooms that require special invitations. As part of her research for this book, Barb pretended to be a twelve-year-old girl on the popular meeting site, www.ICQ.com. Almost immediately, she was invited by someone into a private chat room. She claimed she didn't know how to get into it, and her helpful new friend walked her through the process. Then he wanted to know if she wanted to have sex over the Internet. When Barb wrote back that she didn't know how to do that either, he obligingly explained, "Tell me to unzip my pants, tell me to take out my penis . . ." An adventurous child, looking for new thrills or even just for information, could end up in an upsetting situation. As we saw in Chapter 3, even if a predator never appears in person, sexually explicit online conversations could be overwhelming or inordinately disturbing to your child.

Granted, ICQ is known for such unsavory relationships—unlike MySpace, Friendster, Xanga, Bebo, and Facebook, it's been barred from most public libraries because of its reputation as a sex site. But basically, chat rooms are where your children meet strangers—strangers whom they can't see and don't know anything about. We're not saying they shouldn't go there—lots of healthy and special-interest teen socializing takes place in chat rooms, too—but we are saying that you should remain available to them for all the support and help they need.

We suggest finding out whether your kids are even interested in chat rooms. If they are, invite them to show you how they work. Have them teach you how to enter a public chat room and then, if they know how, a private chat room. Kids love to know things that their parents don't know, and by letting them take the lead, you'll have a chance to express your values and concerns in the form of questions and comments rather than as a lecture. Your child will feel more secure knowing that you actually do understand this kids-only world, and he or she may be more likely to come to you in the event of trouble.

Do review your kids' profiles with them, and help them understand what might happen if they include certain identifying information. They shouldn't mention school names, for example, street names, or any physical descriptions of themselves, other than age. Tell them that you'll review their profiles until you're sure they're old enough to be left unsupervised. Reassure them that you trust them not to do anything wrong, but explain that they might still make mistakes. Give them the message that if they do get in over their heads, they can come to you—that you can tell the difference between them wanting to do something bad and inadvertently getting into trouble. You might say something like the following:

> Honey, I expect you to make mistakes sometimes—we all do, and it's fine that you're still learning. If you do something with serious consequences, then some discipline or punishment may happen, but I promise to be as flexible

and understanding as I can so you will always feel like you can come to me. You're my child, and I love you, and the most important thing is that if you feel scared, upset, or disturbed by *anything*, tell me and we'll work it out to-gether.

## The Benefits of Blogs

A blog—short for Web log—is essentially a live journal on the Internet. Anyone can start one, and, judging by the current state of the Internet, just about everyone has! You can find a number of free sites to host your blog—try www.blogspot.com, or just Google "blogger"—so it costs you nothing but time and energy to share your weekly, daily, or sometimes even hourly thoughts with the world. We'll never forget the online blog we saw that chronicled, in real time, the final episode of *Friends*. You felt as though you were right there with the blogger, watching TV with her.

Other blogs, of course, take on more serious topics, includ-ing politics, history, the arts, and a whole host of special inter-ests. Sue is partial to knitters' and gardeners' blogs, where she finds tips on hand-dyed yarn and fertilizing annuals. There are a number of literary blogs whose focus is to review new books. Sports, science, gay and lesbian issues, movies—you name it, there are blogs that focus on it, as well as on the more personal, "Today I got up and fed my cat" kind of information.

Many, probably most, blogs are anonymous, and a few are deliberately deceptive. Some blogs aren't open to the general public and you need to offer a password before viewing them. More often than not, though, blogs are posted for all the world to see. Blogs can include text, links, photographs, video clips, and other digitized information. Most blogs allow space for people to comment, and sometimes a lively discussion—or even several discussions—will continue as part of the blog. It's a semi-public, semi-private forum, kind of like a permanently published journal or an ongoing memoir. Teenagers love it, because it helps them bridge that public-private gap: they write the blog at home, alone, and then, when someone reads it and comments, they feel that wonderful sense of connectedness: "Someone is interested in my thoughts! I matter."

As you can see, we're big fans of blogs for both children and teenagers, and if your kids want to blog, we suggest that you encourage them—with a few well-chosen words of warning.

**Remember that this is a public form.** It may feel like a diary, but it's a diary that anyone with a computer can read. Even if your kid's blog is anonymous, has he or she included information that might reveal an identity to classmates, family members, or other interested parties? Remember, too, that colleges and corporations sometimes ask for blogs as part of their admissions and hiring decisions. So be careful: what you write could come back to haunt you.

**Remember that comments can be hurtful as well as helpful.** To a vulnerable child sharing his or her thoughts, a blog may feel like a sacred space, vulnerable and intimate. Then some random reader shoots off an e-mail saying, "This is just stupid—you are so lame!" and the child is devastated. That's the price for going public—but it may not be a price your child was ready to pay. Make sure your child really does understand what "public" means, and then be there for him or her if the public response is not so good.

**Be aware of how demanding a blog can be.** Like other forms of Internet use, blogs can have a slightly addictive quality.

Once you start writing, you may not want to stop, or you may feel compelled to return to your blog each day. That's not necessarily a bad thing—for budding writers, it's terrific discipline—but help your child balance other activities and interests with blog time.

We'll talk more about blogs and special-interest/special-needs kids in Chapter 7.

## Forums

Forums are kind of a cross between chat rooms and blogs. A forum is a Web site that anyone can join. Once you've signed in, you choose a screen name, and then you respond to one of the many discussion questions running on the forum. You can usually read forums without signing in, but to contribute, you have to be a member.

In theory, you're supposed to choose your own screen name and stick to it, though people do sometimes fake identities and pretend to be other forum members. In theory, forums are supposed to run according to the best principles of Netiquette: be polite, keep to the topic, and allow others to express their opinions. Forums always have an administrator, and if he or she feels that these rules aren't being followed, action may be taken, including the closing down of entire discussion areas. Forums are usually pretty good about policing themselves and sending away anyone who doesn't want to stick to the topic or who begins to "speak" inappropriately. If you've been on a forum for a while, you begin to feel as though other forum members are your friends, and there's a real feeling of community.

Pretty much any topic you can think of now has a forum—go ahead, see for yourself. Enter a topic into Google plus the word "forum" and see what you come up with. For kids with special interests, forums are terrific, and we're all for them. The only con is that children might think that online is the only place that people congregate to discuss issues, so make sure that your forum-happy child participates in real-life group activities as well. It may require more skill to find people who share your interests in real life, but that's an important skill to learn.

If your child is below the age of fourteen, we think you should be there when he or she signs up for a forum. Read the terms and services for membership and make sure your child understands what they mean. You should probably flip through the forum, too, and make sure that it's appropriate for your child. And of course, make sure your child knows what information to include—and not include—in his or her profile. No last names, addresses, geographic clues, or school names, and certainly no social security numbers or financial information (no legitimate forum will ask for those anyway).

When your children reach fourteen, we think they can have carte blanche to enter pretty much any forum that interests them. However, don't let the topic drop—this may be a big part of your children's life and so it should get talked about. Some sample forum questions:

"How did your forum go today—anything interesting come up?"

"Is everyone behaving well, or did you have to discipline someone lately?"

"What's the most interesting thing you all talked about this week? What's your opinion about that?"

## Keeping Track of Your Child

Just as you can't follow your child from home to school to choir prac-tice, so do you have to let your child have a little space and freedom online. But just as you'd watch for warning signs with those other activities, so should you keep an eye out for possible danger signs online. If you have a happy, bubbly kid who suddenly clams up and seems depressed, find out what caused the change, and don't ne-glect online causes—maybe your child had a disturbing conversa-tion in a chat room or read something upsetting on a blog. Often, children won't tell you what's bothering them until you ask the right question—so make sure to include a few questions about Cyber-world.

## YouTube

YouTube is a Web site that allows users to view video clips as well as to post their own clips on the site. The site is changing so quickly that it's hard for us to make solid recommendations as we write this: by the time this book appears in print, the rules may already have changed. At this point, though, we're not recommending YouTube for kids or teenagers; there are simply too many disturbing, violent, and sexual images avail-able with no kind of filtering system. YouTube, Google Video, and Yahoo! Video have all been criticized for allowing graphic violent material to be posted on the Web with easy access for everyone, but perhaps by the time this book appears, better controls will be in place.

Meanwhile, our recommendation is to put your kids on the honor system: ask them to avoid YouTube, or at least, to watch it only with you. As with all other aspects of Cyberworld, keep your kids talking about this site, even if they're not watching it, because their friends almost certainly are watching it and are talking about it at school. Find out what your kids' assumptions are and help them understand why you're being stricter than the other parents (if you are).

If your kids have heard about a really cool clip that they want to see, watch it with them. That way, you have the chance to weigh in, and your kids know that *you* know a little bit more about their world. That way, too, your kid won't be flipping through YouTube, finding out how to make a bottle rocket out of Mentos and Coke (which was there the last time *we* went to the site!).

## Keep Those Conversations Going!

Just as you did about e-mail, get your kids talking about their Web site experiences. Here are some questions that can help you learn more about what they're doing online and that offer you chances to express your own values, concerns, and questions.

**1.** When you see a pop-up, what do you do?

**2.** Do you Google everything you want to know something about?

**3.** What would you do if you saw an ad for a free sweepstakes?

**4.** What if you saw a diet product advertised on a Web site? What if it was advertised as a natural or herbal product?

**5.** What if someone told you they'd set up a Web site and wanted you to contribute? What would you put on it?

**6.** What would you do if you found out a friend was meeting people in person whom he or she had met online?

**7.** What would you do if you found out a friend was going online and pretending to be someone else? What if that other identity was a real person, someone you both know? What if it was a total fantasy?

**8.** What if you knew someone was copying or downloading material from a Web site and pasting it into a school paper as if he or she had written it?

As we've seen, text messaging, e-mail, and the Internet offer many wonderful opportunities for your child—even if they also pose some troubling concerns. In all cases, your focus should be on maintaining communication with your child, who is likely to know more about Cyberworld than you do. You, however, are the one who knows what your child needs—so keep listening, keep learning, and keep following your instincts. That's one aspect of parenting that Cyberworld will never change.

## PART II

# HOW CYBERWORLD
# AFFECTS YOUR
# CHILD'S
# DEVELOPMENT

f you're going to help your children get the most from Cyberworld—providing maximum support while setting appropriate limits—you need to know how the electronic world appears to children at various stages of their development. Concerns that made sense when your child was six are replaced by new challenges when he turns ten, fourteen, or seventeen. And Cyberworld may seem quite different to a calm, focused child than to one struggling with attention-deficit disorder, Asperger's syndrome, or persistent anxiety.

Cyberworld can also be a godsend to a wide range of special-needs children: helping lonely kids connect with others who share their interests, opening up new vistas for wheelchair-bound children, enabling children with developmental disabilities to learn at their own pace.

In this section, we help you match the challenges, dangers, and opportunities of Cyberworld with the particular age, personality, and abilities of your child, offering specific suggestions for understanding and responding to your child's needs. In Chapter 5, we relate the challenges of Cyberworld to pioneering psychologist Erik Erikson's developmental stages, helping you identify parenting solutions appropriate to different ages. In Chapter 6, we provide a comprehensive look at Cyberworld challenges and solutions for children with a wide range of disorders and disabilities. And in Chapter 7, we help you see how Cyberworld can enrich the life of your special-needs child, including gifted kids, children from cultural backgrounds that differ from their classmates', and children with unusual interests.

## CHAPTER 5

# YOUR CHILD'S DEVELOPMENT

One of Sue's most cherished memories as a child was being held by her mother during a thunderstorm. She vividly remembers sitting in her mom's lap, neither of them saying anything, just listening to the sounds of the storm. For Sue, the experience was a profound lesson in the healing powers of silence, she and her mother sharing a wordless appreciation as they simply listened together.

We can't help but be concerned that today's generation of kids gets less and less of that silence. Between television, radio, iPods, and computers, is there a moment they're not plugged in, staring at a screen, or bombarded with words, music, and images? The most creative periods of our day, we've found, are the down times—those silent moments when nothing much seems to be happening and our minds are free to wander. But what about children who have little or no downtime? How do they find the places "in between their thoughts" that allow them to come up with new ideas?

We believe that silence, creativity, and the space to do nothing are crucial for your child's development. So are the key values of empathy, connectedness, and compassion. But children deal with these issues differently, depending on how old they are. So in this chapter, our basic focus is to help you understand how the Internet affects your child's emotional and cognitive development, and to help you ensure that your kids get what they need to grow up into well-developed human beings.

## Erik Erikson and the Developmental Stages

One of the areas where we'd like to see a lot more research is in the ways that Cyberworld interacts with the different stages of children's emotional and cognitive development. The pioneering psychologist who identified developmental stages from infancy through adulthood was Erik Erikson, and his work continues to be the gold standard for teachers, therapists, and other helping professionals. To our knowledge, no one has yet related the classic Eriksonian stages of development with the challenges and opportunities of Cyberworld, so we're going to make a start in these pages, bearing in mind that a great deal more research needs to be done.

Erikson, by the way, was inspired by his work among the Lakota Sioux in the 1950s. Although the Sioux lived in great poverty, they had managed to preserve many aspects of their traditional society, and Erikson could see that they had provided young people with a number of ways to understand what their social roles should be. Working with the Sioux, Erikson came to realize that until very recently, traditions had provided children and their parents with clear guidelines for what children were supposed to do at particular ages—when they were old enough to help with certain chores, when they were expected to work alongside adults, at what age they could marry.

In modern society, though, roles became more fluid and traditions no longer served as reliable guides. Is a five-year-old big enough to walk to school by himself? That depends on where he lives. Is a ten-year-old mature enough to spend her own money? That depends on her family's income, history, and values. At what age can children date, socialize, engage in sexual relations? Again, the answers vary widely, with few coherent social traditions or even role models to guide us: what worked for our parents may not have applied to our own childhoods, and our childhoods are an imperfect model at best for the Cyberworld of our children. Disintegrating communities and the increasing influence of mass media make these decisions even more difficult.

So Erikson decided to come up with his own guidelines, based on his understanding of children's universal needs. He believed—and we agree—that all five-year-olds are struggling with certain cognitive and emotional tasks, whether they're doing so in a traditional Lakota tipi or a totally wired suburban duplex. No matter who we are or where we live, from infancy through our early twenties we all share certain developmental tasks, though these tasks may take very different forms depending upon our families, culture, and environment. Accordingly, Erikson identified particular issues that defined each stage of life.

Perhaps our hardest challenge as parents is that while our children are growing up in Cyberworld, we didn't. So we can't always tune into our own memories as a guide for parenting our kids, but we can turn to Erikson's stages to remind us that, in some ways, our children need exactly what we needed. Let's take a closer look at how the life stages that Erikson identified can provide a concrete, hands-on guide to helping our children cope with Cyberworld.

## Ages 3–6: Initiative vs. Guilt

Think about your three-year-old—how proud he is of his new ability to move around the world, how excited she is by all the cool things she now can do. Starting at age three and continuing through age six, children are experiencing the thrill of a new autonomy, when expanded cognitive skills and physical abilities enable them to consciously take initiative rather than simply responding to their parents and other caretakers: Hey, what a cool-looking cloth hanging from that table. Wonder what'll happen if I pull on it? Wow, it slipped right off in my hand and then that big bowl fell down! So *that's* what happens if I do *that!* Who knew?

Of course, taking the wrong kind of initiative can lead to guilt. "Oh, *Molly!*" sighs the mother. "You *know* you aren't supposed to pull on the tablecloth. Look, you broke my favorite bowl—and you could have gotten hurt!" Molly sees her mother's distress, and, unlike a younger child, she realizes that she's the cause of it—her and her precious initiative. She had an idea, she took action, she followed through, and *this* is the result!

Certainly, little Molly can have positive experiences with initiative as well—in fact, it's your job as parents to set up as many of those as possible. "Look what happens when I make Mommy a picture!" Molly crows. "She smiles and hugs me and looks so happy! That was *me! I* did that! I like when that happens—maybe I'll draw another picture tomorrow and make that nice thing happen again!"

As you can see, some types of initiative relate to interpersonal activities—hitting brother or sister, making Daddy a present, bringing Grandma a favorite book and asking to be read to. Others relate to the outside world—pulling on that tablecloth, climbing the stairs, building a really *high* tower with your favorite blocks. But the basic dynamic—initiative vs. guilt—is always in place, as little Molly learns that Mommy, Daddy, and maybe Teacher applaud her for climbing the stairs and building the tower *(good* initiative!) while they rebuke her for hitting other children or breaking things, even accidentally. "You're old enough to know better" is a constant refrain for the three- to six-year-old—and an appropriate one, because for the first time in her life, she *is*.

As you can see, the initiative vs. guilt phase is the time in children's lives where they need to become secure in their ability to lead and to make decisions. They need to find out what happens when they decide to do something that affects the people and objects in their world. They need to learn the difference between "good initiative" and "bad initiative," and to start taking responsibility for their own choices and behavior. When a baby slaps us or even bites Mommy while she's nursing, we may not like the feeling, but we understand that the baby didn't do it on purpose. When a three-year-old slaps her little brother or throws a cup at Daddy, we understand that she *did* do it on purpose. However gently, our job as parents and teachers is to train her to choose differently next time: to say "I'm mad!" instead of hitting; to put the cup down instead of throwing it.

---

### A Word About Guilt . . .

In Erikson's opinion—and ours—*guilt* is what children feel when they are punished for taking initiative. "I shouldn't have brought water out to the sandbox and gotten my clothes all muddy. I'm a bad person."

*Remorse* or *regret* is what children feel when they understand the consequences of their actions. "I shouldn't have brought water out to the sandbox. Now my clothes are dirty, and Mommy will have to do extra work washing them. I wish I hadn't done it. I won't do it again."

It's a fine distinction, but an important one. We're all for helping your child see that certain actions—hitting, being careless, disobeying—may have unpleasant consequences, including Mommy's anger or Daddy's disappointment. But try to convey that what you object to is a particular behavior, not the taking of initiative in general.

---

As all these examples make clear, initiative vs. guilt is a very concrete, hands-on, physical kind of stage, in which the child is learning an enormous amount from her moment-by-moment experience in the physical world. So where does Cyberworld—and, for that matter, TV, DVDs, and all our electronic media—fit in? How do they help or hinder a child in this stage of development?

### Cyberworld Challenges for This Phase

**Children need to figure out their own ways of doing things, but computers, electronic games, and media tend to offer stan-**

**dardized, prepackaged approaches that offer less scope for ini-
tiative.** Children aged three to six are physically capable of sitting in front of a TV set, a DVD, or even a computer. Children
at the upper end of this age range can certainly create computer art and write e-mails, while children of all ages can play
electronic games. And for parents who are busy, stressed, or
overwhelmed, the temptation to park the kids with something
that keeps them quiet is well-nigh irresistible. But is it a good
idea?

Alas, the answer is no. A child sitting quietly with a plastic
bowl, taking off and putting on the cover, or making messy
mud pies in the sandbox is fulfilling his developmental tasks; a
child pushing buttons on a keyboard or passively watching an
electronic show is not. The first child is engaged in an open-
ended set of explorations—"What if I push the cover this way?
Will it still fit?" "What happens if I mix the sand with lots and
lots and lots of water—oops! The mud won't stick together!
Maybe I should use less water." He is setting his own agenda,
taking his own initiative, and learning from the results. (And
if you point out that he's gotten mud all over his new trou-
sers when you specifically asked him *not* to bring water out to
the sandbox, he'll learn a little bit about guilt, or, ideally, remorse.)

A child who is playing an electronic game, though, is engaged in a far more limited exploration. Yes, he may learn that
pushing the red button makes the cow moo, while pushing the
green one makes the rooster crow. But that's a very limited set
of results—only a few things can happen, and they're already
predetermined by the computer. It may look like the same
kind of quiet, self-generated play as the mud pies or plastic
cover, but in fact it's worlds away. The cyber-kid is learning to

follow directions, not to take initiative, and an important part of his development is being compromised.

That's even more true for the child watching TV or videos. We're not saying that you can *never* leave your child alone with electronic media, but you should be aware of the compromises you're making every time you do.

Now, what about the child who's writing, reading, or drawing on the computer? Is there anything fundamentally different between the electronic and hands-on versions of those activities?

Again, our answer is, regretfully, yes. The nature of computers is to limit how you do things by setting out a consistent set of possibilities. Hit the "s" key and you'll always get a lowercase "s." But try to print an "s" or write one in cursive, and you can't quite be sure *what* you'll get at age five or six, unless you practice, practice, practice. So even the simple act of writing becomes an opportunity for expressing initiative—"I want to press down *this* hard, and curve my letters *that* big"—as well as a chance for the child to assess the results of that initiative: "Wow! That last *s* looked just the way I wanted it to! So I guess I should always press like that. And isn't it cool that I'm getting better at making on the page what I see in my head!" Choosing from a predetermined set of computerized possibilities just isn't the same. It doesn't matter that when the kid grows up, he'll spend 90 percent of his time on the keyboard and save the handwriting for a note or two—it's not the content but the process that is important here.

Now, let's not go overboard. If you have a learning-disabled or physically challenged child who can produce beautifully written stories on the computer but must struggle for hours just to print a few words, it's no contest: put her on the com-

puter! You're the parent, you know your kid better than anyone, so if you can see ways that the computer is of benefit, go
for it. But please don't confuse the results you see (that beautifully printed story) with your child's experience (the hours
spent trying to shape the letters). All things being equal, kids
need to test themselves against physical and human obstacles
in this stage, and for most children, the computer makes things
both too limited and too easy.

The virtual, elusive, abstract qualities of Cyberworld are
meaningful and perhaps even fascinating to us, but they're just
not what a three- to six-year-old needs to learn about. Children
need to interact with the physical world. Even sitting on the
kitchen floor with some pots and pans is a wonderland of possibilities: things to fit, to put on, to take off. The pioneering
cognitive psychologist Jean Piaget points out that this is the
age when children learn all sorts of mysterious facts about their
physical world. For example, that tall skinny glass *looks* bigger
than the short, fat one, but hey!, they both hold the same
amount of water. These are the kinds of lessons that a child can
learn only in the real world, where there are limits and consequences, and not in the virtual world, where the computer pro-
grammer or games designer is capable of portraying virtually
anything, no matter how fantastic or unlikely.

Children with perceptual and physical disabilities, by the
way, need even more of this real-world immersion than other
children do. They need above all to find out what their bodies,
minds, and perceptual apparatus are capable of. What does distance *mean?* It's the difference between how far you can walk
and when you get tired. What does it take to keep from stumbling or to keep from falling when you do stumble? What can
your arms do (aka gross motor skills)? What about your fingers

(aka fine motor skills)? You can learn some of this on the computer—but only a very little.

**If children are isolated by their use of computers and electronic media, they miss vital opportunities for cooperation, collaboration, and leadership.** A central task for this phase of development is learning how your actions affect other people. What happens when you hit? What happens when you say "please"? What happens when you share? What happens when you say "Mine!"? Can you get everyone in the room to help you make the biggest tower you've ever seen? Is it fun to play with Angela when she offers you one end of the jump rope? Would you rather make a picture with Brendan or draw one by yourself? Did you just hurt Brendan's feelings by saying "No"? How can you make him smile again?

As you probably already know from your own experience, children ages three to six need lots of social time with both children and adults. Learning how to "play well with others" begins at this phase; before that, kids are engaged in "parallel play," with each child making up a separate game and taking a kind of abstract comfort in the presence of other people. In this phase, though, children begin to learn and create games that actively involve others: throwing and catching a ball, inventing fantasy games, doing puzzles together, playing board games and other activities that involve taking turns.

Certainly, children can play a computer game with their friends or watch a DVD together. But again, these scripted situations offer far fewer opportunities for negotiation, creativity, collaboration, and leadership. The child may be learning to follow rules and not make waves, but he or she is not being given the chance to genuinely take initiative.

# Cyber-Exposure: How Early Should Children Begin?

We've heard some parents worry that if they don't immerse their children in Cyberworld early on, the children will miss out on valuable training. In a society where cyber-skills are so crucial, parents may think that the more early practice their kids get on the computer, the better.

We don't agree. Little children need concrete, sensory experiences, not the abstractions of Cyberworld. Children younger than six often become obsessively involved with certain activities, and that's fine if the activity requires physical effort and produces a concrete result—removing and replacing the lid of a jar, for example, or digging and refilling a hole. It's not so good when the repetitive activity is passive and abstract—staring at a screen or pushing a button, which even for adults can become a hypnotic, mind-numbing experience.

So feel free to expose your children to a second language; to get them a pet or introduce them to animals; to take them on nature walks or let them help you garden; and to surround them with art, music, storytelling, and books. Any of these experiences might stimulate your child's senses and imagination while perhaps laying the foundation for a lifelong passion or at least a kind of comfort level. But leave the computers, movies, TV, and other electronic media for later. If you want your children to learn the basics of how to use a computer, write programs, or otherwise penetrate the mysteries of Cyberworld, wait until they're at least six years old—secure in the knowledge that within a week or so, they'll probably know more about computers than you do!

## Parenting Solutions for Ages 3 to 6

→ Limit children's total daily computer and video game time to no more than forty-five minutes.

→ Make a point of putting them in situations where they have the chance to take initiative, especially unstructured play.

→ Monitor them while they're on the computer—don't leave them alone for much longer than a minute or two, especially if they have Internet access.

→ Encourage them to talk with you about conflicts they're having with their friends, and show them how to appropriately and politely resolve conflicts.

→ Help them develop empathy by inviting them to imagine other people's points of view: "How do you think Robin felt when you said you didn't want to play with her?" "I wonder what Martin thought when you said you didn't want to share?" Be aware that these are not the kinds of issues that are likely to come up in e-mail.

→ Discuss mass media with them in age-appropriate ways. In our opinion, no child below the age of six should be watching anything that you haven't also seen, and ideally, you'll watch it *with* your child, so that you can both raise and answer questions. After all, most of the media made for children is done by companies whose main goal is to make money, not to educate your child. And even if the DVD or TV show is a model of early-childhood learning, you still don't necessarily know what your children are taking away from it: they may be anxious, upset, puzzled, or simply have drawn an incorrect conclusion that you never would have expected. We'll never forget the son of a friend of ours who looked at the picture on the paint can and said to his mother, who had been painting their house all summer aided only by a female babysitter, "Mommy, you *can't* paint the house—the picture shows a man doing it."

Part of the challenge of raising kids these days is the omnipresence of mass media and the riveting nature of TV, DVDs, and computer screens. Research shows that there is a hypnotic quality to the flickering light that is physically very hard for many of us to resist, at any age. And there's a fundamental difference between the messages that kids get from human interaction, however problematic, and the ones they get from media and books. Human interaction is something *you* can affect, while media messages are impervious, which gives them a kind of power. So make sure your parental voice trumps the media's voice. Your child needs to learn by actively interacting with you, rather than by passively absorbing information.

## Ages 6–12: Industry vs. Inferiority

As they get older, kids learn a sense of self-worth from what they do. Accomplishing tasks successfully—especially tasks they've chosen and developed themselves—gives children pride in what they've done and who they are. Their goal in this stage is to develop a sense of industry, or competence, and to avoid the inferiority that comes from feeling helpless or incompetent.

The three- to six-year-old is excited just to be taking initiative; the six- to twelve-year-old wants to actually accomplish something. To us, it's one of the greatest tragedies of Cyberworld and the modern world in general that any child between the ages of six and twelve ever says, "I'm bored," because left to their own devices kids this age would *never* run out of things to do. The world is so full of places to explore, trees to climb, holes to dig! There are sports to master, and clothes to sew, and games to invent, and new tasks, skills, and challenges at every turn.

Paradoxically, this is why we're so concerned about the way kids this age are overscheduled: filling their days and nights with French lessons and soccer practice and riding school and drama club, however worthy these activities may be, deprives children of the chance to identify and master skills for themselves. Once again, they're put in the position of being passive learners, living up to others' tasks rather than setting and mastering their own. The boredom sets in when no one else is directing them.

At the same time, Cyberworld and Media World conspire to fill up a child's every free moment with passive stimulation—music, DVDs, games. Between the busy "work" life of lessons and homework and their media-ridden play life children seem to be learning only two activities: *produce* and *consume*. This may well prepare them to fit into the adult world, but it's not necessarily serving their developmental needs. Where is the time to create, to master one carefully chosen skill by practicing it for hours, to invent something new, to choose a task or invent a project and then bring it to completion? Children are given bits and pieces of these activities, but almost always in contexts where there's a set agenda and an authority figure in charge.

Now, certainly, in traditional society, children were subject to all kinds of authority. But they had the chance to master this

Eriksonian stage because they were actually doing real work. They helped the grownups feed the animals, tend the crops, mend the fishing nets, gather the berries—whatever the society did to survive, children aged six to twelve were involved in it. They learned the lesson of industry vs. inferiority with a vengeance, because they understood from a very early age that their own industry was crucial to their community's survival.

Later generations had a version of this with farm chores or household chores, work that had to get done so the family could survive. And, on a more negative note, many generations of children were set to work in factories, mines, and mills, also out of economic necessity.

Certainly, today's middle-class children have the opportunity to learn about industry vs. inferiority in almost magical ways, as they are offered experiences, lessons, and activities that would have seemed like paradise to earlier generations of kids. But this new set of opportunities may result in a confusion about who the industry is for—their parents, their teachers, or themselves?

Having said that, we must admit that this is probably the stage where Cyberworld is most in tune with children's developmental needs. They may need some support for broadening their skills, interests, and leisure activities beyond Cyberworld, and they may need some help developing their friendships and social life in this context (see Chapter 10), but Cyberworld itself offers many opportunities for six- to twelve-year-olds trying to master this stage. Of course, a few challenges remain.

## Cyberworld Challenges for This Phase

**The insubstantiality of Cyberworld may work against a child's need to see his or her effect on the surrounding world.** The computer has so come to dominate our world that the physical world sometimes seems to recede. Children who spend every spare minute online, IMing friends, and checking their MySpace accounts are not learning how to knit, cook dinner, build a doghouse, put a ball through a hoop. They're not finding out how far they can ride their bikes without getting tired, or figuring out how to organize the local kids into a neighborhood game. The rising national statistics on childhood obesity (see Chapter 8) suggest that children are sitting more and moving less. At least some of that has to do with the computer, the TV, and the DVD player—and it is at least partially a move away from industry.

**If your kids can't share their cyber-experience with you, you may have a harder time fostering their sense of accomplishment.** Children aged six to twelve are engaged in a delicate balance: on the one hand, they need to see for themselves that they've achieved something; on the other hand, they need to see their achievements through the eyes of people they trust, particularly their parents. It can be difficult for a child to share his or her Cyberworld experience with parents who just don't have the same comfort or familiarity with the computer (though we hope, after reading this book, that you'll be better able to bridge some of that gap).

**Cyberworld is such an odd mix of production and consumption that it can be hard for children to be industrious there.** You sit down to do your homework and you're distracted by the "you've got mail" beep. You search for a Web site to answer a question about the Civil War and are distracted by the flashing light of a pop-up ad. You try to be industrious, but you're distracted by all the invitations to respond impulsively—or compulsively: electronic games to play, cool things to buy, more links to click . . . Even adults have difficulty remaining industrious in Cyberworld; for children aged six to twelve the task may be even more challenging.

### Parenting Solutions for Ages 6 to 12

→ Limit children's daily computer/electronic time to no more than forty-five minutes for younger children and two hours for older children—including schoolwork.

→ Make a point of giving your children access to a wide range of activities from which they can choose. Encourage them to develop at least one nonelectronic skill: music, art, theater, model-making, building things, repairing things, sports, hiking, bicycling—activities where they can develop a sense of accomplishment apart from what they do on the computer.

→ Check in on them when they're on the computer, especially when they're online. Even short check-ins or quick conversations can forestall some of the eye strain that can result from sitting too long in front of the computer screen.

→ Encourage them to talk with you about the kinds of activities they like and help them develop a sense of pride in their achievements. This can include their cyberactivities. Have them take you on regular tours of *their* Cyberworld so you can see what you're missing!

→ Encourage them to talk to you about their TV watching

and electronic entertainment, too—along with other real-world topics.

→ If necessary, help them master the problems of impulsivity and compulsivity that plague so many of us computer users. Show them how to use an egg timer or a computer timer to help them budget their time. If you need to follow up, do so in a supportive way, without blame: "Honey, the dinger just went off. I just want to remind you that your computer time is up." If they have a problem jumping from hyperlink to hyperlink, explain the problem in a concrete way ("You seem to have a hard time paying attention—those links are pretty distracting, huh?") and model an alternative ("Let me show you how I research something. I have trouble ignoring those pop-up ads, too, sometimes, and it's sometimes hard to stick with one Web page, but let me show you . . .). Then give them a chance to do it themselves. ("Now you try, and I'll watch" or even, "Now you teach me how to do something on the computer that you know and I don't"—you can be sure there's something!)

→ Help them identify positive "industrious" Cyberworld experiences that have real-world effects: blogs that they can write for other people; using IM or e-mail to plan an event; doing advance research about a place that they then visit.

→ Encourage them to teach younger siblings—and you—what they know about cyber-skills, as well as other skills. The more real-life uses your kids find for their abilities, the more successful and industrious they'll feel.

## Who Are You When You're Not Online?

For your children of all ages, we recommend brainstorming to come up with non-cyber ways of spending time alone and together. What can they do alone, with their friends, or with you that doesn't involve video, TM, cell phones; that costs no money or minimal money; and that doesn't involve being entertained or using an electronic product? Ask them, what can you do that doesn't involve iPods, movies, phones, pagers, malls, or gyms?

Here's a list we came up with, in no particular order. You and your kids may like these ideas or you may have some new ones of your own. Bear in mind that you may be creating a monster—some of these activities are so fun and satisfying, they may become just as addictive as Cyberworld!

Go bowling. Go to the library. Read a book, magazine, or comic book. Do a crafts project. Write a story or a poem. Paint. Collect. Just talk with a friend. Go for a walk. Build something. Spend time in a park or nature area. Hike a nature trail. Try wall climbing. Whittle. Ride a bike. Redecorate your room. Go to a museum. Take up bird-watching. Climb a tree. Do a crossword puzzle, Sudoku, or a brain-teaser. Put a jigsaw puzzle together. Play badminton, tennis, or volleyball. Go fishing. Go to the beach. Go beachcombing. Play bocci or *boules*. Play cards, charades, or a board game. Cook something. Garden. Just dig in the dirt. Invent something. Search for stuff with a metal detector. Sew, knit, crochet, or do needlework or bead work. Learn how to make your own jewelry. Try a scientific experiment. Make a model. Take up pottery. Go rollerblading or visit a skating rink. Sit and daydream and do nothing for a while . . .

## Adolescence: Identity vs. Role Confusion

When your kids are teenagers, they're trying to figure out who they are and who they might become. They have a lot of confusing choices to negotiate, including their sense of their sexuality and gender, as well as their potential college major, the work they'd like to do, and what kind of life they intend. More immediately, who will they be friends with, go out with, dress like, be like? Who, finally, *are* they?

Of course, this problem of the teen years is one of modern society—maybe the last couple of centuries or so. In traditional societies, there was no adolescence. Most cultures around the world have never even had a word for this time in a young person's life; why should they? There were children, who needed care, and then there were young people, who apprenticed and got married and continued to live in an older person's household, compound, or community. The transition from childhood to adulthood was far easier, and often marked by an initiation ritual with a clear-cut "before" and "after."

Now, however, we've got this confusing time when young people are too old to be cared for as children and too young to take their places in the demanding world of adulthood. A great deal of recent research indicates that adolescent brains may not be fully developed; the latest studies suggest that our brains continue to mature into our early twenties. In more structured societies, where young people took direction from their elders even after they were married and had children of their own, it may not have mattered exactly when a brain was fully developed, but in our world, it's crucial. Teenagers just don't have the maturity to figure out all the complicated choices that most adults have to make each day.

So there are two senses in which adolescence is a time of identity vs. role confusion. One is the aspect of this phase that Erikson observed among the remnants of traditional Sioux society and believed he'd find among all teenagers: the need to answer basic questions about who you are and where you belong. "I am a baker, the son of a baker," might be a traditional answer to that question. "I am a woman, so I will have children," might be another. In this context, the years between twelve and seventeen are devoted to understanding what the identities of "baker" or "mother" involve and to mastering the skills you'll need to fulfill them.

In traditional societies, the threat of role confusion came when someone didn't want to or wasn't able to live up to the identity expected of him or her—the rebels, misfits, wastrels, and iconoclasts, the ones who never married or couldn't do the work that others did, the ones who made alternate choices or had unacceptable desires. They might be penalized by being denied full adult respect and status, regardless of their age. In many traditional societies, for example, an unmarried man or woman is treated almost as a child, without adult rights and privileges. Those who struggled with role confusion might never achieve adult identities.

Today, kids have lots more choices, yet they still have to master some of the basic skills we associate with adulthood: finishing their schooling, earning a living, socializing and eventually dating, often getting married, perhaps raising children. They also have to master the internal issues: Who am I? What do I believe in? What kind of life do I want for myself? What work will fulfill me? What kinds of relationships will make me happy? Do I desire people of the opposite sex, the same sex, or both? Do I want to have a child, adopt a child, or perhaps raise a stepchild? Will my work be important to me or just a paycheck? Am I part of my community or do I want to remain an outsider?

Today's teenagers struggle with these identity questions and more—and it's all the harder for them to come to terms with these issues when they are largely isolated from all the places where society's actual work gets done. In middle-class families, teenagers are unlikely to be married or raising children. They usually can't get jobs that bear much relationship to the work they want to do later on. They can't even earn enough money, most of the time, to make a serious difference to their family's income. Yet they are supposed to be preparing for a time when they'll do all those things. How?

On the one hand, we've got all those teenagers guided by the overwhelming need to sort out identity vs. role confusion. And on the other hand, we have Cyberworld, a type of virtual reality that seems to promise everything while maintaining the teenager's constant sense of unreality. You talk to people you never see. You spend money without handling either currency or the item you're purchasing. You don't make things that you—or anyone—can touch. You *kind* of feel as though you have an impact on your world—look at all those responses to your blog or that string of comments you inspired in your forum—but that's just type on a screen and often it, too, feels unreal. The gap between you and your *real* life seems wider than ever, even as you also have the tantalizing sense that everything that could turn you into an adult is right there, just beyond the screen.

Now, back in real life, what's your teenager actually doing? He's trying out a bunch of different aspects of his identity, maybe wearing weird clothes and using a funny vocabulary, or taking up new hobbies and dropping them just as quickly. She's figuring out who her friends are—but her friends are changing, too. She may be drawn to online relationships at this point, precisely because she has a chance to try out different identities without having to endure the consequences, the way she has to do in the real world. That seems like a plus—chances to experiment and take risks—except that the sense of unreality continues, because without the social support of real-life consequences, he never really finds a way to integrate the changes into his personality: he can play the role, but he doesn't feel like it's really *him*. Stuck in Cyberworld, your teenagers can never really be sure what difference they make to anyone, no matter how many friends they have on MySpace, no matter how many e-mails clog their inbox, no matter how many comments reach their blog: it's all just words on a screen.

As we try to understand what the teenage years are like in this modern age, we should recall that adolescence is also preparation for the next developmental phase: intimacy vs. isolation. Intimacy isn't just sexual intimacy: it's the ability to share your true self with a friend, colleague, or loved one. The price for not achieving intimacy is isolation: no one knows who you are or really connects to you, while you hide your true self and avoid meaningful relationships. If kids don't master identity vs. role confusion—if they never find out who they really are—they will have a tremendously difficult time sharing themselves with another person in an authentic, intimate way. Fearing to connect, they'll remain isolated. Indeed, this is the fate of many college students, not to mention a cliched portrait of the computer-centered nerd who can play Dungeons and Dragons for hours online but fears ever talking to a real person.

So what's the solution? Obviously, you don't want to keep

your children out of Cyberworld entirely—that would be a terrible disservice, especially as cyber-skills become increasingly important to jobs, schools, and adult socializing. Instead, you need to back up the cyber-portion of your teens' lives with some solid, real-life experience: meaningful work, genuine friendships, in-person dating.

For example, it's crucial that your teenagers learn about conflict resolution—how to fight and then make up with friends and loved ones. We'll talk more about that in Chapter 10, but meanwhile, let's remember that e-mail can be a terrific part of that, giving children the opportunity to speak without interruption or to get their thoughts in order. E-mail is not enough, though: real problem-solving is achieved only by talking things through. You can help your children learn this skill by engaging with them yourself, so that they find out what it's like to express feelings, listen to a loved one, and work out a painful conflict.

It's also vital that your children begin to explore the areas they'd like to study and the work they'd like to do, so they have some sense of who they are in relationship to these dreams. If your daughter wants to be a doctor, can she volunteer at a lab, hospital, or nursing home? Will she answer the "Who am I?" question by saying, "I am someone who likes to help people," or "I am someone who likes to look at cells under a microscope," or even, "I am someone who faints at the sight of blood"? The more real-life chances she has to answer that question, the better, because these are the questions she *can't* answer while sitting at her computer.

Being part of a group is also a vital part of forming an identity, and one that gets too often neglected in our individualistic society. Joining a religious organization, a community group, or a political-action group can be a fabulous experience for a young person. Who am I? Someone who cares about global warming, community empowerment, fighting racism. Who am I? Someone who speaks up at meetings, whose ideas hold people's attention, who's shy in big groups but good one on one, who likes to stuff envelopes but not to make phone calls.

Moreover, the social experience of working things out with real people, face-to-face, helps reveal another aspect of identity. Who am I? Someone who is part of my neighborhood, my ethnic group, my city, my country. Someone who is just myself but also more than myself—proud of my participation in this bigger entity. Again, that's not something your child can find out in Cyberworld, even if part of his political or religious work involves e-mailing, doing Web-based research, or designing flyers with a computer graphics program. To help a teenager resolve his developmental questions, there has to be some arena where the teenager sees firsthand the impact her work has had on her world.

## Cyberworld Challenges for This Phase

**If teenagers are working out their sexual/relationship issues online, they're missing an important component of intimacy and relationship-building.** Sure, you can establish some level of communication through e-mail, IM, and TM. But there's a level of intimacy that comes from physically occupying the same space, an intimacy that really can't be created long-distance. Teenagers, in particular, need that physical contact with one another to integrate their sexual feelings with their emotions. And they need to have some sense of how these new physical and emotional responses actually relate to the person who's inspiring them. What's the difference between being attracted to your classmate Sandy and turned on by a sexy photo of a hot rock star? What's the difference between fantasizing about Sandy and actually getting closer to the real person? And how do these new sexual and emotional feelings affect you and your identity? These questions can only be answered in person.

**If they're taking on fantasy identities, they're probably avoiding troubling issues about their real identities.** To some extent, fantasy and role-playing are an important part of building an adolescent identity. That's part of why theater and creative writing are so useful for teenagers: these activities give them a chance to try out different aspects of themselves, to imagine new aspects of their personality, new desires, new interests. But when teenagers literally pretend that their fantasies are true—when they communicate with other people in disguise—they may be running away from their true identities. "Who I am in real life isn't good enough," they seem to be saying. "I don't feel confident enough, sexy enough, or spiritual enough. If I pretend to be someone older, more experienced, more religious, maybe then I'll be 'good enough.' " Instead of resolving the identity vs. role confusion issue, cyber-teens may be delaying it by pretending to be someone they're not.

**If children are maintaining their friendships primarily through IM and TM, they may not be learning how to share their ups and downs, challenge each other, and brainstorm solutions together.** A huge part of adolescence is developing the friend part of your identity. What kind of friend are you, anyway? Are you loyal or fickle, or some of both? Do you like lots of friends or just a few close ones? Do you challenge your friends or let them slide? Do you share both bad times and good times with your friends or do you hide your joys, your sorrows—or both? Do you get envious easily? Are you the jealous type? Do you compete with your friends? Are you easily angered? Easily placated? These are only some of the identity questions that center on friendship—and none of these questions can be satisfactorily answered if the friendship is primarily conducted through the computer rather than in person.

**If children's sole "work experience" is homework, done primarily in Cyberworld, they may not be learning how to work with groups, master concrete skills, or have an impact on the world they live in.** Part of developing a work identity is finding out how you work with others. Do you take the lead, prefer to follow, or like to do some of both? Do you dig in and argue for your point of view or do you give in easily and let others' views prevail? What kinds of work situations do you enjoy and which would you rather avoid? Again, you can learn some of this on the computer—but for fully exploring a work identity, it's crucial to have other experiences as well.

## Parenting Solutions for Adolescence

→ Limit children's daily computer/electronic time to no more than two hours, including schoolwork. If this is not realistic because of the amount of homework your kid has, limit his or her non-homework electronic time to thirty minutes a day during the school year, and one hour on vacations and holidays.

→ Make a point of putting your children in situations where they can try out different identities—in real life, not online. Let them visit friends and relatives in other cities so they can enter communities that don't already know them. Help them develop different circles of friends, so they can try out different personalities with each group. Encourage them to charge ahead into new situations where they can learn new things about who they are.

→ As always, check in to see what they're doing online— and make sure they know you're doing this!

We'll let the man who inspired Erikson, the founder of psychoanalysis, have the last word. Sigmund Freud said that the definition of a good life was to love well and to work well. Cyberworld can be a portion of that, but never all of it. Make sure your children learn to love and work in the real world, too.

## CHAPTER 6

# EMOTIONAL AND LEARNING DISORDERS

I f your child struggles with emotional or learning disorders, you already know how contradictory Cyberworld can be. On the one hand, cell phones, Web-based research, and e-mail can open up a whole new world to your child, a world where he or she may feel more like other children or empowered in exciting new ways. On the other hand, for children with cognitive and emotional disorders, Cyberworld can be tough: the weird spelling, the abbreviated interactions, the multiple distractions, the infinite number of seductive links to follow . . . These are challenging for all of us, children and adults alike, but if your child has difficulties reading, writing, or receiving information; paying attention; coping with depression or anxiety; or forming emotional attachments, Cyberworld may seem daunting indeed.

Don't worry: we're here to help, and we promise you that for every cyber-problem you've encountered, there is indeed a cyber-solution. It may take a bit of time, persistence, and creativity—but what doesn't?

## Keeping It All in Perspective

We're going to start by assuming that your special-needs child has already been diagnosed and that you're familiar with his or her educational and emotional needs. If not, we urge you to seek help from a psychologist or other professional; what's in this chapter is only intended to supplement a larger and more complete view of how to help your child learn and grow. We also recommend that your child get regular physicals, especially if he or she struggles with problem behaviors or erratic emotions and mood swings, since many symptoms result from the body's misfiring. For example, thyroid malfunctions are often misread as sluggishness or depression.

Because the *Diagnostic and Statistical Manual of Mental Disorders* 4th Ed., Text Revision *(DSM-IV-TR)* is what most professionals are currently using for diagnosis and treatment, that's the basic reference work for this chapter, too. (As you probably already know, *DSM* is the comprehensive list of emotional, cognitive, and behavioral disorders used by insurance companies, educators, therapists, health professionals, and just about anyone else in the helping professions.) When the next edition of this work, the *DSM-V*, appears in 2011 or 2012, a lot of definitions, diagnostic criteria, and recommendations may change, and some clinicians are already basing their work on the current research rather than on the last edition of *DSM*. But because schools and insurance companies are still using the published edition, *DSM-IV-TR* is the one we use.

Now, here's the most important thing we'll say all chapter, so listen up: *You know your child better than anyone else.* That's right. You. Not his teacher, not her counselor, not any professional who comes in to help, no matter how caring or effective or well-trained. The folks who are part of your kid's team are invaluable, and you should always listen to them with an open mind—and that goes for grandparents, aunts and uncles, and any other caring adults who might indeed pick up some things you missed or suggest some ideas that seem new to you. Now that you're reading this book, we're part of that team, too, and we'll do our best to offer you some new approaches.

But in the end, you are the one who needs to decide what's working and what isn't. You may not have an advanced degree, but you love your child and you're there every day, and you're entitled to "go with your gut." You probably have already figured out that not every solution works for every child. The best you can do is listen to your instincts and to your child, and be willing to try, and fail, and try again. Like all parenting, caring for a special-needs child is a process of trial and error. We all wish our kids came with a manual, but alas, none of them do, and this book isn't that magic manual, either, much as we wish it were. Still, we do have some good ideas that you may want to try—so read on!

## For All Special-Needs Cyber-Kids . . .

• Help your child decrease his or her stress levels as much as possible.

• Help your child increase his or her coping skills.

• Find other ways to measure achievements besides grades—don't hold your child to unattainable goals.

• Pick your battles; accommodate your child's quirks whenever possible.

• Set your limits and feel entitled to them; you're allowed to have things *your* way, too.

## Setting Up Your Child's
## Electronic Environment

First things first. Let's get your child settled in an electronic environment that will provide the least amount of distraction and the fewest obstacles to being calm, focused, and on-task.

**Choose a separate area for the computer.** Ideally, you'd have your child in his or her own room, facing a screen into the corner—nothing to look at but the screen. If that's not an option, try to block off the computer area for your child—perhaps with a portable wooden screen—and keep others out of the room during computer time if you can. That doesn't mean you should let your children use the computer completely unsupervised: make sure to set time limits and to check in on them periodically.

**Keep the walls around the computer bare.** Lots of special-needs children go into sensory overload fairly quickly, so let's reduce or eliminate any sources of stimulation in the work area. If your child likes to collect things, enjoys books, or responds well to art, that's terrific, but ideally, none of these enticing objects should be within his or her sightlines while sitting at the computer, especially if he or she has problems paying attention.

**Create a quiet environment.** Many special-needs kids are hypersensitive to sound, including those struggling with autism, Asperger's syndrome, and ADD/ADHD. Choose a quiet room if you can, and perhaps tack some cork on the walls to keep the sound out. A rubber mat or some felt pads under your child's chair will keep it from squeaking or scratching along the floor. If you can, set up your child's work area away from vents, so the sound of the heat or the a/c coming on doesn't startle him or take him off task and so the air flow doesn't distract him.

**Try to light the room with natural rather than fluorescent light, and with floor lamps rather than overhead lamps.** Even though most of us are not attuned to it, fluorescent lighting and some overhead lighting emit a slight hum; this, too, can be very distracting for some children.

**Make sure there's plenty of fresh air.** Maybe add a plant somewhere out of your child's sightline for extra oxygen. You want to encourage your child to breathe deeply and work calmly, which will be harder to do in a stuffy room.

## Establishing a Study Routine

Most of us do better when we've got a clear routine—and that goes triple for most special-needs kids. So we suggest that you create a study-starting routine that you and your child perform in exactly the same order each night. Such rhythms are very reinforcing—and in some instances comforting—and help to establish discipline, concentration, and focus, not to mention easing the anxiety of anxious children while energizing kids who struggle with depression. Here's a sample routine, though of course, you and your child can come up with your own.

**Turn off all the phones in the room and lower the volume on any answering machines within earshot.** *No distractions* is your goal—and hearing a ringing phone or a voice leaving you a message is highly distracting, even for an adult. Your child can check his or her messages when the homework is done.

**Turn off any music that's playing and put the iPod away in a drawer that can't be reached while sitting at the desk.** Otherwise, reaching over to put on those headphones "for only a minute" can be way too tempting. If your child takes a music break, he or she can get up, go across the room, listen, and return when the break is over—clear boundaries, clear tasks.

**Turn off the overhead light and put on the floor lamp.** Especially if you have fluorescent lighting, the slight hum it may make can be distracting for your child. And you don't want too much light when viewing a computer monitor anyway.

**Check to make sure there's paper in the printer and replace any ink cartridges that have run low.** Now is the time to tend to these things—not in the midst of a demanding task.

**Lay out any books and other materials you'll need close at hand, stacked in the order you'll use them.** Now your child's books are ready for action—and your child is already ordering and organizing the evening's work. If your child has trouble with that kind of organization, you can be the coach: "What will you do first? Okay, then get your history book out. What will you do when you've finished your history assignment? Great, then let's put your science notebook underneath your history book so it will be right there when you need it! What's next?"

**Go to the bathroom.** Yup, let's just get this out of the way so the next thirty to sixty minutes can be focused indeed! This also can be a soothing activity for anxiety-prone children: first, they set up, then they get a little break, and *then* they start work. Knowing they can leave the work area if they want to means they may not feel so anxious about staying.

**Shut the door.** That's your child's signal: now the focus is on the work, not on any of the other people in the house.

**Set the timer for your first break.** We all need regular breaks when working on the computer (for more on the importance of breaks, see Chapter 8), but it's easy to get drawn into that flickering screen and lose track of time. Special-needs children can benefit from timers to remind them when they need to stop, stretch, and maybe get a healthy snack or run around the block to discharge some built-up energy. Choose a timer that doesn't have a loud ticking sound and whose alarm isn't—well, alarming. You can also install a timer/message reminder on your computer if you find this works better.

Having set up this routine, support it with break-time rules such as the following.

**No phones, including cell phones.** It's too easy to get drawn into a long, distracting conversation, and when you realize you have a text message, it's really hard not to check it out. All of this communication has the potential to raise anxieties, depress mood, or simply start your child's brain off in a whole new direction. Break times are for giving your brain a rest—not for inspiring it with new preoccupations!

**No TV or DVDs, and probably no reading.** Obviously, this one's your call: maybe your child is capable of watching only five minutes of a favorite show or briefly dipping into a favorite book. But we'll tell you the truth: neither of *us* has that kind of self-control! Our TV and reading breaks always stretch into thirty minutes minimum, and sometimes we never do get back to work. So you and your child may need to figure out together some realistic ways to enjoy breaks while not drifting out of homework mode entirely.

**No e-mail or computer games.** This one's important: your child's break time is for getting *away* from the computer, not for switching to a new cyber-activity. This is a health issue that's important for all children, not just those with special needs (for more detail, see Chapter 8), so help your child understand the importance of physically leaving the computer for five to ten minutes before returning, refreshed, to work.

**Get some physical exercise: stretching, time on the exercise bike, a quick run around the block.** See Chapter 8 for more on this suggestion, which again, goes for all children.

**If you eat something, make it a healthy snack and eat it away from the computer.** The goal is always to be in full work mode in front of the computer. If your child sits there and reads for pleasure, has a snack, or chats on the phone, there's not such a strong association between *computer* and *work-focus*. Help your child build that association so that just sitting down in front of the screen triggers his or her brain for action. (For more on healthy snacks, see Chapter 8.)

## Chunking: Working Bit by Bit

All children can benefit enormously by learning how to chunk a task into smaller steps, but this technique is vital for most special-needs kids. An assignment that can feel overwhelming as a big picture—*Find out how to make a terrarium*—becomes manageable when broken down into discrete tasks:

1. Find out what elements go into a terrarium.
2. Choose one element. Find out where to get it.
3. Choose another element. Find out where to get it.
4. When all the elements are ready, what's the first thing you'd do?
5. What would you do next?
6. What would you do last?

You will almost certainly need to model this kind of chunking for your child, and be prepared to chunk assignments over the course of several years—some children don't master this skill until they get to college. But if your child knows that you'll help him break down apparently overwhelming assignments, he'll approach his schoolwork with far more optimism and calm.

How does this apply to Cyberworld? In our experience, the electronic media make chunking both easier and harder. Harder, because of the proliferation of links, cross-references, and multiple answers to a search: learning-disabled children can easily become overwhelmed by their own search results. But Cyberworld can also make chunking easier, because if your child learns to ignore the siren song of links and extra search results, she can use a search engine to help her answer each individual chunking question that you have helped her prepare.

## Impulsivity and the Internet

A wide variety of special-needs children struggle with impulse control and excitability, and sometimes we feel as though Cyberworld was specifically designed to make this problem worse. Not only are there numerous visual and auditory stimuli— literally, bells and whistles, along with flashing lights and high-speed video—but there's the constant possibility that behind every link lurks an exciting new site. When children are old enough to understand that some of these sites are sexually explicit, or that they can have racy conversations with IM or in chat rooms, the excitement builds.

If your child needs help relaxing in Cyberworld, here are some suggestions:

**Explain that you've installed filters to reduce the possibility that he or she will stumble on a sexually explicit site—even accidentally.** The same goes for gambling sites or any other forbidden fruit that you think might excite your child. (And you may want to choose stricter filters than you otherwise would.)

**Choose a really strict filter to get rid of pop-ups, advertisements, and other extraneous features.** Cyberpatrol and Net-Nanny are really good for this. (See Resources for more information.)

**Steer your child away from IM and suggest that he or she answer e-mail on a non-e-mail program and then paste it in.** Knowing that someone might be standing by, waiting for a response, can create an uncomfortable level of excitement for some children, not to mention anxiety among children who can't read, write, or type quickly.

**Practice going from link to link with your child.** Help her learn to slow down and focus on the site she's found before clicking compulsively on the next link. The goal is to interrupt her impulses with calm and conscious thought, so work with her to develop some strategies for slowing down—perhaps a ritual of taking three deep breaths before clicking on any link or posting on the (otherwise blank) wall a question she always asks herself: *Am I ready to leave this site and go to the next one?*

## Guiding Your Special-Needs Child Through Cyberworld

Okay, those are the all-purpose suggestions; now let's get specific. We're assuming that you'll be turning directly to the section that affects your child, but if your child has multiple diagnoses or if you're parenting more than one special-needs child, you may find yourself reading several sections. Don't be surprised to find some overlap: we tried to make each section as complete as possible.

### LEARNING DISORDERS
### Disorders of Written Expression

These are the kids who will have a real problem with text messaging and e-mail abbreviations. Since they already have trouble with phonics, spelling, and grammar, they'll find it challenging to switch back and forth between the alternative language of electronic communication and the more correct forms of standard English.

If you do allow them to use e-mail, require them to spell out every word and use proper capitalization, punctuation, and complete sentences. Encourage them to use the spellcheck feature and to correct anything that the spellcheck brings up. If they object, simply say, "I am happy to give you the privilege of e-mail, as long as you respect this boundary." You know best whether you should put your child on the honor system, but even if you do, we suggest checking his or her e-mails periodically as yet another way to monitor progress.

TM presents more problems for these children because there are so many more abbreviations, less punctuation, and no capitalization. We think it's worth taking a firm stand: your child must either spell out everything correctly or forfeit the privilege of text messaging. (As you saw in Chapter 2, we're not so crazy about text messaging anyway.) With TM, you'll really need to put your child on the honor system—monitoring his or her messaging just isn't feasible—but you might spot-check by TMing your child yourself once in a while and having your child TM you back.

Now, what if your child gets teased for having to write everything out? That's your chance to work with your child on what we call refusal skills. Help your child practice what he'll say to friends who want to know why he's not using common acronyms or leet speak. Role-play with your child and let her explain why she does things differently. Here are some sample explanations and retorts you might suggest:

> You know I'm in a special class for my writing. This is all part of that.
> My folks are pretty strict. It's either this or nothing!
> I know my long messages may be more work for you, but they work better for me. Thanks for understanding.
> This is the deal I have with my parents. That's just the way it is.
> Hey, I'm getting better grades now, so it's totally worth it.

If your child is cooperative and is making progress, you might loosen up a little and allow some acronyms, but no alternate spellings. (Acronyms are abbreviations based on the first letter of each word, like "lol" for "laugh out loud." Alternate spellings are when a word is spelled differently than in standard English.)

| Acronyms: Okay | Alternate spellings: Not okay! |
| --- | --- |
| LOL (laugh out loud) | u for *you* |

| | |
|---|---|
| ROFL (rolling on floor laughing) | c-p for *sleepy* |
| OMG (Oh my God) | r for *are* |
| TTFN (ta-ta for now) | cyo see you online |
| TY (thank you) | cul8r see you later |
| BRB (be right back) | tlk2ul8r talk to you later |
| HAHAO1/2K (ha ha only half kidding) | K for *okay* |
| TMI (too much information) | Tks for *thanks* |
| BTW (by the way) | |
| NALOPKT (not a lot of people know this) | |

It may also be helpful for your child to do searches, which won't work unless the terms are spelled correctly. Many search engines will ask "Did you mean [correct spelling]?", which might actually help your child improve his or her spelling. Help your child feel comfortable coming to you if a search goes haywire: "If you come up with something crazy, no problem, come to us—even if your timer hasn't rung yet! We won't call it a break!"

Finally, children with difficulties writing may have trouble beginning, continuing, or ending conversations for a variety of language-related reasons. Both on e-mail and in real life, they may struggle with limited vocabulary, errors in tense, difficulty recalling words, difficulty producing sentences at their grade level, and difficulty expressing ideas. You might help them make a list of some conversational remarks that they can post by their computer while they're doing e-mail:

| Starting Out | Continuing | Signing Off |
|---|---|---|
| What did you do today? | What do you think? | I've got to go now. |
| Did you hear about . . . ? | Wow! | See you tomorrow! |
| What did you think of . . . ? | That's cool. | Later. |

## Reading Disorders

Kids who already have trouble reading may find electronic text especially frustrating: the letters are smaller, the text size varies, and the graphic displays and nonstandard layouts can frustrate even a skilled adult reader. Pop-ups, ads, banners, and other electronic distractions only add to the confusion.

If your kids struggle with reading, you might encourage them to download electronic text and work with it on paper, possibly helping them manipulate type size, margins, line spacing, and other features to make the physical experience of reading easier for them. They might also want to use the boldface feature to make the text easier to read. (By the way, this kind of text manipulation is *much* easier in WordPerfect than in Word.)

If your child does need to manipulate and/or print out modified electronic text, turn this apparent disability into an opportunity. Teach your child some new computer skills, or better yet, hire a college kid or "computer geek" to teach your child, treating the whole occasion as an advanced computer class rather than as one more example of how frustrating your child's disorder can be. Instead of feeling disordered, your child grasps that she's mastered a whole new set of valuable skills that she learned from people who didn't have her disorder and yet used these skills anyway. Plus, her classmates never need to find out that she's compensating for her disorder in this particular way.

Meanwhile, you can experiment, too, to find out which typefaces, colors, and fonts are easiest for your child to read. Show your child how to prepare homework in that font and then convert it at the last minute to whatever the teacher requires. That goes for e-mail, too: very few kids know how to manipulate their e-mail program, but yours can be one of the few!

Many reading-disordered kids do better when they can actively interact with the text, using highlighters, underlining, and making notes in the margins. Again, this is better done with downloaded text and hard copy, at least until children become comfortable with electronic formats. And again, this is an opportunity for you (or a hired helper) to show your child how to use specialized electronic features—highlighting, underlining, comments, and the like.

Slow readers may well feel frustrated using IM or entering chat rooms, as their friends and fellow "chatters" wait impatiently for them to respond. So you might want to discourage that kind of cyber-activity. If your child insists, give him or her a ten-minute window to try it out, perhaps while you observe. Remember—and help your kid remember—that anybody could be frustrated by another person's expectations of a quick response, so normalize this experience and decide with your child whether IM and chats are a good idea for *him*. E-mail is fine, because children can read and respond to it at their own rate. If the acronyms seem to be slowing your child down, encourage the use of the acronym translator at the bottom of the www.teenangels.org Web page.

> **TIP** Specifying particular fonts and colors for Web pages can be especially helpful for children who struggle with reading disorders. Here's what you do:
>
> 1. In the Tools menu of your Internet browser, click Internet Options.
> 2. On the General tab, click Accessibility.
> 3. Change the settings as needed.

## Processing and Receptive Difficulties

Children with processing and receptive difficulties may need more time than others to answer questions, absorb text, or respond interactively. Encourage them to find ways to control the flow of electronic information so that they can work in their own time, and do what you can to prevent pop-ups, banners, and other electronic interruptions.

These children need extra time, both because they process information more slowly and because anxiety can really disable their responses. You already know that these children need to spend more time doing homework than their classmates, so work with your child, her teacher, and any specialists on your team to figure out realistic amounts of time for doing homework and being at the computer. Help your child schedule what needs to get done when, and show her how to figure out what's most important, in what order the assignments should be done, and how much time she should spend on each one.

These types of children often have difficulty switching from one topic to the next: either they can't leave an old topic, can't begin a new one, or both. So check in on them regularly to see how they're doing. They need structure, boundaries, and positive reinforcement, and they'll do much better with that type of oversight. If you feel frustrated by focusing on your child's homework to this extent, consider hiring an older kid or college student as a tutor or monitor—not so much to teach your child as simply to sit nearby and check in with him every fifteen minutes or so, just to keep him on track.

These children need lots of help in coping with their own frustration, because everything is so mysteriously difficult for them. They know they're of normal or even above-average intelligence, and yet they can't do what their classmates or siblings can manage easily—and that hurts. Support their process by encouraging them to take regular breaks, eat something between study sessions, stretch or exercise, and perhaps do some deep breathing, which has a wonderful calming and focusing effect. (See Chapter 8 for some suggestions about yoga and computer health.) You and they may both be tempted to "wrestle the problem into the ground" by having them sit at the computer for hours until they're done—but resist that temptation. It will only frustrate everyone, and it doesn't teach your child how to establish good long-term work habits. We also know that anxiety affects performance, so help them achieve that calmer state. They need breaks, movement, and breathing, so that when they're focused, they're really focused.

With regard to the Internet, sit down with your child and help her get used to navigating it. But let her find her own way; give her some time alone to sit and process, rather than standing over her shoulder and distracting her.

We suggest that you discourage IMing and TMing, given how frustrating the acronyms and alternate spellings may be.

Maybe your child will get better after some chat room practice, though, so be prepared to experiment. If your child has trouble answering quickly in IM, TM, or chatrooms, teach him or her some holding phrases to normalize the need for more time:

Be right back.
Let me think about that. (By the time the other person has read those words, you've bought yourself the time you needed.)
Tell me more.
Cool.
Wow.

Chat rooms are especially challenging, because many chatters don't like sending or receiving long responses all at once. The protocol is to send a sentence or two at a time. This might be hard for a receptive-disordered child, so suggest that she jot down a few notes to keep track of her thoughts. She might get used to phrasing her answers in stages, too:

I have two thoughts about that. The first is . . . [send the message]
And the second is . . . [send the message]

This allows the sender time to organize and plan what she has to say, while also reserving the time and attention of the receiver.

Children with receptive disorders often have difficulty with multiple meanings and multiple spellings, so you can imagine how difficult they find the jargon-laden world of IM and TM, with its alternate spellings, acronyms, and inconsistent use of language. (Again, the acronym translator at the bottom of the www.teenangels.org Web site may help.) On the other hand, when kids are motivated, they can accomplish extraordinary feats. Perhaps your child will love chatting so much that she'll master some challenges that in other contexts would have left her baffled. So give her a chance to excel if she can—but help prepare her for frustration, just in case. We suggest starting with a ten-minute time limit so that she knows an absolute end to her frustration is in sight:

> Honey, I know all your friends are hanging out in chat rooms, and I'd like you to have a chance to do it, too, so let's go ahead and start you with ten minutes. And if you really like it, and you're doing okay with it, I'll be willing to expand that amount.

Then take it slow and see how it goes. As far as e-mail, suggest having your child ask his friends to use the spell-check, perhaps blaming it on you:

> Please don't use shorthand or initials—just spell everything out. It's *so* much easier for me.
> My mom and dad won't let me use e-mail unless everything is spelled right.

We suggest starting all these activities with a ten-minute limit and the willingness to move up to an hour in slow stages, knowing you may never get there. On the other hand, be prepared for some surprises. It's remarkable what kids can do when they really *want* to communicate!

## Idioms, Images, and Metaphors

Some children have special difficulties with idioms and other figurative language, especially children with receptive disorders, Asperger's, and autism. Barb once supervised a child whose foster
mother used to punish her son by sending him to stand quietly in a
corner for a few minutes. To warn him, she once said, "I've got a corner right here with your name on it"—and was then surprised to see
her child diligently checking out every corner in the house. When he
came back and told her he hadn't found his name anywhere, she
thought he was mouthing off, but he was really struggling with Asperger's and his lack of ability to think in figurative terms.

Translating phrases like "fingers crossed" or "bad hair day" is
hard enough for a literal-minded child in the context of an ongoing
conversation, where there are lots of cues to help figure out what's
going on, including smiles and laughter to indicate joking or teasing.
On e-mail, as we've seen, even nondisordered children have trouble
sorting out irony, sarcasm, and hyperbole. So if you've got a literal-
minded child, help prepare him or her for what e-mail and other
cyber-communication might be like:

> You may see a lot of things that won't make any sense to you, so I'd
> like you to come to me when you get nonsense sentences from
> your friends. These words and phrases may almost feel like an-
> other language—but I can help you navigate.

### ATTENTION DISORDERS
### Attention-Deficit/Hyperactivity Disorder (ADHD)

Kids with ADHD are easily overstimulated by Cyberworld.
They need help in slowing down, focusing, and controlling the
flow of information. So do what you can to minimize elec-

tronic distractions, such as e-mail announcements, pop-ups, and other interruptions. Encourage them to focus on only one task at a time. And set a timer so that they take frequent breaks to avoid overstimulation.

Healthy, high-protein, low-carb/low-sugar snacks are very helpful for ADHD kids, as is vigorous exercise. Make sure your kids take protein and exercise breaks, so they can return to work refreshed and focused.

Sometimes taking notes by hand while looking at an electronic screen is a helpful way of slowing down the flow of information and making it your own. Writing down questions you have is also a good way to focus.

### Helping ADHD Children in Cyberworld

→ Limit distractions around the computer to help them focus.

→ Chunk down tasks that need to be accomplished into short steps (see page 194 for details).

→ Schedule lots of breaks that include healthy food and vigorous exercise.

→ Structure is vital: set a schedule for every work session and review it with your child.

→ Use timers as needed.

→ Monitor them as needed; children with this disorder often lose track of time or underestimate how long a task will take.

**TIP** Many programs have reminder pop-ups as part of their alarm function—little balloons that you can program to appear at specified times, with notes in them like "Five minutes till dinner," "Pace yourself," and "Time for a break!" If your child won't be distracted by these interruptions, consider using them as friendly reminders. They might even save you a few trips into your kid's room at homework time. Work with your child to figure out what's helpful and what's just annoying.

## Talking to Teachers

Many schools now post homework assignments on the Internet and/or on a voicemail recording. Show your child how to check her assignments and make sure she knows how to print them out. Double-check her until you're sure she's able to handle this part of her school responsibilities, which may not happen until college.

Many teachers now provide their e-mail address to parents, so we encourage you to communicate with your children's teachers directly—always being respectful, of course, especially of their time. Think of how many e-mails your child's teacher gets each day and then limit your e-mails to brief notes setting up a meeting—perhaps once or twice a semester—to see how your child is doing and to find out how you can support her progress at home. Use the "read receipt" function so you can wait more patiently for the teacher to get back to you.

**TIP** To find the receipt function in your e-mail program click on Tools, then on Options. Click on the receipts tab and request a read receipt, then when you send an e-mail, the recipient will be asked to check a box acknowledging that he or she has received it. While you're waiting for an answer, you at least have the comfort of knowing that the e-mail was received.

We also suggest providing your child's teacher with a one-page overview of your child's strengths, what he needs to work on, and anything that might be useful in soothing or calming him, if necessary. For example, one autistic boy we knew would start rocking himself when he felt anxious, but as soon as someone asked him a question about his older brother, he came out of his dissociative state and began talking normally.

Finally, make sure your child's teacher knows about your child's progress in Cyberworld, as well as any specific concerns you've developed as the year continues.

## MOOD DISORDERS
### Bipolarity and Depression

If your kids struggle with mania or manic phases, you might follow the same recommendations as for ADHD. Although the diagnoses are different, many of the cyber-problems and solutions remain the same.

If your children are coping with depression, help them take exercise breaks, eat healthy snacks, and make sure to have plenty of social contact. Try not to let them become isolated in Cyberworld: even healthy adults can wake up from a period of several hours online, wondering where the time went and feeling a bit lonely or depressed from the extended isolation. Also make sure that staying online isn't keeping your kids from getting enough exposure to sunlight and/or a light box, which can be crucial to preventing or overcoming depression, especially in the winter. (See Resources for more on light sources and light boxes.)

Be aware if your child is becoming obsessed with negative

or depressing domains, such as Web sites or blogs that focus on sad poetry. Most teens like to explore the newly discovered dark side of life, especially through poetry and music, but for a depressed child, a bleak version of Cyberworld can come to seem more compelling and overwhelming than CDs or books—the combination of meeting real people online and yet never actually seeing them can make it seem as though the world is full of depressed people who all agree that suicide is the only way. Some chat rooms even focus on death and suicide to the point where they even post ratings on the best way to kill oneself. You should be aware that your depressed child is visiting such sites and steer her away from them.

On the other hand, Cyberworld can be wonderful for depressed kids who overcome their sense of isolation through writing e-mails. Writing a journal is also a terrific tool for depressed kids, who may find it easier to record their thoughts electronically than by hand. And sometimes the effort of reaching out from journal to blog—making the blues public, so to speak—is a way to begin to connect, find self-worth, and create a new identity as a positive, effective person.

Bipolar and depressed children often need to learn how to accept compliments, how to handle conflicts, and how to become more assertive. E-mail can be a terrific practice forum for these issues, since there's usually a time lag between responses. If your child gets a compliment via e-mail, for example, you can work with him on ways he might accept it gracefully rather than downplay or deny it. Try role-playing with your child to portray what a person receiving a compliment might say, and then help him compose an e-mail that contains his own version of a response. Suppose your child tells you that he got an

e-mail from a friend saying, "You looked really good today."
Some sample replies might be:

> Thanks!
> Do you really mean it?
> What about me looked good today?

What you want to help your child avoid is "No, I didn't," or
"Don't say that—why are you making fun of me?!" These might
be his automatic responses in person, but because e-mail doesn't
take place in real time, he has the chance to try something different.

Likewise, bipolar and depressed children often have difficulty asserting themselves; they frequently need work on what
we call their refusal skills. Again, you can role-play different
situations with them in which it's important to say no, set limits, or agree to only part of a request, and then coach them on
applying these new skills via e-mail, where the pressure to give
in is mitigated by the gap in time and space. Help them choose
from responses like the following:

> "No."
> "Not right now."
> "I'd rather not."
> "I can do part of that job, but not all of it."

You can also have a conversation about your child's fears:
"What's the worst thing that could happen if you refuse?"
Then talk together about ways your child might respond in a
worst-case scenario.

Finally, depressed children often need extra support in coping with change and with bad news in general. They are often highly sensitive, and it can be disturbing to them to be assaulted by TV news reports, headlines, and other reminders of the world's tragedies and horrors. If your child responds this way, choose a start page that doesn't force her to confront new information, opinions, and events every time she sits down at her computer. Help give her a sense of proportion about bad news, perhaps suggesting that she read some "bad news" stories online and then search for stories about topics that she'll find inspiring—people making positive changes or helping others, to balance her view of the world.

Generally, if you're caring for a depressed child, you know what is likely to trigger his or her depression and the signs that he or she is heading into a funk. You'll probably want to formulate your own plan of action to head off a depressive episode, and you'll know best whether that plan includes extra time online e-mailing sympathetic friends or limited time online if your child feels more isolated there. Either way, remember that it's one of your child's developmental tasks to recognize and cope with his own depression, developing lifelong strategies for dealing with it. Help him figure out where Cyberworld fits into his vision of caring for himself.

## Common Warning Signs of Suicide

Although teenage suicide is rarer than it used to be, it's still the third leading cause of death among U.S. teenagers. The vast majority of depressive episodes among teenagers don't lead to suicide attempts, but if your child is struggling with depression, you'll want to keep an eye out for the following warning signs:

• Appearing depressed, hopeless, desperate
• A preoccupation with death
• Making statements such as "Nothing matters" or "I wish I was dead"
• Using drugs or an increased use of drugs
• A loss of interest in his or her appearance or a change in hygiene
• A lack of interest in the future, such as college or other long-term plans
• Giving away prized possessions
• Any change in eating or sleeping habits
• An unwillingness to accept praise

## ANXIETY DISORDERS
### Generalized Anxiety Disorder (GAD); Social Anxiety Disorder (SAD)

If your child suffers from GAD, he or she may find the Internet very helpful, as it offers ways to connect to other people without feeling watched or judged. Help your anxious child build on experience with virtual contact to develop real connections in live situations.

Typically, children with GAD and SAD have trouble concentrating—their anxiety makes it difficult to focus. However, one of the things we're finding is that Cyberworld actually enhances anxious children's ability to pay attention, especially when they're interested in something—and the Internet is full of things to be interested in!

Like depressed children, children with GAD may be highly

sensitive to bad news, change of any type, and information about events they can't control. As with depressed children, you might choose a start page that isn't linked to news headlines, so that your child doesn't have to face bad news every time he turns on his computer.

Beyond the news aspects of Cyberworld, though, generally anxious children often respond badly to unmonitored, unstructured time online: there's simply too much change, and the speed of information flows too fast for comfort. Help them pace themselves as you monitor their level of anxiety. Once again, you know your child best: she may actually calm down online because she has a list of assigned or self-generated tasks to complete: *find out the lyrics to that song I liked, write Jenny an e-mail, look for some blue slippers like the ones Cecy has,* and so on. She may actually find it soothing to sit in one place and take care of so many different little chores. So make your cyber-decisions based on your child's actual responses to time online.

Children struggling with social anxiety disorder worry excessively about ridicule, humiliation, and embarrassment to an extent that goes way beyond ordinary shyness. You'll want to avoid being overprotective with this type of anxious child and help him socialize online as a way of practicing for more intense in-person encounters. This is one of the few circumstances in which we wholeheartedly support chat rooms, since they offer such good practice for protected social interaction. Here's where it's actually good to remind your child of the no-consequence culture of the Internet; if things don't work out in one chat room, there's always another, and another, and another—and you'll probably never see or hear from the people in those earlier chat rooms again. Although we believe in teaching children empathy and compassion, they do need to learn that it's not the end of the world if they hurt someone's feelings or if a friend is mad at them—and chat rooms can be a good place for children with SAD to develop a slightly thicker skin.

## Obsessive-Compulsive Disorder

Cyberworld can be super-seductive for kids with OCD, who can get locked into a feedback loop, obsessively jumping from one link to another, feeling unable to stop until they "reach the end" or find an elusive piece of information. Or they may fall into an information-gathering frenzy, in which they obsessively need to track down every single link relating to a particular idea. (Again, as somewhat compulsive Internet researchers, we can relate!)

Work with OCD kids on setting limits, and don't let them use Internet alone until you and they feel secure that it won't trigger their anxieties. Keep a keen eye out for signs of distress, and help them set goals for their online activity that they can be sure to achieve. OCD children need to learn that their behaviors can be controlled and how to be accountable for their actions, so make sure your rules for their Cyberworld activities are clear and that the consequences for breaking those rules are also clear.

Like many children—and adults—kids with OCD often lose track of time online because they get obsessive about following something, so timers can be especially helpful to them. You might, for example, arrange for a pop-up to appear on your child's screen every five minutes, reminding him to check himself: is he calm, focused, and making conscious choices? Or does he need to find some way to interrupt the feedback loop he's fallen into? You can also work with your child on conscious self-soothing strategies to employ whenever the pop-up appears, such as employing self-talk techniques like "I'm getting stuck here again because I'm anxious about getting done. I'll make a note to come back to this later and move on for now."

## Post-Traumatic Stress Disorder (PTSD)

If your child has been diagnosed with PTSD, or if she has witnessed or been involved with any type of traumatic event, be aware that she may be especially sensitive to her Cyberworld experience. On the Internet, all sorts of things can pop onto your screen without any notice, and even your start page can show you something that triggers your sense of being unsafe. We recommend choosing a start page for your PTSD child very carefully, and again, setting clear limits on time spent in Cyberworld, at least until it's clear that your child feels safe there. (The Google search page is a great choice: it contains no flash animation or disturbing news, and it cues your child to get ready for work.)

On the other hand, time in Cyberworld could be just what your child needs for a bit of desensitization to the often disturbing and unsafe nature of our world. You'll have to be the judge of whether Cyberworld is reducing or exacerbating your child's anxieties, and set your cyber-rules accordingly.

 **To change your child's homepage, particularly if he or she finds the news disturbing or all the choices distracting:**
    **1. On the Tools menu, click Internet Options.**
    **2. On the General tab, the first thing you will see is the**

**Homepage setting, which you can adjust to choose a site that has no headlines or news of current events.**

## AUTISM AND ASPERGER'S SYNDROME
### Autism

Many autistic children who self-stimulate or engage in repetitive, obsessive behaviors can benefit from the use of a basic computer. Your child may even be nonverbal, yet might blossom in front of a computer. We don't have all the answers yet with this population, but we are finding that these children are learning all the time, even when they don't appear to be—even when they're nonresponsive, rocking back and forth, or making self-comforting noises. Autistic children tend to be visual thinkers, which means that their ability to navigate and manipulate in Cyberworld sometimes boggles the mind. It's almost as though their nonverbal minds work better in Cyberworld than others' do.

So see what happens when you expose your child to Cyberworld: you may discover that you've enhanced his communication skills and also helped him deal with the rest of the world more appropriately. We've seen autistic kids with computers whose attention spans improved, who became more motivated to participate in activities, and who even initiated or asked for time on the computer.

If your child has trouble manipulating a mouse, consider a computer with a touch-screen window. If you do use a mouse, get one with a cord so that it won't be misplaced, dropped, or thrown. Children may be bothered by the glare of the screen, so adjust its angle and the lighting, and perhaps install a filter over the screen to reduce the glare. If you find that your child is startled by sounds the computer makes, mute the computer. And as we suggested earlier in the chapter, try a rubber pad or felt tips under his chair to buffer startling or distracting sounds.

## Asperger's Syndrome

Like autistic children, Asperger's kids are highly visual thinkers, and they, too can potentially benefit from Cyberworld a great deal. Your Asperger's child may need extra processing time and extra help in deciphering the wondrous world of technology, but we think the potential benefits are well worth it.

Your first step is to help your child find ways to slow down as she encounters the enormous amounts of information suddenly available at her fingertips; kids with Asperger's can easily become overwhelmed if left to their own devices online. Their tendency, as with most things, is to move too quickly and to fall into an information-gathering frenzy, so you can see that Cyberworld is both ideally suited to their special gifts and highly problematic for their special challenges. Help them learn to *slow down*, to monitor themselves, and to take breaks. Again, timers, including timed pop-ups, can be extremely useful, as these children may need to be reminded to "check themselves" as often as every five minutes so they can finish tasks like homework in reasonable time frames.

With regard to e-mail, IM, and chat rooms, kids with Asperger's may need a lot of help in starting, continuing, and ending conversations, so check out the suggestions on page 200. They may find idioms and acronyms daunting (see page 198), so help them find some strategies for identifying and resolving their confusion. For example, you might work with them to translate acronyms with the translator available at the bottom of the www.teenangels.org Web page. You might also teach them a repertoire of standard neutral responses to use when they don't understand something:

"That's awesome."
"That's so interesting."
"How did that happen?"
"Tell me more."
"Wow."

Asperger's children tend to become deeply involved in any topic that interests them. Help your child learn how to limit her detailed responses so that the other children have a chance to participate in the conversation.

Because an Asperger's child often has such difficulty with conventional social interaction, he may appear uncaring, inattentive, or even rude. You might help him learn how to navigate conversations more easily by going with him into a chat room and observing together the chats of other children. You can role-play online chats with your child, perhaps using some real-life chats in which each of you takes turns playing different people.

E-mail and the social connection afforded by the Internet can be terrific for Asperger's kids as a way of building relationships in a structured, limited situation. Eventually, your goal will be to help them use the social skills they learn online to create more comfortable and effective real-life relationships.

## Reactive Attachment Disorder (RAD)

Children with this disorder can find themselves using the Internet to keep people at a distance—choosing to e-mail friends rather than spending time with them, for example, or making friends only online rather than in person. Don't let them use the Internet to avoid real contact; instead, work with them to use electronic communication to create a bonding experience.

RAD children may get from Cyberworld a buffer that makes them feel safer developing empathy and consideration as well as collaborating with others. Be aware that children with RAD often try to manipulate friendships to their own advantage and against the best interests of their friends, so you might want to monitor your child's ee-communication to help him or her learn more about treating others with caring and respect.

### BEHAVIOR DISORDERS
## Oppositional Defiance Disorder (ODD) and Conduct Disorder (CD)

Children who struggle with these disorders often have trouble with aggressive and hostile behavior, which in some cases can be inflamed by certain types of online games and video games, so notice the effects of online activity on your child and steer him or her away from anything that has a disturbing effect.

ODD and CD children also need to learn how to accept consequences and follow rules. Often, they'll follow the links online just to see what kind of trouble they can get into—or simply how far they can get. You can use a two-pronged strategy: rely on filters to your best extent, but then make it very clear what the consequences will be if your limits are not respected. It's crucial to be absolutely consistent with these children, because they're all about testing your limits. Try not to get drawn into a battle of wills, but stick to your guns nonetheless. It's also helpful to explain why you think the rules are needed, to give lots of positive reinforcement for every day they're followed, and to write a contract with your child that you both sign. Role-playing and role-reversal can sometimes help children with these disorders learn to develop sensitivity to the feelings of others.

Cyberworld can be challenging for special-needs kids, but it can also greatly enhance their schoolwork, their socializing, and their sense of power and efficacy. Taking the time to find out how your child works best in Cyberworld may require a lot of effort and energy, but we think both you and your child will be glad you did.

## CHAPTER 7

# KIDS WHO REALLY
# NEED THE INTERNET

Martin is a bright, lively ten-year-old with environmental sensitivity—severe allergies that frequently keep him confined to a hospital or to his room at home. He's an only child, and his parents have decided to have Martin's mother home-school him rather than let their son miss numerous school days because of doctor's appointments, hospital visits, and bad allergy days. Martin's illness keeps him more isolated than either he or his parents would prefer: despite his long bouts of solitary time, Martin is a social kid who enjoys playing chess and card games, chatting about the science-fiction books he loves, and hearing about his father's work as a building contractor. Martin's parents are interested in learning how Cyberworld can expand Martin's world, so that he can have more of a social life with children his own age.

Thirteen-year-old Kim was adopted at the age of two from a Chinese orphanage. Her American parents live in a somewhat rural part of their state, and Kim is the only Asian child in her school. Kim's parents went to China with a large group of area parents, all of whom adopted children from the same orphanage, but the nearest child leaves at least fifty miles away—too far for casual play dates—and isn't a good enough friend for regular overnights. Kim is happy and well-adjusted in her American life, but her parents want her to understand her heritage and to have access to children who share her experience of being adopted. They feel that as Kim becomes a teenager, this issue may take on more importance for her, and they want to know how Cyberworld can help Kim make this cultural connection.

Petra is a highly gifted sixteen-year-old who's fascinated by molecular biology and fond of Russian literature. Those two interests are her passions, but she's got a wide range of other interests as well: drama, horseback riding, fencing, politics. Petra is in the top track at her suburban high school, but she's often frustrated with her classmates. "They never want to get into anything serious," she complains. "All the girls care about is boys and clothes, and all the guys care about is girls and sports." Petra does have a few good friends to hang out with, but her parents sense her frustration, both intellectually and socially. They've considered sending her to private school, but they're not ready to let her go so soon. How can they use Cyberworld to enrich Petra's world?

These are only some of the children we've encountered whose need for cyber-resources runs especially deep. On some level, of course, as we saw in Chapter 1, all children need the Internet. But beyond this general need are some more urgent special needs that apply in particular to three groups of children, who are especially likely to benefit from the limitless options of Cyberworld.

## Children Who Are Physically Restricted or Isolated

The Internet is a godsend to children like Martin, opening up a whole new world of possibilities even while they are confined to a wheelchair, a hospital bed, their bedroom, or any other limited environment. Cyber-communication through computers, cell phones, and other electronic devices gives isolated children a measure of independence in making friends, staying connected, and exploring new worlds.

Kids who are disabled, wheelchair-bound, or environmentally sensitive often feel very isolated, incapable, or overly dependent. Worse, they can come to believe that they're the only ones with limitations. So it's very empowering for them to find others in similar situations elsewhere. Perhaps there's not another child "just like them" around the block, but if they can communicate with similar children through e-mail, IM, and perhaps even a Web cam, they may feel less ostracized and more enfranchised.

For kids who are partially isolated and partially mainstreamed, working with classmates on computer projects helps everyone feel like they have something in common. Your children can also use cyber-methods to stay connected to their classmates.

Sometimes children with physical disabilities feel self-conscious about how they look, speak, or behave. They may feel more comfortable beginning relationships by e-mail or in a chat room, where no one has to know how "different" they are. We urge you to use these initial anonymous connections as a bridge to fuller and more authentic relationships: having children send pictures, communicating by Web cam, and with your oversight, eventually meeting the people to whom they feel especially close. Thanks to Cyberworld, their appearance doesn't have to be the first thing someone knows about them.

It's not only disabled children who are isolated. Children who live in rural or remote areas may also find it difficult to socialize with other children outside of school. And children who are being homeschooled often miss out on even that much contact. For isolated children everywhere, Cyberworld can bridge the gap and make new connections possible.

As a result, isolated children may need more cyber-time than other children do. You can use the guidelines we offered in Chapter 5 as a starting point, but for an isolated child, you may want to modify or expand them.

On the other hand, isolated children should ideally have as much face time as possible with other kids and adults. Especially as children reach their middle-school and teenage years, they need wide-ranging access to people who aren't part of their family, people who represent the larger community. They need to develop the skills they'll use later in life: cultivating friends, networking, maintaining their values among people who don't necessarily share them, negotiating relationships, and balancing their own individuality with the needs of a group. If the best way for your child to get this experience is through Cyberworld, more power to you all. But if there are real-life alternatives, we urge you to supplement cyber-time with some face-to-face interactions.

Real-world connections are especially important for children who are being homeschooled. If your kids aren't leaving for school every day, find other ways to get them out of the house as much as possible. Have them do their homework in a library rather than in their bedroom. Sign them up for swim classes at the local Y. Involve them in some after-school or summer programs—sports, crafts, drama, music, Scouting. Your children need to be out in the world, interacting with people, and involved in organized children's activities not just in one-on-one time with their friends, though of course, they need that too. But it's important for your homeschooled children to participate in structured activities, learning to cope with people they haven't necessarily chosen to be with, cooperating with people they don't necessarily like or agree with, dealing with conflicts, and perhaps even seeing past superficial differences in order to form closer bonds than they realized were possible.

## Children from Other Cultures

We've seen the benefits that cyber-communication offers to children like Kim and the rest of her generation: Chinese adoptees who are often the only Asian and/or adopted child in their immediate environment. You may have similar concerns if your family has emigrated from another country or even another region of the United States, so that your children suddenly find themselves in a place where there are few others of their culture. Happily, you and your children can use the Internet to find and stay connected to other kids from similar ethnic or national communities.

One of the best advantages of Cyberworld is the way it transcends the boundaries of time as well as space. Long-distance phone calls across the globe, or even across the nation, can be tricky, as the time difference, cost, and sometimes technical difficulties with reception make it hard to communicate. E-mails, though, are free, easy to read, and nonintrusive. You can send or receive them at any hour of the day or night, without fear of inconveniencing the person you're writing to. Just knowing that someone else is out there can help lessen a child's feeling of cultural isolation.

Foreign-language newspapers, originating either in the United States or in your child's country of origin, are another terrific way to stay connected to a home culture, as are culturally specific Web sites. You can also order a whole host of culturally specific products online: books, magazines, musical offerings, food, clothing. Finally, as in Kim's case, you can start to create a network of people who share your child's experience, whether as adoptee, speaker of another language, or participant in another culture.

Kim's parents, for example, helped form a local support group among the other parents with whom they went to China. The group had yearly reunions at a centrally located summer camp, and encouraged the children to do Internet searches not only on Chinese culture in general, but also on the specific province from which they'd come. The kids began e-mailing one another during the year and looked forward to their summer reunions. Many of them mastered the ability to send each other pictures of their family, friends, even their pets. Some of the children established more intimate friendships— and all had the security of knowing they were part of a group.

## Children Who Have Unusual Interests or Talents

Maybe your son is a huge devotee of classical music or adores chess or, like Petra, has a near-fanatical interest in molecular biology. Perhaps your daughter is an expert on obscure jazz from the 1920s, or enjoys rare comic books, or is a huge fan of Olympic-level bobsledding. If your child is gifted, focused on a particular talent, or fascinated by an unusual topic, the Internet offers him or her a virtual community of similar souls—the type of community that you used to have to grow up to find.

For children in any of these unusual situations, the Internet and other electronic communication offers a significant way of overcoming isolation and the sense of being "the only one in the world like me." With your help, they can locate other people who share their interests, their situation, or their point of view, perhaps by forming a Listserv or special e-mail list, creating a Web site, or starting a blog. They can keep up with associations and other groups online; discover books, magazines, and other resources; and maybe even find mentors, role models, or teachers who can help them learn and grow.

As in other situations, we suggest trying to move your children from the virtual to the real as much as possible. Can they visit the friend they made in California? Can you help them travel to the museum they've discovered or allocate part of a family vacation to attending a special event? The more you can assist them in developing genuine relationships—with all of the responsibilities, demands, and rewards that a relationship can bring—the more you'll be helping them bridge the gap between Cyberworld and the actual world.

## Ways to Stay Connected

### Web Cams

Although for those of us who grew up with dial phones, a Web cam sounds like the ultimate sci-fi invention, they're not very expensive these days, and they're fairly easy to set up. You just plug it into the right port on your computer and within minutes you can start broadcasting. Very user-friendly! You can even let your child figure out how to set it up and how to access the program on your computer that will activate it—that's what cyber-kids are for!

## Getting Up to Speed: Web Cams

A Web cam is just what it sounds like: a camera that sends images over the Web, using basically the same technology that allows for instant messages to be transmitted. With a Web cam, your child can speak directly to a person in another location in real time, with your child's image appearing on the other person's computer screen. If the other person also has a Web cam, you'll get a visual two-way conversation. If the other person has a microphone feature, he or she can reply by voice only, and your child will hear it on his or her computer speakers. It's also possible to simply type a reply that appears in the IM program.

As with IM and pretty much all electronic communication, Web cam images that you receive are saved automatically by your computer unless you've programmed your computer to delete them automatically. Web cam images can therefore also be forwarded to anyone you choose, even if you don't have a Web cam yourself. (It's the same principle as electronic photos: you need a digital camera to take the photos, but once they're on your computer, you can just forward them, even if you don't have a camera.) And, like e-mail or digital photos, anyone who receives these images can forward them on ad infinitum.

We generally recommend against Web cams except in the case of isolated children, or perhaps to occasionally keep in touch with distant family members or loved ones. Ideally, children will be focused on face time, not Web cam time, but if face time is limited for the reasons we've mentioned, a Web cam is an excellent substitute.

Still, don't set it up in the bedroom. Let's face it: children just don't realize the way an electronic image can live on to haunt you. What middle-school boy could resist waving his butt around in front of the camera? No big deal—he's just sending it to friends, right? But if one of those friends sends it to another, who sends it to another, and so on, that borderline obscene image can make the rounds in school and even show up later when the child is older. It's not the kind of thing any boy wants to be shown at school assembly, for example, or have e-mailed to a college admissions officer by a friend, enemy, or neutral bystander who happens to think that kind of thing is funny. Help your kids realize that anything they do or say on a Web cam can be recorded at the other end and then forwarded on ad infinitum; there's no way to know who's seeing it or keeping it.

For geographically isolated kids, Web cams are also appropriate, and if you monitor the interactions, your child can use it to supplement both her schooling and her socializing. Just keep the camera in a public place that your child knows will periodically be monitored—why put temptation in her path?

## Digital or Video Recordings

A wonderful way for children to keep in touch is to make videotapes or digital recordings and send them by e-mail. Many cell phones now have live-action recording capacities, and while we normally don't think children should have access to these cameras—again, with impulsive use, too many images can come back to haunt them—this is a terrific way for isolated or special-needs kids to record and share visual information. Or, of course, they can use a Web cam, DVD recorder, or video recorder and download the electronic image onto their computer. Children can also burn CDs and send them by regular mail, or they can burn CDs from the digital information that a friend sends.

Your children can make a kind of visual journal or photo album to share with friends, or they can document a science experiment, musical performance, crafts project, or other achievement to send to school or to a group they've discovered online. If they're interested in filmmaking or drama, they can also create a film and share it with friends, teachers, or fellow filmmakers.

## Listservs

A Listserv is kind of electronic newsletter that goes out by e-mail to everyone whose name is on a list. Often, a Listserv is posted online for everyone to read, but to send messages to the Listserv, you have to join; instructions for joining are usually posted as well. You don't need a profile to join a Listserv, but the moderator—who supervises the Listserv—will have your name, e-mail address, and perhaps some other information as well. Typically, the moderator can prevent any Listserv member from sending out information that he or she deems inappropriate. For example, if a Listserv is devoted to, say, science, and a member wants to make a political announcement, the moderator might refuse to send it out. On a political Listserv, a moderator might refuse to send arguments that seem offensive or inappropriately personal.

Listservs work in a wide variety of ways, and often there are different options to choose from with regard to how you receive the messages posted to the Listserv. For example, you can request to be on the list for every single post as it occurs, or often you can elect to receive Listserv postings in a digested format daily or weekly, to keep the barrage of single e-mails down.

Your child might want to join a Listserv that goes to people in her special-interest group or create her own Listserv, which is easily done on Yahoo! For example, your child might go to www.groups.yahoo.com and search under Find a Yahoo! Group for a particular topic that interests her. Or she can create her own group by clicking on "Start your group," where she'll find step-by-step instructions on how to start one. Your child may want to announce that he or she is forming a group of adoptees in your area; of people who are interested in Lithuanian culture; of children suffering from environmental sensitivity who like science fiction; or any other category, large or small. Somehow, through the magic of Cyberworld, people seem to discover one another, and perhaps your child will end up moderating a significant Listserv. If not, he or she can try a new topic tomorrow—that's the beauty of Cyberworld. It's a great way for your child to explore his or her interests—even on multiple topics.

## E-mail Lists

An e-mail list is like a Listserv except that only one person posts on it: the administrator. Barb administers a local e-mail list, for example, that goes out to a group of therapists and counselors in the area, all of whom are interested in special-needs children. If someone is looking for, say, a specialist to work with a six-year-old Asperger's child, that person e-mails

Barb with a request, and she posts it to her network, including the person's e-mail address so replies can go directly to him. Your child can join an e-mail list that relates to his special interest or start one of his own with like-minded children.

## Forums, Blogs, and Special-Interest Web Sites

Forums are Web sites devoted to a particular topic that offer participants the chance to express opinions, ask questions, and engage in discussion. We discuss them extensively in Chapter 4, so if you think your child might enjoy joining a forum, turn to page 102.

Blogs are also a kind of special-interest Web site. The blogger keeps an online journal, often about a topic of special interest—politics, photography, literature, and so on—and usually includes opportunities to ask questions, make comments, and engage in online discussion. For more on blogs, see page 148 in Chapter 4.

Other special-interest Web sites often allow questions and comments as well. Or your child might start his or her own Web site. Most Internet service providers provide you space for one or two free Web pages, or you can go to www.angelfire.com and get a free Web site. Angelfire is very user-friendly, and they'll help you pick colors and even design the page for you. The only problem is that the Web addresses are usually so long and complicated that unless you send the link, no one will visit it, unless by chance it turns up on a topic search. You can buy a domain name (for example, www.[yourchild'sname].com) by doing a search for "domain name"; you'll find several companies that will host a Web site and help you in setting it up. Costs vary widely; so shop around. You can also buy a Web

site–building program (check out Resources for some suggestions).

By the way, lots of political activism these days takes place
on the Web. If your child is interested in an issue, such as the
environment, racism, free speech, or a particular political can-
didate, he or she may be able to hook up with like-minded
people online, working from home to send e-mails and even to
make phone calls. Help your child find a group that you trust
and approve of, and work with him or her to get involved. It
can give an isolated child a wonderful sense of connectedness
and empowerment to take action to change his or her world.

## Chat Rooms

Your child might enjoy some social time spent in a chat room,
especially if he or she doesn't have many opportunities to hang
out with other children face-to-face. For more on chat rooms,
see page 144 in Chapter 4. If your child struggles with a learning or emotional disorder, check out our recommendations in
Chapter 6 as well. Look around and help your child find some
good general-interest or special-interest chat rooms, but do keep
monitoring them—chat rooms can change overnight from fun,
age-appropriate spaces into unsavory or even dangerous environments.

## Cell Phones, Text Messages, and Instant Messages

We've discussed these electronic devices extensively in Chapters 2 and 3. For now, let's just remind you that these are excellent ways for your child to keep in touch with a person he
or she has already met face-to-face, at an adoptee's reunion, a

special-interest camp, or any other far-flung place. Help your child develop creative and satisfying ways of combining face-to-face meetings, real-time phone calls, instant messaging, and e-mail/TM.

## E-mail Pen Pals

If your child is looking for more intimate, ongoing long-distance relationships than are available through chat rooms, forums, and blogs, developing an e-mail correspondence with one or more pen pals is a terrific way to go. Your child might begin the process by going to the kinds of blogs and forums where he is likely to meet like-minded people. Help him note the e-mail addresses of people whose opinions he enjoys.

Another potential source of e-mail pen pals is the book, movie, game, and product reviews on Amazon.com and other consumer sites. Often, people will review several items, giving your child a chance to identify that person's interests and personality. If your child is a huge Ursula LeGuin fan, for example, and she finds someone who's given rave reviews to all of LeGuin's books—particularly someone who identifies herself as a fellow teenager—perhaps your daughter would like to initiate a correspondence with that reviewer.

Your children may be able to figure out this process by themselves, but you can certainly offer suggestions to get them started and even walk them through the process. Sit with them as they enter a forum and then suggest, "This kid sounds a lot like you—would you like to e-mail her?" Often, a forum contributor's e-mail address will either be posted or hyperlinked to his or her screen name. If not, your child can write the forum for permission to e-mail a contributor directly; probably, the moderator will then e-mail that person with your child's request to correspond.

Your child may want to start this process without your help. In this kind of protected context, we think it's fine for her to send e-mails without your supervision. We hope that you've set up enough good communication for her to come to you if anything disturbing happens—but that's equally true for all her cyber-activities, and all her real-life activities, for that matter.

If your child does need a little help, you can coach him. Encourage your child to write a brief initial e-mail rather than a long one and to keep it light. That way, if he doesn't get an answer, he won't take the rejection so personally. Help him understand that people are busy, e-mails often feel anonymous, and if he wants to make some online friends, he needs to keep trying until something clicks. If he's spending more time online than with people, point out that this try and try again philosophy would be exactly what he—or anyone—would need to do to make friends in person. Sometimes things don't work right away, especially if you're looking for people to match particular interests. You just have to keep trying and not take it personally.

Point out, too, that there's power in numbers, and urge him to send off several letters at once. Also help him see that by reading what someone else wrote, your child may feel as though he knows that person and they already have a relationship, which makes a nonresponse seem like a real rejection. In reality, though, the two people aren't acquainted, and your child has no idea whether the person not writing back is even a nice person. Or perhaps 130 people wrote to him; can he answer every e-mail? You might steer your child to reach out to people whose comments on forums or blogs netted fewer responses.

If your child does send several e-mails, suggest that he use a basic template that he can cut and paste into his e-mail program, inserting some individual detail in each letter. Point out that the people he writes to may know each other or have their own e-mail correspondence, so his e-mails might end up being seen by more than one person. If so, he'll want to be sure that no one got quite the same e-mail. For example:

> Dear Randy: I really liked that thing you said about how frustrating it can be to miss so much school when your allergies act up. I live in South Carolina, and I'm having the same problems you're having. I'd like to talk about it if you would. Here's my e-mail address. I hope I hear from you. Your friend? Cyrus

> Dear Sandy: In your blog comment, you said you keep in touch with your classmates by e-mail. I do that, too! I live in South Carolina, and I'm having some of the same problems you're having. I'd like to write about it if you would. Here's my e-mail address. I hope I hear from you. Cyrus

> Dear Andy: I really liked that thing you said about how exciting it is to turn on your computer and get lots of e-mails! I live in South Carolina, and I'm having the same problems you're having. Would you like to talk about it more? Here's my e-mail address. I hope I hear from you. Take it easy! Cyrus

Suppose your child does begin an e-mail correspondence and is then stumped for things to say. Help her see that she can begin conversations by e-mail just as she would with the people she knows. Asking questions is always a good idea:

"What's your favorite TV show?"
"I love *The* OC—did you see it last night?"
"Who's your favorite band?"
"Do you like your teacher?"

See page 200 for more suggestions on starting, continuing, and ending conversations online.

The new kinds of connections people of all types are making through Cyberworld are really remarkable. Sue has a friend who, in 1992, went to a forum to discuss the soap opera *General Hospital*. From this anonymous beginning emerged a group of ten friends, all grown women, who have never met but stay in contact with one another. They are picky about who they let join their group and boot people who don't follow their rules. Your child may create or discover a similar community online and a whole new world will open.

## PART III

# PARENTING
## CHALLENGES

So how do you bring up a child in Cyberworld? What are the day-to-day ways in which Cyberworld intersects with the four major areas of your children's life: health; schoolwork; friendships and family life; and sexuality and dating life?

In our experience, virtually no aspect of a child's life remains untouched by Cyberworld. Her health is affected by the number of hours she spends on the computer, the positions in which she sits, and the regularity of her break times. Such key aspects of health as her sleep, weight, fitness, exposure to sunlight, and tendency to experience depression are also affected by her relationship to Cyberworld.

What about schoolwork? Your child probably does a significant portion of his schoolwork on the computer, especially as he gets older. He likely conducts much if not all of his research online, yet he may not know how to evaluate Web sites for bias and reliability; how to distinguish between helping his classmates and simply e-mailing them the answers; and how to tell the difference between cut-and-paste plagiarism and online research. Just as you need to help him learn how to take notes and write an outline, so do you need to guide him in his relationship to cyber-information and its deceptively easy exchange.

Friendships, as we've seen, are affected by the restricted

communication of text messaging and instant messaging, and are shaped as well by the limits and possibilities of e-mail. Family life, too, is greatly affected by Cyberworld, which has the tendency to send every single family member off into a separate corner, focused on his or her cell phone, e-mail program, or Internet hookup.

As for teen sexuality and dating, Cyberworld plays an increasingly potent role. What do you tell your son about Internet porn? How do you guide your daughter through the online dating opportunities offered by MySpace and other social-network sites? How can young people learn empathy, compassion, and respect for one another in the often anonymous and no-consequence world of the Internet?

## CHAPTER 8

# HEALTH AND PHYSICAL FITNESS

Joey was only sixteen years old, but already he'd been diagnosed with high blood pressure and sleep disorders. His doctor prescribed medication but also suggested that Joey's parents take him to a counselor, since it seemed highly likely that his physical problems were related to his stress level. Concerned, his parents came to Barb.

As she talked to Joey and his parents, Barb quickly realized that Joey's frequent late nights at the computer were a huge part of the problem. Staying up till midnight, one, or even 2 a.m. caused Joey to oversleep in the mornings, so that he was often late to school or even missed school altogether. She suggested that Joey's parents set a curfew. "Check each night to see if there's any light shining out from under his door," Barb advised them. "Once a person gets in the habit of staying up, it's very hard to accommodate an earlier bedtime, so Joey will need a lot of help resetting his sleep clock. It's important for you to help him be consistent in going to sleep by eleven."

Joey's concerned parents were only too glad to follow this simple step. When their son's room appeared to be dark each night, they breathed a sigh of relief that all was well.

And yet, his late, groggy mornings continued. Frustrated, the parents returned to Barb. "Maybe he's stuffing a towel under his door to block the light?" she suggested. She met with Joey a second time and identified as well the "excessive reviewing" of video games that's a common problem among teenagers: after watching online video games for hours, the images burned themselves into Joey's brain, and he saw them even with his eyes closed. These troubling evocations of violence and destruction worked their way into his dreams, further disturbing his sleep.

Once Joey's parents grasped the full extent of the problem, they were able to work more directly with their son to limit his computer use. The first thing they did was they took away that towel! Then, following Barb's recommendations, they made sure their son took a ten-minute break for every ninety minutes that he was online. They limited his total daily computer use, and they helped him find ways to get sixty minutes of vigorous physical exercise each day.

Before Joey had gotten so involved with the computer, he used to love to ride his bike, so his parents worked out a schedule with him: first, a forty-minute open-air bike ride each day after school, before he even started his homework. They realized that after sitting all day, Joey needed that movement, oxygen, and downtime to revive and recharge. Then, after every ninety-minute session on the computer, Joey did a ten-minute stint on the exercise bike in the basement. His parents also made sure Joey did a gentle stretching routine after he turned off the computer, which he was now required to do by 10 p.m.—an hour before his bedtime, so that his brain had time to calm down from all the electronic stimulation.

The combination of breaks, vigorous exercise, and that

calming hour before sleep made a world of difference in Joey's sleep habits. He began sleeping more deeply and restfully, and the combination of improved sleep and more exercise seemed to help lower his blood pressure as well. He felt calmer, more alert, and more optimistic—all common effects of improving sleep and exercise. He was able to get his homework done more quickly and efficiently, leaving more of his allotted computer time for play. Joey's parents were enormously relieved—and Joey was happier, too.

Over the years, we've seen kids encounter a number of health risks in Cyberworld. Because this is such a new area, we don't always have substantial studies to back up our observations, but our clinical experience and the studies that do exist lead us to believe that Cyberworld threatens children's health in a number of ways, most commonly:

→ sleep deprivation and disturbed sleep
→ increased tendency to situational depression and more triggers for clinical depression
→ obesity and high blood pressure
→ breathing problems, including increased difficulties with asthma and allergies
→ carpal tunnel and tendonitis

We don't want to alarm you—but we do want to alert you. And certainly, if you're following the time limits we suggested in Chapter 5, you're already well on your way to heading off major health concerns. In fact, if you want a simple, easy-to-remember formula for protecting your children's health in Cyberworld, here it is:

## How to Protect Your Child's Cyber-Health: A Basic Formula

**1. Time Limits:** Follow our age-based recommendations for computer time limits:

**Aged 3–6:** 45 minutes
**Aged 6–12:** From 45 minutes for younger children to 2 hours for older children, including schoolwork
**Teenagers:** 2 hours total, including homework

If this isn't feasible due to the amount of homework your child has, limit your teenager's non-homework time on the computer to thirty minutes during the school year and one hour on vacations.

**2. Breaks:** Have your child take a ten-minute break every sixty minutes if he or she is under the age of fourteen; every ninety minutes if fourteen or older. These breaks ideally would include vigorous exercise or stretching, but at the very least, they should get your child's eyes and brain away from flickering electronic lights, while getting your child's body out of the sitting position.

**3. Exercise:** Make sure your child engages in vigorous exercise at least sixty minutes a day, in increments of at least ten minutes each. You can send your kids out to play for sixty minutes at a time; or they can do six ten-minute stints of weight-lifting, jogging, biking, walking, and the like—or any combination in between, so long as their bodies are moving vigorously for a total of sixty minutes a day.

If that's all you do, in most cases, you'll be fine. But if you're looking for some more detail, read on. We'll offer you several more cyber-solutions for keeping your kids happy, healthy, and physically active.

TIP  **Use pop-ups or a manual timer to remind your child to take breaks. Interrupt his or her computer time yourself if you sense that your child is ignoring the timer. We all know how easy it is to become cyber-obsessed, so start building this new work rhythm into your child's own internal clock: sixty or ninety minutes of work, ten minutes of break. After a few weeks of practice, your child may not even need a timer—he or she will be instinctively looking for the chance to stretch and move.**

## Excel with Exercise

There are lots of different recommendations out there about exercise for kids, but we'll go with the 2005 USDA and Department of Health and Human Services Guidelines, as explained on the surgeon general's Web site in 2006: sixty minutes of moderate to vigorous exercise for all children two years and older, on most, preferably all, days of the week. (Adults, by the way, are supposed to get thirty minutes minimum of daily or near-daily exercise.) In our opinion, at least half an hour of your child's exercise should be continuous. It's okay to break up the remaining thirty minutes into three ten-minute segments taken at various times throughout the day.

Again, use your judgment: if you think your child would benefit from more exercise—or, for some reason, should get less—that's your call. But a number of experts have pointed out that children are becoming increasingly sedentary, with disastrous results for their health and development, and our observation bears this out. Your kids need to move—often, regularly, and vigorously—and their involvement in Cyberworld often mitigates against this. So notice whether your child is getting this kind of daily exercise, and take action if he or she is not. Your child may rail against your attempts to "control every facet of his life," but his health will improve and he'll feel better—though he may not thank you for it!

By the way, don't give in to the temptation to skip the exercise during that week before the big test or when the homework is especially heavy. That's when exercise is needed most of all, to blow off steam, get oxygen to the brain, and keep your child relaxed and healthy. (The same goes for good sleep—numerous studies have shown that skipping sleep to study makes your child more likely to freeze up on a test and forget what he or she has learned.) We're horrified at the way recess has been cut in the service of academic learning—these days, with so many "extras" like music and art already having been cut, the only thing left to eliminate in a strapped school system is recess, and so children are kept sitting at a desk for hours at a time, with no movement to release stress and revive their brains. It's a scandal—or it should be—and we hope you'll do everything in your power to change that practice at your own school system. Meanwhile, don't compound the error: get your kids moving, every day, for sixty minutes.

By the way, if your child has been diagnosed with ADD/ADHD, you should make extra sure that the problem isn't simply that he or she needs a bit more time to run around and release that excess energy. Sue has several supposedly hyperactive clients who only need a bit of physical exercise (and perhaps a bit less sugar) to restore normal levels of attention and concentration. Why put your child on medication when it may just be that he or she needs recess? Don't expect the prescribing psychiatrist to ask about this, either—so many of them are very medication-focused and don't often take into account diet, exercise, and lifestyle—but we've seen it, and we know. Movement is key.

Now, how do you get a sedentary child to start that vigorous exercise? Here are some suggestions.

**Make exercise a part of your child's daily routine and build in some positive reinforcement.** Don't expect your child to add one more thing to an already crowded schedule, especially if exercise isn't something she enjoys. Help her restructure her schedule so that exercise is a natural part of it. If that means giving up another activity, so be it—even if your child balks. You're the parent; it's your call. The improvement in her health, mood, and well-being—as well as in her schoolwork—will be ample reward. You might even decide to join your child in that regularly scheduled exercise.

If your child isn't already participating in after-school sports, our recommendation is to build in some exercise time right after school—*before* he or she sits down to homework. After a day of sitting in school, your child should not go right on to several hours at a computer. Integrate into his schedule an hour of biking, walking, skating, or some other vigorous outdoor sport, perhaps supplemented with a bit of weight-training or another indoor activity.

**Help your child find something he or she likes.** Work with your child to find a kind of movement that he or she will enjoy. Does she prefer to do things by herself or with a group? Is he competitive or does he like to work slowly and calmly without pressure? Has she always liked to dance? Would he like to learn to swim? Are there classes that might tantalize him, such as yoga, tai chi, or martial arts? Would she enjoy gymnastics, folk-dancing, or maybe a class in African dance? Encourage your child to participate with you in choosing something to try out, say, for two months, with the agreement that you'll reevaluate then. Make it clear that doing nothing is not an option, but that your child can be an active participant in choosing what to do.

**Integrate chores and pleasure.** This doesn't work in every household, but it may be that you have chores or errands for your child that would count as part of his or her exercise for the day. Do you need him to run to the store for you? Can she work off some excess energy raking leaves or vacuuming? Housework, yard work, and errands can be perfectly good exercise, and there's no reason why your child can't enjoy a mix of work and fun while moving and breathing.

**Be a good role model for them.** Okay, so you're the parent. You're allowed to ask your child to do things that you no longer have to do. But when it comes to exercise, it's hard for kids to be more disciplined than their parents: if you're living a sedentary life, they may have trouble being active. Certainly, making a deal with your child—"I promise to do my half-hour walk each afternoon if you pledge to do your one-hour bike ride"—will involve you with each other in healthy ways while modeling for your child your genuine commitment to exercise. And if you and your child take that walk together, you've created yet another opportunity to spend quality time listening to your child.

## Exercise Quickies—Some Ways
## to Get Your Child Moving

• Say, "Why don't you take your bike out for ten minutes?"—and then suggest some places to go.

• Take a fun family trip to a place to run and play, or just go alone with your child—to the beach, the park, a nature preserve, or a hiking trail.

• Ask your child to run an errand for you.

• Say, "Why don't you go out back and shoot some hoops? I'll watch and count how many baskets you make in ten minutes."

• If you have more than one child, encourage them to play together.

• Take a class with your son or daughter—yoga, exercise, swimming, martial arts, surfing. Let them choose, with your approval, and make that your special time together.

• Encourage your younger child to skip rope or play hopscotch.

• Say, "Your turn to walk the dog!"

• Say, "Hey, put on some music you like and just dance in your room—no one will come in."

• Find some active chores: gardening, vacuuming, raking, weeding, shoveling snow, taking out the garbage ... Or have your child wash or clean out the family car.

# Sleep

As we've seen, sleep problems can be caused by the flickering screen of the computer, which stimulates the part of the brain that regulates sleep and wakefulness. The obsessive quality of electronic communication can also make it harder for your child to turn off the computer and begin the process of relaxing into sleep. The National Sleep Foundation recommends these basic daily sleep requirements for children, adolescents, preteens, and teens:

→ Preschoolers: 11–13 hours
→ Elementary school students: 10–12 hours
→ Preteens: 9–11 hours
→ Teens 8½–9 hours

The temptation is to let your child skimp on sleep to study, but honestly, that's one of the worst things you could do. Not only does it create poor work habits that your child will struggle with for a lifetime, but it also genuinely interferes with your child's ability to learn. All of us need sleep to retain information—numerous studies have shown that people remember far more of what they've learned when they're well-rested—and a child or teenager's growing brain is particularly vulnerable to the detrimental effects of inadequate sleep.

If your child is one of those lucky souls that can snap off the computer on schedule and fall asleep five minutes later, that's terrific, but children often need calming rituals to make the transition from work to sleep. If your child needs help leaving Cyberworld for Dreamworld, here's a sample bedtime ritual for that final hour before bedtime:

**9:30 p.m.** Turn off the computer. No more electronic stimulation of any kind—no TV, DVDs, or computer games. Music is okay, unless your child becomes extremely wound up. But no caffeine, which you'll find in many sodas, tea, and coffee, not to mention chocolate. Caffeine has been tagged as a real culprit with regard to negatively affecting children's sleep cycles.

Not only can it shorten their sleep time, but it may reduce the depth of their sleep and adversely affect their dream state. In fact, if your child is having sleep problems, you might cut out the caffeine starting at 6 p.m., at noon, or altogether—try it as a month-long experiment (you may not see results much earlier) and then evaluate with your child whether reducing or eliminating caffeine has helped your child feel more rested and alert. The incentive: many people do better on *less* sleep when they go without caffeine.

**9:30–9:35:** Do a relaxing set of stretches to release tension and slow breathing. Vigorous exercise performed within an hour of bedtime will actually make your child less sleepy, but stretching can be a terrific way to let go of the day's tension.

**9:35–10:00:** Take a relaxing bath or shower—warm, but not too hot. Your child will need about half an hour between the bath and bedtime for his or her body temperature to return to normal, also important for good sleep. And bathing at night might allow for getting up a little later, especially if your child's day starts really early.

**10:00–10:10:** Say goodnight to Mom and Dad. If your child is young enough for a bedtime story or bedtime reading, this would be the time (and then, of course, this wind-down hour would be taking place much earlier in the evening). The goal is to let go of the day's worries and the next day's stresses, so any way your child can accomplish that is terrific. Some kids need to talk through what they're going to do tomorrow and arrange the next day's clothes and books before they can finally let everything go. For other kids, that kind of preparation should have been done right after dinner—it's too anxiety-provoking now—and this is the time for a simple hug and kiss good night.

**10:10–10:30:** Bedtime reading, perhaps while listening to music. Writing in a journal or even writing a letter would also be all right, but by hand, not on the computer.

We believe strongly in children getting enough sleep, but we also want them to get *good* sleep. So ideally, your child should turn off the computer one hour before bedtime and get a full night's sleep. If that's just not possible, we think the best compromise is to let your child stay up half an hour later, but to keep that half-hour free of computers, TV, and electronic games. Losing thirty minutes of sleep might be a good trade-off if the remaining sleep time is deeper and more peaceful.

## "I Can't Get It Out of My Head . . ."

As we saw with Joey, electronic games can work their way into your mental vision, so that you can't get the images out of your head. Any repetitive action replays itself in your dreams, though you may not realize or remember this. A friend of ours describes similar experiences from her waitressing days—seeing the orders and the menus over and over in her semi-sleep and dreaming states—and she's also described it happening on her few trips to a casino, with images of gambling recurring obsessively as she lies in bed that night. Likewise, a friend of Sue's stayed up late one night as a teenager, playing Minesweeper, an early video game, for several hours during a snowstorm. That night, she couldn't sleep and kept seeing the images over and over again even when she shut her eyes.

One twelve-year-old boy Barb spoke with—we'll call him Dylan— recently got a program for Sudoku, the popular Japanese logic/number placement puzzle game. He played it for hours at a time after finishing his homework and found it increasingly harder to go to sleep right away. When he did get to sleep, he ran Sudoku scenarios in his dreams throughout the night. He discovered he was waking up more tired than when he went to bed. Taking the advice we've outlined in this chapter, Dylan changed his gaming habits and saw positive results almost immediately.

No one knows exactly why this kind of reviewing occurs, but one theory points to dopamine levels, which are stimulated by electronic games, gambling, and any high-stress situation—including, perhaps, waiting tables. Be sensitive to the possibility that your child is having this reaction, especially if he or she doesn't seem well rested even after a good night's sleep. Help interrupt the obsessive quality of Cyberworld by insisting that your child take regular breaks, interrupting any intense viewing with exercise and deep breathing.

## Depression

There are two types of depression: situational, which occurs in response to a particular event or life condition (the death or prolonged illness of a loved one, a divorce, another traumatic change), and clinical, which is overwhelmingly determined by a person's brain chemistry and sometimes seems to have no obvious cause. Clearly, there can be a continuum between the two: if your child has a tendency to depression, a painful situation that a nondepressed kid might shrug off—say, a friend's rejection—could trigger a depressive episode.

If your child has a tendency to depression, or if situations in his or her life seem to be triggering depression, we urge you to seek out a good therapist and, if necessary, a physician who can prescribe medication. But you may also find that altering your child's relationship to Cyberworld makes a great deal of difference. Lack of exercise, insufficient exposure to sunlight, isolation, and disturbing material encountered online can all trigger or aggravate depression—and changing one or more of these factors may well make a difference. Here are some specific suggestions.

## Improve Diet, Exercise, and Sleep

Follow the recommendations we've made for regular, vigorous exercise—they are triply important if your child is depressed or has a tendency to depression. The same goes for our sleep suggestions—lack of sleep is literally depressing. Happily, sleep and exercise reinforce each other: more exercise leads to better sleep; better sleep can give your child more energy to exercise. You should also speak with a nutritionist about an anti-depression diet or find one of the useful books written on this topic, perhaps *Potatoes Not Prozac* by Kathleen DesMaisons or *The Chemistry of Joy* by Henry Emmons, MD, with Rachel Kranz.

## Sunlight

Many people become depressed as a result of insufficient exposure to sunlight, so that their so-called seasonal affective depression (SAD) intensifies in the winter and eases in the summer. Spending too much time in Cyberworld might also deprive your child of access to full-spectrum sunlight, so consider buying bulbs or a light box that mimics the sun's healing light. (For more information, see Resources.) Do what you can to expose your child to at least ten to twenty minutes each day of actual sunlight (protected by a 45 SPF sunblock). Ideally, your child won't wear protective eye gear—though he or she should obviously avoid staring directly at the sun. However, the sun's full benefits often enter through the eyes, so try to give your child some sun time without glasses, contact lenses, or sunglasses—or at least expand his or her sun time to twenty or thirty minutes.

## Isolation

One of the most troubled foster children that Barb supervised was a depressed sixteen-year-old boy who got deeply involved with online games. He became obsessed with one particular game and played it night after night, alone in his room. Barb was concerned about how isolated this young man had become and suggested that he go to a local bookstore where young people gathered every Saturday morning to play this game: at least that way, he'd be in the company of other people as he played.

The boy was thrilled to find out that other people "in real life" were as enthralled with the game as he was, because even though he'd found other people his age online who played this game, he'd been secretly concerned that he might be perceived as too old for it. At the Saturday event, though, he happily found several players his own age and even made a friend. As a result of these social experiences, he became noticeably more able to talk about his feelings, and gradually began making friends at school as well.

We consider this young man's story a classic example of how crucial it is to break the isolation that often comes with Cyberworld and to find creative ways to work with rather than against a young person's interests. Isolation is truly bad for your child. The more he isolates himself, the more at risk he is for self-destructive behavior, including cutting himself, suicidal thoughts, and perhaps even suicidal actions. We don't want to alarm you, but we do want to impress upon you the need to help your child find real-world connections. If he insists that his cyber-friends are all he needs, work with him to turn those online friendships into real-life relationships. We're not suggesting that you focus your worries on the possibility of suicide, but we are suggesting that you take seriously your child's depression and the isolation that breeds it.

## Overcoming Cyber-Isolation: Some Suggestions

• If your child has trouble making friends his or her own age, maybe relationships will be easier with younger kids: babysitting, volunteering at a daycare center or neighborhood program, helping out with a Scout troop or local club.

• Some children do better in more adult situations: perhaps your child would flourish with a part-time job, a serious volunteer post at a hospital or service organization, or as a volunteer with a political group or campaign.

• Children who like online games and fantasy can enjoy live Dungeons and Dragons groups (in our area, there's one at the local Books-a-Million store), fantasy book clubs, and other real-life meeting places for fellow enthusiasts.

• Perhaps your child would benefit from adult friends or mentors. Is there an aunt, uncle, grandparent, or family friend who would enjoy spending time with your child? Is it possible to hook your child up with a local teacher, artist, minister, or other professional who might tutor your child or help him learn more about a special interest or profession?

• Many isolated children find it easier to relate to animals than people. Can your child volunteer at a local animal shelter, vet's office, farm, or animal-rescue agency?

## Obesity and High Blood Pressure

A sedentary lifestyle can lead to obesity, while high blood pressure may be aggravated by stressful online activity, including cyber-bullying and other electronic activities about which children feel guilt or shame.

Barb has been saddened to observe the daughter of a colleague who, at age sixteen, was of normal weight and attractive, though somewhat isolated and lonely. Now, five years later, the young woman is more than fifty pounds overweight and rarely leaves her room. Her hygiene has degraded, and she's found it difficult to keep a job even as she refuses to go to college. She has an active Internet life and insists that her online acquaintances are her real friends—she even claims to have an Internet boyfriend, though in real life, she's never met him; nor has she ever had a real-life physical relationship. She organizes her job search around positions that will either let her work from home on her computer or that require her to start work at 5 a.m. so she can stay up all night chatting.

Clearly this young woman is an extreme case, and there are other family issues shaping her choices; "Internet addiction" isn't the only culprit. But she's fallen into a vicious cycle: spending hours sitting before a screen has created a weight problem that eats away at her self-image; lacking self-confidence, she isolates herself further.

If your children are getting their sixty minutes a day of vigorous exercise, they don't need to worry about becoming obese, particularly if you're following our recommendations for limited computer time and, most importantly, regular breaks. If you feel that obesity is a problem for your child, though, see if there are ways that your child's relationship to Cyberworld is contributing to an unhealthy situation.

> **TIP**  Encourage your child to drink 8 to 16 ounces of water—*not* soda, iced tea, or any other beverage—for every hour that he or she is on the computer. (Flavored noncaloric water is okay, as is water flavored with fresh lemon or lime.) Drinking water will keep your child hydrated, and the frequent trips to the bathroom will prevent your child from staring at the computer for hours at a time, unblinking and unmoving.

## Cyber-Snacking

Your children's choice of foods can go a long ways toward combating depression, sluggishness, and obesity—and that goes double for snack foods. Children's stomachs are smaller than adults', and their metabolism generally runs higher and faster, so they need to eat smaller amounts more often. That means kids' snacks aren't just "filler" to stave off those hungry before-dinner blues; snacks are actually a key part of your child's nutritional intake.

At the same time, most children don't pay such close attention to what they're snacking on—a snack is often eaten while watching TV, reading a book, or even working online. As we recommend in Chapter 6, you may want to keep your child from eating and working if he or she has difficulty concentrating, paying attention, or completing work, so as to cement the association between sitting in front of the computer and working with full concentration. If your child works easily, however, there's nothing wrong with snacking at the computer—except for how it tends to blunt your child's awareness of what he or she is eating. Children can consume way more food than they're actually hungry for without even noticing, especially salty or sugary snacks like cookies or potato chips, which already have a semi-addictive quality.

The solution? Save the fun foods for dessert or special treats, and keep all snacks healthy: no sugar, not much salt, no "empty calories." Here are some healthy cyber-snacks, all of which are rich in the vital nutrients that your child's brain needs to remain alert, focused, calm, and cheerful.

    walnuts
    almonds
    turkey
    nonfat or low-fat yogurt (if weight isn't a concern for your kids,
        full fat is fine)
    frozen fruit bars
    cheese (if weight is a concern, try the low-fat variety)
    fresh fruit
    carrot sticks and baby carrots
    fresh vegetables
    microwave popcorn
    seeds of all kinds—sesame, sunflower, pumpkin—roasted with-
        out oil or salt
    whole-wheat crackers
    Kashi cereal

As a general rule, water is a better drink than fruit juice, which tends to be high in calories and to promotes tooth decay. Whole, fresh fruit is better than fruit juice, too, because it includes fiber and will help satisfy your child's appetite more fully.

## Breathing Problems

Breathing problems caused by asthma, allergies, and other related conditions may be aggravated by a lack of activity and fresh
air—and once again, Cyberworld may be the culprit. Being fit
and getting regular vigorous aerobic exercise also helps with
asthma control, so be sure to follow that sixty-minutes-a-day exercise recommendation. You have a choice between a vicious
cycle—more time at the computer creates a sedentary child
more prone to breathing problems and less willing to move—or
a positive one—a fit, active child who loves to move and thereby
reduces the risk of breathing problems. Help your child keep
Cyberworld in perspective to keep breathing problems at bay.

## Carpal Tunnel and Tendonitis

Recent research on the risks of repetitive-strain injuries like
carpal tunnel and tendonitis indicates that an increasing number
of children are complaining of computer-related injuries. As
more children spend more hours on their computers, the childhood risk of carpal tunnel and tendonitis seems to increase. The
best way to fight these syndromes is with regular breaks: ten
minutes for every sixty minutes (under age fourteen) or ninety
minutes (over fourteen) your child spends on the computer.
Some stretching during those breaks is a terrific idea. And of
course, make sure your child uses an ergonomically correct
setup. Make sure your child uses a chair that helps him or her
achieve good posture, supporting the spine and allowing the feet
to rest firmly on the floor or on a foot rest. Check to make sure
that your child's arms extend out at a 90-degree angle and that
his or her wrists have adequate support. And make sure the

monitor is positioned so that your child looks into it directly, not at an angle. If you do an Internet search for terms such as "ergonomics," "children," and "computer," you can find sample diagrams demonstrating good ergonomics, along with additional suggestions to make your child's work space safer and healthier.

Another good suggestion for combating carpal tunnel is to have your child do the downward-facing dog yoga posture, which will get the blood flowing in his or her wrists. See www.yogajournal.com or http://yoga.about.com/od/yogaposes/a/downdog.htm for some good illustrations of this posture, which is a simple stretch that your child will enjoy.

**TIP** Wristwand is a short baton that your child can use for stretching exercises that are especially good to combat carpal tunnel and tendonitis. Encourage your child to do a few moments of Wristwand-type or other stretching during each computer break—it can make a world of difference. Check out www.wristwand.com for more information.

Being a parent requires a fine balancing act between being too complacent and too anxious. What's the difference between "too many" hours spent alone in Cyberworld and "enough" human contact? How do you balance your child's need for exercise with commitments to schoolwork, friends, and other activities? How strict do you *really* need to be about bedtime? These can be tough questions and, as with all parenting issues, there's no one answer that's right for every child. Think about the issues, listen to your child, trust your own instincts, and on the few occasions when you feel that's not enough, get help. That's all any parent can ever do, with or without Cyberworld.

CHAPTER 9
.....................

# SCHOOLWORK

Jamie used to be a bright, cheerful twelve-year-old, but for the past few weeks, her parents have noticed her becoming unusually quiet and withdrawn. Her father takes her out for ice cream one Sunday afternoon and as they walk back from the ice-cream store, casually asks if anything's going on at school. "Oh, no, just the usual," Jamie says, but something in her tone causes his antennae to go up.

"Honey, you know if there's anything bothering you, you can always tell your mom and me," he says. "If you're running into anything difficult, we trust you to handle it—but we want to help."

"So you wouldn't do anything unless I said it was okay?" Jamie asks.

"I can't promise that," her father replies. "But I can promise to listen to what you think and what you want and to take it very seriously."

Slowly the story emerges: some of the kids Jamie knows have started a cell-phone cheating ring and they want Jamie to text them answers during the pop quizzes that are a regular part of their science class. So far, Jamie has resisted, but she's worried that she'll lose all her friends if she doesn't go along. After all, she knows the answers—it's not as though she herself would be cheating. What difference does it make to her if some other kids take the easy way out?

Jamie's dad congratulates her on sticking to her guns so far and thanks her for being so honest with him. "Of course, I think cheating is wrong no matter who does it or how it happens," he says calmly, although inside he is furious that cell phones are being used in this way and that his precious daughter is being pressured. "And if you get caught, no one will care whether you were giving the answers or getting them. So you'd fail the class along with the ones who didn't even study. Plus, schools are more and more worried about cheating these days, and many of them add an extra cheating mark to that F that a college or employer might see. So texting the answers to one little biology quiz could mean that you'd have a hard time getting into the college you want. The information might even be something a future employer would have access to. Do you think that's worth it?"

Jamie and her father continue to talk. It's clear to Jamie's dad that if he can't trust his daughter, he'll have to solve the problem by confiscating her cell phone. But at the end of their conversation, he decides that he can trust her and that it's a bad idea to punish her in advance for something she hasn't even done. He doesn't want to violate his daughter's confidence or get her into trouble with her friends, but now that he knows students are cheating, he doesn't feel comfortable doing absolutely nothing about it.

Then Jamie's father has a brainstorm and suggests an interim solution to the immediate problem. He offers to call the school principal, along with Jamie's mom, to let the principal know that they've heard rumors about cheating, although he has no proof of it and no specific names to give her. He'll simply suggest that the principal announce to the entire student body that teachers will now be watching for cell-phone cheats. He promises Jamie that she won't be put on the spot or referred to as a tattletale.

Jamie makes a token protest, but her dad senses that she's actually relieved, and in the end, she agrees to the plan. She even suggests that she could tell her friends that she heard her parents talking about "this rumor they heard" and that she wanted to warn them to stop cheating before they get caught.

Jamie's dad understands that by opening up to him, Jamie was asking for him to reinforce what she already knew about right and wrong: after all, she could have been cheating all along and he'd never even have suspected. She wanted to do the right thing and she wanted his help—she just hadn't wanted to come right out and ask for it.

So the most important lesson, he realizes, was that if he hadn't made the time to hang out with his daughter, he never would have known about any of this. Jamie hadn't come to him or her mom and said, "Hey, folks, we need to talk." She hadn't even responded the first time he'd asked her if anything was wrong. Only after he'd persisted had she slowly opened up. As Jamie became a teenager, she was likely to become even more reluctant to talk with or spend time with her parents, so he and Jamie's mom would have to become extra-committed and extra-creative about finding ways to hang out with their daughter. There might be other times in the next six years that Jamie would want to come to them—but they'd have to find ways of making it seem as though they had come to her. By taking her seriously and involving her in the problem-solving process, Jamie's parents made real progress in keeping the lines of communication open.

As Jamie's story makes clear, Cyberworld offers your child a whole new set of temptations and challenges that nobody who's now old enough to be a parent ever had to face. The child researching a paper the old-fashioned way—plowing through a pile of books and magazines—may feel occasionally confused about how to take notes, organize information, and create an outline. But the child who turns to online resources has a whole new level of distraction to deal with—cyber-gambling, pornographic photographs, offers for free stuff, flashing banner ads, colorful animations—and that's just after clicking on the first link. What about all those hyperlinked key words in the midst of online articles or the hypertext at the bottom of the page promising additional research opportunities? It's all too easy to end up wandering from one intriguing Web page to another, forgetting the piece of information you were trying to track down in the first place.

Children doing homework online must also sort through a great deal of misinformation. Although published books can certainly distort the issues, they have at least been approved by a publisher and a librarian. Anyone can post "information" on the Web—and even adults have trouble sorting the wheat from the chaff.

And then there are all the issues that relate to cheating: cell-phone texting, e-mailing your friends the answers, cutting and pasting information from the Web into your own work without references or acknowledgments, and even going to one of the many online sites that sell papers on various topics. The sites even suggest that you order a paper that falls within or just above your normal grading range and instruct you to add a few sentences of your own to make the whole paper look more authentic!

In this chapter, we'll talk you through all of these cyber-challenges and offer you some hands-on solutions. Let's start with one of the most pressing concerns that your child faces, perhaps without even realizing it: sorting through the information on the Web.

---

### Getting Up to Speed: Doing Internet Research

If you're not comfortable doing online research yourself, you may want to get some practice in before helping your children with their Internet-based homework. The best way is to choose a topic that interests you and try to find out more about it. Either of the following books can walk you through the process:

• *The Internet for Dummies,* 10th ed., by John R. Levine, Margaret Levine Young, and Carol Baroudi

• *The Rough Guide to Internet 12*

---

## Evaluating Web Sites

Your children are probably going to rely on the Web for much of their research, so teaching them how to evaluate Web sites is a key part of helping with their homework. Here are some helpful steps in walking your child through the evaluation process:

### Model the Process

We suggest sitting with your child at the computer and doing some Web searches together, either for actual homework assignments or simply on questions that interest you both. Talk through your own evaluation process for each Web site that comes up and invite your child to do the same. Modeling your thought process is the best way to help your child develop the right balance of healthy skepticism and willingness to learn:

> Now, first, I look at the suffix of the Web address. This one is ".edu," so I know the site has some kind of connection to a college or university. That makes me think it's probably reliable, but wait a minute. Here's a sentence that lets me know a professor has created this site all by herself. So she's probably well-informed—but not necessarily. Maybe she's a professor of biology and this is a Web site about politics—let's check. Now, even if she is an expert in the field, I might not agree with her, so I'm going to see what I can find out about her biases and background before I go any further. Here are some clues I've noticed . . .

Obviously, you'll need to tailor this process for children of different ages. We suggest sitting down with your child at the beginning of each school year and then periodically throughout the year, demonstrating your evaluation process and asking your child to demonstrate his or hers. Yes, it's time-consuming, but in Cyberworld, this kind of evaluation is an essential skill both for school and for adult life, and you can't assume your child will learn it alone. If you don't feel confident teaching this process, or if you feel your child won't be receptive to your guidance, we urge you to find another adult mentor or even to hire a trustworthy college student who can help your child evaluate cyber-sources.

Of course, if your child's teacher is making this kind of evaluation a regular part of the curriculum, that's terrific, but in our experience, most of them don't. That may change as Cyberworld becomes more familiar, but most teachers these days are still working with pre-cyber curriculum and textbooks, and they simply don't have the time to model this kind of research process to their students. Nor do they have the resources to help their students do hands-on computer research while the teacher supervises. So you need to make sure your child is getting this background somewhere, from you or someone you trust.

Even if your child is lucky enough to get this basic instruction from a teacher, you should remain involved in the process. As you review your child's homework throughout the year, ask about the sources she chose or the sites he found. Invite your child to keep sharing his or her thought processes with you, giving positive reinforcement for good choices and making suggestions if you think your child seems too credible, careless, or confused. Cyberworld can be overwhelming even for an experienced adult researcher—we ourselves were struck, as we prepared the material for this book, at how many conflicting biases, statistics, and recommendations were out there, and at how difficult it often was to sift out the sources we trusted from those we didn't. Your child will be dealing with this aspect of Cyberworld for the rest of her life, so give her a good start and keep offering her support. It's one of the most important gifts you'll ever give her.

## Site Suffixes

One of the first steps in evaluating a site is to look at the suffix:

**TIP** The suffixes ".gov," ".mil," and ".edu" are available only to government divisions, the military, and educational institutions, respectively. The names of commercial Web sites are sold to individuals and businesses, and when you buy one, you're allowed to decide whether your Web name will be ".com," ".org," ".net," or ".biz." Be very careful about these suffixes; often, pornography companies will mimic a site name but change the suffix. For example, www.crazygirls.com is a useful Web site for teenagers, but www.crazygirls.org is a hard-core sex site.

**.gov—government agencies.** Government agencies are good for official statistics and for finding out the official position on an issue. These are the most reliable Web sites for basic information, and they're excellent for the kinds of reports usually assigned to elementary and middle-school children, with reliable information on such topics as population statistics, information about the states (capital, slogan, state flower, and the like), national parks, and other relatively noncontroversial topics in social studies, health, and science. Government Web sites tend to stay away from controversial topics and they usually don't express overt biases, but help your child think about the relationship between the site's official nature and the information included there: What information can the government present better than anyone else? What information might the government not be the best source for?

**.edu—educational institutions.** This is the suffix used by colleges and universities—but it's also used by professors and staff people at those institutions. So you get both highly reliable data and more subjective, but possibly still useful, information. Help your child become aware of possible biases from these sites while also grasping that Web sites with these suffixes are probably more reliable than those maintained by unaffiliated individuals. For example, if your child is seeking information for a report on snakes, an .edu suffix probably indicates that the information comes either from an official college or university department or from a professor. Thus, they're probably more reliable sources than the .com Web site maintained by an individual who just happens to have a special interest in snakes. Point out that some .com Web sites are even maintained by children. .Com sites are not necessarily unreliable—but in most cases, an .edu site is probably better. On the other hand, professors have their own biases, and they may set up Web sites on topics in which they're not necessarily experts. So help your children—especially your older children—evaluate whether .edu really does indicate expertise.

**.org—organizations.** These can be sites maintained by large, well-known organizations who are major authorities on their topic—such as the Red Cross, the National Kidney Foundation, or the American Heart Association—or they can be the sites of minor groups who may or may not be reliable sources. Younger children won't necessarily have the basis for distinguishing, and even high school students might not be able to evaluate the difference between, say, a major national group and an obscure community organization, let alone to detect the political biases affecting groups of all types. "Biased" doesn't necessarily mean "wrong," but you still need to take it into account: think of how sites maintained by, say, the NAACP and the American Heritage Foundation might be at odds about such topics as affirmative action, even though both are large, well-respected groups. Encourage your child to check out his or her .org sites with you or with a teacher to help evaluate their reliability.

**.mil—military.** Clearly, a .mil site would be best for statistics about the Armed Forces or for anything official about the military: rules, regulations, polices, and the like. Share with your children your own sense of how reliable or biased the military is likely to be on other issues.

**.com—commercial.** This is the catchall suffix used by commercial entities but also by many individuals. Again, help your child think through the relationship between the Web site owner and the information that's included. Suppose your child is doing a report on the environment and wants to find out about the miles-per-gallon rates of cars over the past decade. He may need help sorting out the difference between objective information ("Our mileage rates have been steadily increasing") and other opinions that may be presented as fact ("We're doing all we can to preserve the environment"). This kind of scrutiny is even more important when a site is maintained by an individual, whose biases and perspectives may not be apparent at first viewing.

**.biz—businesses (or commercial use).** This suffix also indicates private, commercial use, though individuals don't tend to have addresses with this site. Your child can rely on sites with this suffix for specific information about the particular business that operates the site—for example, prices, product specifications, where items are sold, and so on—but you should make sure your child understands all the ways a business might be biased in the kinds of information they include or omit. Again, help your child distinguish between fact and opinion.

**.net—network organizations.** Sometimes this suffix indicates another type of organization; other times, it simply denotes a commercial ISP. Earthlink, for example, is a network, so any individual or group who sets up a Web site through this commercial ISP is likely to have .net at the end of the address. For all practical purposes, your child should ask the same types of questions of the .net suffix as he or she would about the .com.

There are also suffixes that identify a Web site's country of origin. Some of the most common are .ca for sites originating in Canada, .fr for those originating in France, .de for Germany *(Deutschland)*, and .uk for United Kingdom. Help your child think about the relationship between a country extension and a site's content. On what topics would information coming from a particular country be more reliable? On what topics might it be less reliable? Also alert your child to the possibility of nonstandard spellings or misspellings, grammatical oddities, and other language-based problems. There is a translation feature on many search engines that will translate Web sites from other languages, but in our experience, these translations are often bizarre and difficult to understand, and your child should be prepared for that as well.

## Helpful Questions

Here are some useful questions for your child to ask about Web sites as part of his or her evaluation of the site. Again, we think this process is best taught by modeling: sit down with your child and do a search on a topic that interests you both.

Then work with your child to answer such questions as the following:

→ Who created the site? Are there any sponsors or affiliated groups besides the main author?

→ What are his or her credentials? Do you trust him or her as an expert on this topic? Why or why not?

→ What's the date? Is it recent enough to make this site reliable, or do you need to find an update somewhere? Can you trust some types of "old" information (historical dates, for example) and not others (population statistics, perhaps)?

→ Who's the intended audience? How might that affect the information on the site? How does that affect your own evaluation?

→ Does the site offer complete and accurate information or argue for one particular perspective? How does the answer to that question affect your evaluation?

→ Can you back up the information on the site with other Web sites? Does it fit with information in other printed sources?

→ What are the links on the site? How do these links affect your evaluation of the site's author or sponsor? You should be looking for three factors: 1) how up-to-date the links are (because they'll tell you how often the author checks the site); 2) how reliable the links are (because they'll tell you about the author's judgment); 3) what bias, if any, is shared by the links (because they'll help you evaluate the author's bias, and that will help put the information into perspective, especially if you share or actively disagree with that bias).

## Studying the Studies

As your child gets older and more sophisticated, help him or her evaluate studies and research data with questions like the following:

• Who conducted the study? Does the study have any built-in biases? For example, is it a study of a drug funded by a pharmaceutical company or an opinion poll funded by a political campaign?

• How many people were studied? Does that seem like a large enough number to you?

• When was the study conducted? Has it been superseded by more recent research?

• Can you think of alternate explanations for the study's results? For example, if the study says that African-American children did worse on a test than white children and concludes that the black children were not as skilled in that area, does that seem correct to you or can you think of another reason why even skilled black children might have done worse on that test?

**TIP** Many libraries—public, academic, and specialized—post lists of recommended Web sites. An especially useful site is the Librarians' Internet Index: http://www.lii.org. Show your child how to search that site by keyword.

# Don't Forget the Library!

However much your children rely upon the Internet, we think they should also know how to use a library. They need to remember that not *everything* worthwhile is on the Internet—at least, not yet!—and they need to feel comfortable exploring a library's resources. If they go on to college or for other types of advanced training in the arts, design, or technical fields, they'll be using libraries at least as much as Cyberworld, so let's start polishing those skills now and keep renewing them every year.

Your children's relationship to the library starts in preschool, when they can attend special children's programs and browse around for the books they want. You can also help them choose videos, DVDs, and music from the public library. We recommend that your preschool and elementary school–age children visit the library at least once every two weeks for an hour minimum.

Middle-school children should be visiting the library at least once a month, for a two-hour minimum. They can browse for books, and you should also show them how to use the computer catalogue, the Dewey decimal system, and the Library of Congress system. Once they know how those systems work, which they may well have learned in school, have them help you find books. There's nothing kids enjoy more than showing their parents how much they know. You can even have races with your children: they give you a list, you give them a list, and whoever finds all the books on the list first wins.

You can also reserve, request, and renew books, movies, and music online, so show your children how to integrate library and Internet use. Many research librarians now also specialize in cyber-research, so make sure your children know that librarians can help them with both books and cyber-resources.

Your high-school children need to know how to do library research, so they, too, should be visiting the library at least once a month for a two-hour minimum. If their curriculum isn't already requiring some regular library visits, come up with a fun research project—with or without their input—and help them sharpen their skills. Or again, if they already know how to find things, have them demonstrate their skills to you. You're not only reassuring yourself that they know how use a library, you're showing your kids how highly you value library skills—and that's important, too.

Ideally, you'll encourage your children of all ages to complete a school assignment using the library at least once a month, whether or not they're also doing online research. We know this means blocking out your own precious time to take them to the library, but if you can manage it, we think it's worth it. Explain to your kids that you want them to be creative and that you don't want them to be limited by what anyone chose to put online or by what comes up on a search engine. "Do you want anyone else—besides me!—to have control over you?" you might ask them. "I want you to have access to as many sources of information as possible, so that no one can tell you what to think."

## Try a Library Scavenger Hunt!

Turn a library visit into a treasure hunt. For younger kids, you might give them the title and Dewey decimal number of a particular book, and challenge them to locate the book. You can hide a note or a gift certificate inside and then tell them there's a special letter in the book that you want them to retrieve. (You might give the librarian a heads-up first.)

Slightly older kids might enjoy a more complex variation: hide notes in six books, with a single word on each note. Together, the six words make a sentence. The treasure-hunt aspect of the game can be fun for all of you and that fun will rub off on their associations with the library.

Middle school–age children can be given a scavenger hunt–type list and a time limit, and you can encourage them to play alone or with friends. A time limit might make the game more fun. Here's a sample list that you might use to challenge your children:

**1.** Find a book with the Dewey decimal code 898.05.

**2.** Find an item in the A/V department with the word "stone" in its title.

**3.** Bring back the microfiche of a newspaper page from a city with a "u," "v," or "w" in its name, whose date adds up to less than twenty. Make sure the word "blue" is somewhere on the page, either in an ad or in an article. (Give your children a quarter for the microfiche machine.)

**4.** Ask a reference librarian to help you find the name of the original building on the site of that Starbucks downtown, and find out what they did in that building, too.

**5.** Bring back the titles of the three latest CDs available in the collection.

**6.** From the library's picture collection, find an image that includes a boat and a duck.

**7.** From the library's map collection, bring back a map of a country with "z" in its name.

**8.** From the "new selections" list, bring back the titles of one novel, one nonfiction book, and one photography book.

(You can do the same kind of scavenger hunt at a natural history or art museum. It gives children a wonderful sense of ownership—the museum is their playground and they become familiar with its contents in a whole new way.)

After your library scavenger hunt, take the kids out for ice cream and discuss with them the differences between the Internet and the library. You might make a formal list of pros and cons for each type of research or simply chat informally. But remind them that the library is there for them when they need it.

## Multitasking vs. Single Focus: Keeping Your Child on Track

As we've seen throughout this book, Cyberworld encourages multitasking—and that's not necessarily the best formula for doing good work. Consider these additional cyber-challenges to schoolwork:

→ not completing tasks because of online obsessions: from e-mails, IMs, and multitasking, to chat rooms, pornography, and gambling

→ the temptation to TM friends while you're supposed to be studying or even attending class

→ difficulty dealing with the distractions of being online— especially for children who have problems with attention and/or impulse control

You may also be concerned with how much harder it is to monitor your child's activity while he or she is supposed to be doing schoolwork. How do you know if that busy typing sound is a paper being written or a chat room correspondence?

Here are some cyber-solutions we suggest:

**Monitor your kids' work on the computer, and encourage them to separate electronic tasks.** Help them learn not to e-mail or IM while they're supposed to be doing homework, and encourage them to find other ways to minimize electronic (and other) distractions. This is especially crucial for younger children, who tend to be very responsive and distractible. And of course, as we saw in Chapter 6, it's crucial for many special-needs kids.

**When you do pop in to check on your children, cast an eye at**

the bottom of your kids' screens to see how many windows are open and which ones. If you feel they're looking at too many unrelated topics, work with them to narrow their focus. Notice whether they're distracting themselves with IMs, pornography, gambling, or other compulsive behaviors. (Of course, as we've seen, you'll want to filter out porn and gambling sites, but your child may have figured out how to access a few you didn't filter.)

If necessary, have your kids download what they need off the Internet and then get offline. That helps remove the temptation to keep checking e-mail or bounce around among several different screens.

Consider turning off Internet access while your children are doing homework, so that they have to focus on the work and not their cyber-lives. It might even be appropriate to take away the computer—or at least the keyboard—so that your children have to finish their work by hand. This is especially important if you feel they need more reflective time with fewer distractions and more "quiet space."

TIP   You can turn off the IM function on your ISP, or you can program it to turn itself off after any period of time you choose. We recommend taking away the IM function for children younger than thirteen or for especially distractible children. You can give kids thirteen and older more leeway, but work with them to make sure they're not being distracted.

## Keeping Your Kids on Track

It can be difficult staying on track when you're working online. So give your children as much help as they need in organizing and pursuing their work. Check out the getting started ritual we suggest in Chapter 6 on page 191 and see if it's appropriate for your child, too. Help your child figure out what he or she has to do, how long each assignment will take, and when the whole night's homework will be done. Make sure your child gets regular breaks according to the schedule in Chapter 8 on page 246, and check in periodically to make sure everything is working smoothly. Your monitoring can be as simple as a quick knock on the door and poking your head in to see how many windows are up (check the bottom of the screen) or what your child is doing (staring dreamily into space, writing an e-mail, or busily working away).

If necessary, you can use a program like NetNanny or PCTattletale (see pages 117 and 119) to monitor your child more closely. Our recommendation is to let your child know that you're doing this, to make it clear that you're not spying but trying to help.

If your child is having trouble staying focused, explain that you're going to limit his or her access to e-mail, IM, chat rooms, or perhaps even the Internet itself—not as punishment, but to help him or her stay focused. Help your child understand, too, that multitasking is simply not an efficient way of getting things done. Focusing on one task at a time rather than toggling back and forth between two or more tasks is the best way to master information, complete assignments, and remain on track.

# Plagiarism or Research?

Eight-year-old Robbie was confused. He'd been doing online research all evening for his report on the state of Connecticut. He'd found great Web sites that told him the state's population, flower, bird, and motto, and he'd also found a page that summarized the state's history. He'd cut and pasted everything from the online pages into his own word-processing program, arranged it all in order, and formatted it all so it would match. Now his mother was checking over his work—and she was telling him he'd made a mistake.

"But it *is* my work," he protested. "I found it all. I pasted it in. I put in the borders and the titles and the lettering."

"But you've copied it," his mother tried to explain.

"Sure," Robbie answered. "I always copy stuff off the Net. Isn't that okay?"

Robbie's mother was faced with a delicate problem. She was proud of her son's online research, and she had no problem with him copying material as a first step, rather than taking notes by hand. But she wanted him to understand what an original report was—that Robbie's job was to summarize and put things into his own words rather than simply copy what the Web-page author had written.

Robbie still didn't get it. "Why should I use my own words?" he asked her. "The Web site's words are better than mine. If the teacher wants to know about Connecticut, why can't I just find the information she wants and give it to her?"

"She wants to know that *you* understand the information," Robbie's mother tried to explain. "She wants to hear it all in *your* words." Robbie finally agreed, reluctantly, to write his own paper. But Robbie's mother wondered how she could keep the same problem from coming up again.

Even in pre-cyber days, it was hard helping children understand the difference between taking notes and copying outright. Cyberworld, with its cut-and-paste capabilities, makes this concept much harder to grasp. Here are some basic suggestions that can help children of all ages and grade levels steer away from plagiarism and toward research.

**Don't ever copy anything directly from the Web into your own work.** It's fine to cut and paste material from Web pages onto "notes pages," or even to print out entire articles from the Web. But your own assignments must all originate in your own word-processing program. Even if you want to copy a sentence or a quote, you have to type in every word yourself.

Our reasoning for this recommendation is twofold. First, a child who cuts and pastes creatively may not thoroughly read the material he or she has copied from the Net. Asking children to take notes and to type out all quotes rather than cutting and pasting ensures that they will read every word.

Second, children who cut and paste material from the Net can easily become confused about how much original work they themselves need to generate. The author's original words seem so much more eloquent and clear—it's simply too tempting to include long quotes or to change only a word or two. Even if children attribute these quotes to the correct source, they're still not learning as much as if they'd put most of the material into their own words.

Parents of learning-disabled or special-needs children may want to modify this rule to cut down on the typing, but then you'll have to use extra care to ensure that your children understand the difference between copying and writing. And of course, older children who do understand the rules of report writing might be given the leeway to cut and paste direct quotes. But it will be much harder for any child to use his or her own words if the first step in writing is to paste someone else's words onto the page. So if at all possible, stick to this principle even if your kids find keyboarding a struggle.

**Note the source of everything you copy.** If you're taking notes on something you read, the following information should be at the top of every page or on every note card:

| Books | Magazines | Web Sites |
|---|---|---|
| author, title, publisher, publication city and country, year of publication, page number | author, article, journal, volume, number, page number | author, Web page title, organization (if any) full Web address, the date you last accessed it. If possible, include as well the date the Web site was last updated by its author. And if you're printing out a Web page or a portion of a Web page, this information needs to be on every single piece of paper that has Web-sourced material. |

In other words, your child should never be able to look at any part of his or her research without knowing exactly where it came from. This is useful for training your child into good work habits—and it's also evidence that your child has done the work in case a teacher ever has any questions.

**Print out material you've taken from the Web—and mark it up.** This is helpful for a number of reasons. Highlighting, bracketing, underlining, and making marginal notes all help your child make the switch from passive reader to active writer. Your child is not just reading something and thinking, "Yeah, that's what I want to say." Instead, he or she is noticing what's most important, relevant, or interesting, and actively selecting it from the page. This will make it easier for your child to put the material into his or her own words later on. And again, you've now got the evidence that your child went through a thought process and didn't simply copy out material wholesale.

**Appropriately paraphrase material from these sources into your own words.** Sometimes children need a lot of help with this. Instead of coming up with their own words, they are mightily tempted to just parrot the source. If your child is having trouble with this concept, you may need to invest a little time—but it will be worth it in the end. Sit with your child and have him read aloud a sentence that he's decided is useful and wants to copy. "Tell me what this means in your own words," you say. As your child does so, you write down what he says. After you've gone through one or two sentences in this way, switch to, "Now, you write it down, just the way you said it to me." Eventually, you can let your child do his own work, but double-check by asking him to let you compare his research and his homework.

Of course, sometimes your child will want to quote someone. Then you'll need to make sure she knows how to use quotation marks and to copy the quote exactly. She can also copy part of a quote and just put that part in quotation marks. Either way, though, she'll have to find a way to reference the author whose words she's taking.

Unfortunately, this isn't an exact science. Knowing how closely your own words can follow a published source is kind of a gut feeling that you just have to have intuitively. If you've got it, work with your child until he or she gets it, too. If you don't have it, meet with a teacher or a counselor and have them explain it to you—then work with your child based on your own new knowledge. We suggest you visit a Web site that walks you through sample rules such as http://www.lib.berkeley.edu/TeachingLib/Guides/Internet/Style.html.

## Accidental Plagiarism: How Do You Know?

Some child plagiarists are active cheaters, but most children plagiarize by accident, because they honestly didn't understand the difference between plagiarism and research. If you know you've got an honest, trustworthy kid, how can you tell if he or she is accidentally crossing the line? Here are some questions to help you notice the red flags:

• **"How long did it take you to do that?"** If you think your child is working way too fast, based on your understanding of the assignment, maybe that's because he or she is unknowingly taking inappropriate short cuts.

• **"What an interesting piece of information—where in the world did you find that?"** Have your child talk about his or her sources with you. If you're concerned, ask your child to show you the Web pages he or she used. If you spot a problem, gently point it out.

• **"This is a really interesting point—but I'm having trouble understanding it. Can you explain it to me?"** If your child can explain what he or she has written, at least you know they've completed the assignment "in spirit." You may need to follow up with more explanation of the difference between paraphrasing and copying, but your focus will be on the technical problem, not on your child's avoidance of the work.

## Helping or Cheating: How Do You Know?

Just as kids might cross the line with research, so might they inadvertently cross it as they try to help their friends. A child might copy a portion of her own assignment "as an example," or "to show you what I mean," and then discover that her friend—knowingly or unknowingly—has simply pasted it into her own work. In such a situation, it's hard to prove which child originated the work and how conscious the cheating was, so you want to work with your child to prevent these situations.

We have a simple suggestion: tell your child that she can help her friends as much as she wants, as long it's over the telephone and not by e-mail. Reading a friend your version of a writing assignment means that the friend can benefit from your ideas but can't inadvertently use them verbatim. And your child can share anything she likes with her friend from a completed assignment that the teacher has already seen.

The one exception is for assignments, including math, where there's a specific answer to find. In that case, your child can tell her friend how to get the answer, and she can let her friend know if she got the same answer as the one her friend came up with, but she can't tell her friend her own answers, and she can help on only 10 percent of the questions.

Of course, you should back up this rule with a conversation

about the honor system. Help your child understand why it's important for every student to do his or her own work, unless the assignment specifically calls for collaborative work. Even if your child thinks she's being helpful, sharing her answers may limit her friend's ability to come up with her own original ideas. And if your child has made a mistake, she may inadvertently encourage her friend to make the same mistake.

---

### Homework and Cyber-Bullying

A recent *Lifetime* adaptation of *Odd Girl Out,* Rachel Simmons's excellent book on bullying among girls, portrayed a bully who tricked another girl into sharing her homework "just as an example" and then turned it in as her own. When the teacher asked the girls about their identical papers, the bully pressured her target to explain the coincidence by saying that they had worked on the assignment together and hadn't realized that they weren't supposed to turn in such similar work.

If your child seems to be helping her friends in a way that makes you uncomfortable, be aware that some kind of cyber-bullying may be going on. This is another example of why you need to know what your child is doing online, so that if something smells fishy to you, you can find out more and, if necessary, take action.

---

## Papers for Sale

Now, what about the Web sites that actively encourage conscious plagiarism by offering to sell your children papers? We think it's crucial that you talk about this possibility with your child and make sure he or she understands how dangerous it could be.

Your child needs to know that teachers are very sophisticated about these kinds of papers. Not only do they have their own instincts to go on, but now there are actual Web sites, including www.plagiarism.org and www.turnitin.com, that teachers can use to check out questionable homework. Even if your child orders one of these papers "just to see how someone else did it," he or she could inadvertently use a phrase or a source that the teacher or the Web site flags as belonging to a "paper for sale," and that may be enough to convict your child of plagiarism. Help your child realize that he or she is not the first kid in the world to think of using these sites. The teachers know all about this practice—and are way ahead of them.

If you like, demonstrate this by doing an online search with your child. Enter the words "buying term papers" into the search engine and see what comes up. Then go with your child to www.plagiarism.org and show her just what teachers might do to check out her work. Make sure your child understands that plagiarizing a paper could keep him or her out of college in a way that one bad grade could never do. Likewise, a plagiarism scandal could be a factor in future employers' decisions.

We know that you're asking a lot of your children, especially as they reach high school age, and you want to pick your battles. To us, there are three major teen issues that are worth making into a big deal: drunk driving, Internet predators, and plagiarism. The wrong decision about any one of these issues could torpedo your child's future in a way that few other bad choices could. The first two concern his or her physical safety; the third could affect his or her academic and professional future. So here's the kind of conversation we recommend:

> I know you're under a lot of pressure, and you want to get
> good grades. But on this issue, no bad grade will do you the

harm that plagiarizing a paper can do. Honestly, I'd rather you get a D or even an F than buy a paper or copy someone else's work. You can make up a D or an F, and in two years, no one will even remember that grade. A plagiarism scandal can follow you for a long, long time. If you ever feel on the verge of making that decision, please, come to me. I'll work with you to solve any school problems you're facing—and I'll thank you for making a smart decision.

---

### Cover All Bases

Your child may not acknowledge this, but perhaps he has a friend who has gotten away with cheating, and so he *knows* it's safe. Preempt that thought with some of the following what-ifs:

- What if you just happen to have a substitute who recognizes that paper?

- What if your own school just happened to start an in-service training on plagiarism and now your teacher has wised up?

- What if your teacher has taken a while to catch on with your friend but has just now gotten the final piece of evidence?

- What if your friend hasn't been cheating but has only pretended to cheat so people will think he's cool?

---

## Stealing Music? The Latest on Illegal Downloads

For a while, there was a lot of talk about illegal downloading of music and other media from the Internet, but we're happy to tell you that, at least as of this writing, that problem seems to have passed, thanks to litigation begun in 2000 by the Recording Industry Association of America (RIAA), which put music-sharing sites out of business. Colleges and universities across the country issued warnings after the final decision was made that downloading music illegally would be treated just like plagiarism—as a violation of federal copyright laws—and could result in expulsion.

These days, when kids download music onto their digital audio players, they pay for what they take, and sites that try to make free music available to Internet users are immediately sued by the RIAA. And while some experienced computer hackers have figured out how to illegally download movies on-line, most young people don't bother.

Of course, there are many sites that legitimately offer free music, often for a relatively small initial subscription fee. For example, http:/www.aeres.com is currently popular with lots of kids for helping them find free and inexpensive downloads of music and other media. These tend to be legitimate sites, however, and nothing for you or your child to worry about.

Only a few years ago, Internet access was an optional part of children's schoolwork—now it's practically a necessity. Yet due to lack of resources and training, most schools don't teach Internet research skills, just as many teachers don't take the time to help children learn the difference between plagiarism and legitimate online research. If your children aren't lucky enough to attend a school where they're learning the skills they need, we strongly urge you to teach them, or to find someone else who can. Don't neglect this aspect of your children's education—it's just too important.

## CHAPTER 10

# FRIENDSHIPS AND FAMILY RELATIONSHIPS

As Cyberworld has continued to expand, we've both been struck by what a large role it's come to play in family life, and by how disruptive that role can be. One family Barb was counseling—we'll call them the Davises—included a corporate executive father who dashed to check his e-mail the moment he walked through the door; a teenage girl who was continually on her cell phone; and a ten-year-old son whose constant preoccupation was playing Xbox online. The mother came to Barb in despair.

"Even when I'm home at a decent hour and make dinner," she told Barb, "nobody comes to the table. And when they finally do come, nobody talks to anybody—they're just marking time till they can get back to their electronic devices. I feel like my family is falling apart and nobody even cares."

Barb suggested family night, a weekly time when everybody could get together and simply talk. She explained the notion of a family meeting—a forum for bringing up problems and concerns. "You don't have to change things completely," she told the family. "Just tweak it some." When the kids were presented with this idea, the mother expected them to balk. Instead they made a suggestion of their own—family game night. They weren't comfortable with the idea of everyone sitting around and simply talking, but they loved the idea of hanging out together enjoying a family game like Uno. Of course, while they were drawing cards and engaging in heated contests, they managed to chat about their day, their schoolwork, and their friends.

One evening, the daughter let it slip that she was in a school play, which the parents hadn't even realized. They asked if they could attend, which in turn shocked the daughter; it hadn't occurred to her, she said, that her folks might want to come. Although she insisted that she was too embarrassed for them to see her, the parents persisted—and, the girl was pleased with their presence. Family game night had transformed the Davises.

This kind of indirect communication is common with teenagers, and it's why unstructured time with them is so crucial. The kid who won't come to you and say "I want to talk" may be just dying for an opportunity, so you need to provide one that allows your child to save face. That can't happen while everyone is cordoned off in his or her own little electronic world. So in this chapter we'll help you figure out how to keep your kids—and the rest of your family—from being lost in Cyberworld.

## Finding Family Time

Let's start with family issues. We know of two terrific ways to enhance your family life in the context of Cyberworld:

1. Find family-focused activities that you all can share, with or without electronics.
2. Invite your children to share their Cyberworld with you.

## Finding Family-Focused Fun

It can be hard to find ways to bring your family together, but if you're committed to making family time, you've got lots of options. All you have to do is start thinking about what kinds of activities can be shared, as opposed to activities that tend to pull you all in different directions. Here are some examples to get you started. Notice, by the way, that some shared activities include cyber-fun, but as social rather than private time.

| Activities That Bring You Together | Activities That Separate You |
| --- | --- |
| reading a book together | TMing |
| cooking | talking on the phone |
| doing craft projects | sending e-mails |
| sports | surfing the Web |
| playing a game together | solo or online video games |
| watching TV, DVD, video together | watching TV, DVD, video separately |
| going to a movie together and then out for ice cream | kids and adults going to movies separately |
| going for a walk or hike together | children's lessons; paying bills |
| going for a drive together | kids and adults only spending time with friends |
| doing yard work or errands together | separate chores |

We're certainly not suggesting that you and your children drop all solo activities. Especially as your children get older, they'll want and need to spend more time alone, with their friends, and in activities that don't—and shouldn't—include you. That's how they'll prepare for the day they finally go off on their own—and they need to practice flying solo in short trips from your safe and comfy nest!

But although your children are becoming more independent, they still need some family time, as the Davises discovered—time for the whole family to be together and time for each child to hang out with each parent. As you can see from the list, family time can be as simple as making dinner with your son or raking leaves with your daughter. It can be a shared game night, movie night, or even just a trip to the park. The challenge isn't so much in finding the activity as in making the time for it and making it clear to every single family member that this is part of your common life. Adults as well as children can get caught up in work, scheduled activities, social obligations, and a whole range of separate things to do. Committing to some relaxed time together on a weekly basis can be difficult, but, as the Davises discovered, it can be crucial.

### Family Formula

• Once a week, spend at least two hours of family time

• Once a week, each child gets at least two hours of one-on-one time with one parent

We find it fascinating that kids whose parents are divorcing often refer appreciatively to how much more individual time they get with each parent as a result. We can learn from these observations and make that quality time happen while remaining a family unit.

Remember, you can combine any of these times with doing errands, completing chores, making dinner, or taking care of business in some other way. The only requirement is that the atmosphere be relaxed and allows at least some time for each of you to talk.

## Coming Together in Cyberworld

You don't necessarily have to leave Cyberworld to come together. Sit down with your child at the computer and ask him or her to show you something Internet-related. Here are some questions you might ask your children that can allow them to show off a bit and that can also make Cyberworld more of a social experience:

→ "So help me out—if I wanted to find out how to get to [a place that interests you], how could I do that online?"

→ "You know, years ago, I had a recipe for shepherd's pie, but I lost it and I've never been able to find it again. Can you help me look for it online?"

→ "I want to find a pattern for my [knitting, embroidery, crocheting, sewing]—how would I go about that?"

→ "I'm having so much trouble saving and organizing my Favorites—can you give me a hand?"

→ "Aren't Favorites interesting? Let me show you some of the sites I've saved—and then would you like to show me some of your Favorite sites?"

→ "I found a Web site for downloading a free song I want to put on a CD. I've never done that! Can you help me?"

→ "I missed my favorite TV show last night, but I've just seen an ad saying I can download it for free from the Web. Can you help me figure out how to do that?"

Besides bringing the two of you closer together, sharing Cyberworld with your child can help him or her feel valuable, smart, and competent. And who knows? You might learn something, too!

## Communication Is Crucial

As therapists who often work with at-risk children, we're struck by how many tragic situations might have been avoided if only the adults in the situation had been paying closer attention. Whenever we read about a school shooting, for example, we're saddened to think of how many warning signs adults could have seen—but missed. Frequently, the children involved had been looking at disturbing Web sites, sending troubled e-mails and IMs, and otherwise leaving a cyber-trail. We can't help thinking that if only parents had gotten more involved in their children's cyber-lives and their real lives, some tragedies might have been averted—especially since in many of these situations, classmates also had the sense that something was up but never alerted their parents, teachers, or other adults. It's why we keep repeating that same crucial message: *if you want your kids to talk to you, make some opportunities—lots of opportunities*. You can't be sure they'll talk to you, but if you don't create the occasions, you may never hear a word.

## Negotiating Friendships in Cyberworld

Childhood is a time for learning how to relate to others. Sometimes Cyberworld helps with that process and sometimes it just gets in the way. For example, computer games and video games give kids a chance to play together and share techniques with each other. Children need to experience aggression and angry feelings and then handle them in a social context, and computer/video games are a perfect opportunity for them to work out these issues. But it's important for them to be *with* each other when they're processing these feelings. Playing online, at a distance, is not at all the same experience as engaging in competition, victory, and loss with people you can actually see.

On the other hand, Cyberworld also allows shy or awkward children to start with online friendships and online interactive games as a stepping stone to more active involvement with others. And for kids who have trouble handling aggression, the distance of an online relationship can offer a kind of grace period: you can work with your child to find healthy, satisfying ways of coping with difficult situations—and nobody but the two of you needs to know that your child had trouble.

Barb recently worked with one child—a nine-year-old boy whom we'll call Garth—who struggled with Asperger's syndrome and wanted to enhance his social skills. Barb suggested that Garth enter some chat rooms, initially with his parents' oversight, so he could practice talking with other kids. Garth agreed that his parents could use their monitoring program to print out his chats, so we could all look at them in therapy.

It turned out that Garth was often puzzled by responses he got from people online but couldn't reconstruct these conversations by himself. When we looked at the transcripts together, we discovered that Garth had misinterpreted several comments and then responded to them in a way that led other kids to make fun of him. Garth also felt clueless about all the acronyms everyone was using. All three of us gave him some coaching, and his parents found him an acronym translator. Suddenly, Garth was able to engage with other kids far more successfully. He felt more connected, while his parents felt the whole exercise had brought them closer to their son.

Likewise, Cyberworld is the perfect context for encouraging socialization—even from afar—for children who are physically isolated from other children or who can't find children who share their interests nearby. If your kids have the choice, of course, you should help them choose to be with live people rather than in cyber-relationships. Your goal is to make Cyberworld a bridge, not an end in itself.

**TIP**   **If your child has a tendency to avoid challenging situations, encourage him or her to try out new social situations or to play challenging games online. The distance offered by online relationships gives you a chance to build in some coaching and support.**

## Mastering the Skills of Friendship

Children need friends, classmates, and the company of children their own age to learn such skills as

- → resolving conflicts
- → solving problems together
- → setting boundaries
- → staying in touch with friends
- → negotiating time together, time apart
- → sorting through popularity issues—who's in, who's out, and why it matters (or doesn't)
- → expressing feelings
- → building trust
- → evaluating—who can be counted on and who can't

Cast your eyes over that list again and think about how these skills are affected by e-mail and other electronic communication. Let's look more closely at each skill.

## Resolving Conflicts

In most cases, this is a skill that is best learned face-to-face. As we saw in Chapter 3, misunderstandings and quarrels can often fester if not worked out in a personal, immediate way. When two people aren't getting along, e-mail can frequently make things worse, encouraging both parties to posture or to cling to their initial angry positions. Or two people may simply find it too hard to resolve their issues in writing. Kids who are still learning about the written word may not be able to express all their complex thoughts and contradictory issues onscreen—and that goes triple for the smaller screens and shorter messages of TM.

For example, suppose Emily is annoyed with her friend Olivia. "Olivia!" she says angrily. "I was really upset when you left me alone at that party."

"I couldn't help it!" Olivia protests. "Marcy came over and pulled me away—and I couldn't *not* go with her—she was *so* upset!"

"I know!" Emily says impatiently. "But it was *so* awful. Because right after you left, PJ came over, and she was *so* mean to me—wait till I tell you what she said—"

"Oh, no, how awful!" Olivia says sympathetically.

As you can see, that's the kind of conversation that you pretty much have to have in person. Even IM doesn't quite allow for the lightning-fast shift from anger to empathy. Emily needs to *see* that Olivia feels bad for her, not just read some sympathetic words. Olivia needs the chance to stand up to

Emily's anger before she expresses her sympathy. An e-mail or even an IM exchange risks freezing each of these moments into place, instead of allowing the girls to express and then release their feelings. And being in the same room also gives the girls a chance to remember how much they like each other and to put their quarrel into perspective. Comic relief is easier to attain in person, too, with an exaggerated look or a giggle. All things being equal, people tend to move toward conflict resolution, but if you interrupt that process with time delays, you can knock it off track.

On the other hand, sometimes e-mailing each other can be a helpful first step in a conflict. It gives each party time to process the issues and think about his or her own feelings. And if you want to give the other person bad news, it may be easier if he or she isn't hearing it directly but in the privacy of their own home, where parents or other friends may be there to offer support. E-mail is especially good for those times when you're too angry to think clearly. Instead of saying something you'll regret, you can write down a response, take a time-out, and then rethink your answer—or simply walk away.

## Helping Your Child Cope with Conflicts

If your child is struggling with an e-mail conflict, do what you can to help him or her cope with all the complicated feelings that may be involved. Take seriously how much the situation hurts and try not to minimize your child's emotions by saying "It'll pass" or "Soon this won't matter to you." Think for a moment—can you still remember hurtful things that happened to you at age ten, twelve, fourteen, sixteen? We'll readily admit that we can and, in our experience as therapists, we've found that's true of most people. So why tell your child that his feelings don't matter or that her pain isn't real? Even if the pain will pass, it's real now. And the tools you share with your child for coping with it—on- and offline—will also be with your child for the rest of his or her life. After all, we want our children to grow up to be caring adults; shouldn't we model that to our children by being empathic to their emotions?

On the other hand, if your child is upset by something going on in Cyberworld, your job is often to be the calm within the storm. Even if your child always remembers this incident, the intensity of the pain *will* pass, and it's good for your child to have someone around who knows this. You can't help your child if you get as upset as he or she is, so maintain some detachment even as you also affect a nurturing stance. That way you can support your child's feelings while also helping him or her move on when the time is right. Best of all, this sets the tone for a healthy relationship between you and your child even after he or she reaches adulthood—and it helps model for your child a healthy relationship to Cyberworld and all the stormy emotional issues that Cyberworld can raise.

## Solving Problems Together

This, too, is a skill that's best learned face-to-face. If your child is collaborating with a classmate on a school project, for example, the two kids will probably get more done if they work out a plan together. Likewise, if your child is on a committee—let's say to plan a school dance—he or she needs the experience of figuring out what to do with a live-action group where ideas are flying, suggestions are being brainstormed, criticisms are considered, and somehow everyone comes to a decision.

True, committees can sometimes use e-mail to make plans, sample opinions, or divide up tasks. By and large, though, you need the nuances of tone, language, inflection, body language, and facial cues to really get the most from the group process. Often, in both one-on-one and group collaborations, a lot is said by not saying anything—things you might miss online or on the phone. Ever suggest something that's followed by a loud silence? There's no more eloquent way to be told that your idea was a real bomb. E-mail simply can't capture that kind of effect.

## Setting Boundaries

There are both pros and cons to practicing this skill electronically. On the plus side, you may be able to e-mail something you'd be too scared or embarrassed to say out loud. "I can't go to that party because my mother said no" might be easier to write than to say. Sure, your friend may e-mail back, "What a dork!" but that, too, may be easier to read than to hear without all the facial and vocal cues. E-mail may also make it easier for you to speak your piece without interruption ("It was hard for me when you kept me waiting at the mall for a whole hour, and I want to tell you all the reasons why I never want you to do that again"). And with e-mail, if your child needs your support or the support of a friend, there's some time to get it before continuing the correspondence.

On the other hand, taking a stand in person makes a far stronger statement, and both your child and his or her friend will probably experience it that way. You can also put forth your position with more flexibility and negotiate, if necessary, on the spot. This is an acquired skill, but one that's definitely worth building. Expressing yourself spontaneously may seem more genuine and heartfelt, and the immediacy of the situation may call forth thoughts and feelings you didn't realize you had—an experience that may not happen as you sit at your computer and write.

As a parent, your job is to give your child some sense of these pros and cons and to make sure he has the skills to take either route as the situation warrants. When your child grows up, she will sometimes want to set a boundary via e-mail and at other times need to do it in person. Childhood is the time for learning how to do both—so make sure your child has both kinds of practice. We've also seen parents polish their own boundary-setting skills in order to offer their kids a good example, so both parents and children benefited in the long run.

## Staying in Touch with Friends

No doubt about it, e-mail is terrific for staying in touch. Both of us have a much wider circle of out-of-town friends and connections than we'd ever have maintained without e-mail, and we're grateful for it.

We've also seen how helpful e-mail has been to the children we work with in this regard. Recently, Sue counseled a child who'd moved with his family to Charleston from another region. He felt isolated in the south and was going through his own version of culture shock. Staying in touch with his old friends back home by e-mail and IM was tremendously helpful to him as he slowly started to make new friends.

Your child can also use e-mail to expand his or her bonds with local friends and classmates. Children can share a richer world by sending each other links to blogs, Web sites, and forums. They can forward jokes, cartoons, clips from TV shows, pictures of themselves, or items from catalogues. "Do you agree with this guy?" they might write. Or, "This is the sweater I'm planning to buy—what do you think of it?"

We have only two minor concerns about this kind of online bonding. First, you should make sure that your child isn't choosing e-mail over face time. Always, real-life connections should be preferred to online relationships—but if your child can manage both, that's terrific.

Second, if your child is attached to another place—either a former home or a camp, conference, or other environment that he prefers to the place you actually live—then e-mail can sometimes increase your child's sense of missing out and interfere with the bonding process to his actual surroundings. Being in touch via e-mail makes it even more vivid and hurtful that life in another place is going on without you. Or if a friend has moved away, e-mail keeps reminding the child left behind of what he's missing by not being an ongoing part of that friend's life. So again, if you feel that your child is using e-mail to keep from engaging with the places or people around him, you may need to set some limits.

Sometimes, to be sure, your child may resist these limits. One of Barb's clients, a nineteen-year-old college student whom we'll call Mady, recently told Barb that when she was sixteen, she and her family moved from North Carolina to South Carolina. Over the course of the summer, she kept in touch with her former boyfriend, Tim, by e-mail. Every day after school, she came home and dashed to the computer to spend hours chatting with Tim about how much she hated her new school. They even talked about her running away and hiding out at a friend's house in North Carolina.

Luckily, her parents noticed how alienated she seemed and

how absorbed she was in chatting with Tim. They ended up restricting her e-mail and IM contact with Tim, allowing only snail mail and weekend telephone calls. Mady was initially furious over what she viewed as "an attempt to control every facet of my life!" Then she started making friends at her new school. Mady told Barb that she began to feel secretly relieved at being able to blame her parents for quashing her communication with Tim. She even stopped answering the snail mail letters, and eventually the phone calls stopped as well. On her most recent college break, Mady told her parents how much she now appreciated their limits.

## Negotiating Time Together, Time Apart

This can be a tough skill for kids to work out, especially as they get older—and again, there are both pros and cons to doing it by e-mail. Either way, a child needs his parents to model the high-level skill of scheduling different friends for different activities and coping with the hurt feelings of friends who may be left out. Whether a child is speaking or writing, she often needs to convey an assertive yet friendly message like the following:

> This Saturday, I'm going to be spending time with Shelby. I know
> you guys aren't so crazy about each other, so I'm not inviting
> you—but I'll see you Sunday, okay?

The advantage of conveying something like this by e-mail is that people who want to stay connected don't have to deal with each other's bad feelings. Here's how that conversation might go in person:

**EMILY:** This Saturday, I'm going to be spending time with Shelby. I know you guys aren't so crazy about each other, so I'm not inviting you—but I'll see you Sunday, okay?

**OLIVIA:** How can you spend *any* time with Shelby? She's such a slut!

**EMILY:** She is not! She's my friend, and I like her!

**OLIVIA:** Well, if you *like* spending time with sluts, maybe that means *you're* a slut.

Olivia is hurt, Emily is defensive, and in person, the two girls may not be able to keep their feelings in bounds. Here's how they might handle the same situation by e-mail.

**EMILY:** This Saturday, I'm going to be spending time with Shelby. I know you guys aren't so crazy about each other, so I'm not inviting you—but I'll see you Sunday, okay?

**OLIVIA:** How can you spend *any* time with Shelby? She's such a slut!

**EMILY:** Well, I'll try not to turn into a slut by Sunday. See you then, okay? Love you! XOXOX

**OLIVIA:** Love you, too. XOXOXO

Emily may still be feeling defensive, but when Olivia isn't right there in front of her, Emily can take a deep breath and take the high road, especially if she and her folks have practiced just this kind of tactful response. Likewise, Olivia may still be hurt, but when Emily offers to make peace, Olivia can force herself to write an appropriate answer more easily than she'd be able to express such a response in person. Emily can't see the hurt, angry expression that's still on Olivia's face as Olivia types those friendly words—and now Olivia has until

Sunday to calm down and see things differently, perhaps aided by her parents or another friend.

## Sorting Through Popularity Issues—Who's In, Who's Out, and Why It Matters (or Doesn't)

In our opinion, e-mail has vastly complicated the whole issue of popularity, gossip, rumors, and all the entangled relationships of preteen and teenage life. E-mail makes it easier to lie—you're typing something alone in your room, not saying it to someone's face—and that whole anonymous, no-consequence feeling of Cyberworld helps make the pain you may be causing seem less real. E-mail also allows you to forward other people's e-mails, giving you the ability to betray their secrets in a whole new way. And, as we've seen, Cyberworld has taken the possibilities of bullying to an unprecedented level.

In such a context, your child may have more trouble than kids from earlier generations in figuring out what popularity means and why it might or might not matter. Of course, Cyberworld might also give your child more perspective, opening up a world beyond his or her school. But at the same time, it gives expanded powers to cliques and gossips, possibly magnifying their importance.

Still, blogs and Web sites can offer lonely, awkward, or unusual children new avenues for popularity—a popularity that might be felt only in Cyberworld but that might also spread to school or to another real-life community. If your child is struggling with questions about popularity and acceptance, help him define his ethics and sense of responsibility toward others, even as you also help him develop a thick skin and a kind of indifference to other people's opinions. Help your child see the need to pick her battles; you don't need to respond to every-thing with the same level of intensity. And help her find her own community—through Cyberworld if necessary—so that she knows that she belongs somewhere.

## Expressing Feelings

As with so many other friendship skills, practicing this one by e-mail is a kind of double-edged sword. On the one hand, the privacy and sometimes the anonymity of e-mail can allow chil-dren to express more of what they feel than they might other-wise do. On the other hand, this kind of private, anonymous expression can be deceptive. Children may find themselves say-ing things they don't really mean, can't back up, or later regret.

E-mail can be a terrific way for children to practice express-ing their feelings, and if they're doing so in a safe, protected context where they're not likely to hurt anyone else, we're all for it. But we urge you to keep an eye on this part of your child's development so that you can make sure that e-mail is facilitating it, not distorting it.

## Building Trust

E-mail is a terrific medium for building trust, especially for shy or awkward children, who may be able to extend themselves via e-mail and then, with help, make the transition to trust in real life. If your child has an e-mail correspondence with some-one she hasn't met or has barely met, help her find ways to get to know her new friend. Suggest that she ask what her friend is interested in, what her favorite TV show is, her favorite sub-ject in school, the songs or singers that she likes. You can also suggest things that your child might share about herself, including her opinions of TV and movies. This will all give your child a better idea of whether her new friend shares her values and interests. As the children move from an e-mail to a real-life relationship, encourage them to find nonthreatening ways of being together: playing a game, going to the movies, bowling, skating, miniature golf—some structured activity that offers a common topic of conversation without putting anyone on the spot. The new friends can start off with limited time together and then, as their comfort level rises, plan longer days.

## Evaluating Who Can Be Counted On and Who Can't

This is a harder task to accomplish by electronic means, because it's usually more difficult to evaluate someone just based on what he or she writes. It's easy to share secrets and intimate feelings in an e-mail, but does that mean you can trust the person who seemed to open up to you or to whom you felt comfortable opening up? Just as a child may express more by e-mail than she can really back up, so might a child find herself taking another person's expression of feelings far more seriously than is warranted. Certainly that can happen in person, too, but expressions of love, devotion, and "friends forever" might become more intense and far-reaching by e-mail than face-to-face. So evaluating the trustworthiness of friends' e-mails is another issue that your child may need help with.

Help your child identify and then pick up on the red flags that indicate danger, suggesting that a seemingly reliable friend may not be so trustworthy. Your child should learn not to trust someone who has forwarded him someone else's e-mail, who forwards his e-mail to someone else, or who has otherwise used his e-mail against him. Your child also needs to learn to pick up on less obvious disappointments: breaking a promise to chat at 8 p.m., for example, or being chronically late in keeping other appointments. You can help your child learn how to make judgments about reliability and/or trustworthiness based on e-mail as well as face time. In addition, teaching your children how to make these judgment calls lets them know how others might be evaluating them.

## What to Tell Your Children: Conflict Resolution Through E-mail

E-mail can be an impersonal form—but it doesn't have to be. Just as you teach your kids how to talk through difficulties with their friends, so can you help them understand how to use e-mail as part of conflict resolution. Here are some suggestions.

1. *Use I statements:* Rather than telling your friend what he or she has done wrong, say how you feel. Not, "You're always late and it's just rude!" but rather, "I get worried when you don't show up on time, and it seems like that's happening a lot lately." Generally the rule of thumb for effective I statements is "I feel [emotion] when you [their action] and I would like [your desire]": "I feel angry when you are late, and I would like you to be on time," or "I feel hurt when you are TMing someone else while I am with you, and I'd like you to focus on me unless it's a real emergency."

2. *Prepare for communication with a test run.* Before sending a possibly touchy e-mail, write one or two e-mails that are just for you, so you can vent all your feelings. Say anything you want in these e-mails, knowing ahead of time

that you won't send them. In fact, don't even write them *in* your e-mail program—keep them as separate text.

3. ***Think before you send.*** Never send an emotional e-mail without reading it over at least once—several times and several hours later if you're really seething. One of the most useful things about e-mail is that it lets you process your feelings and think about what you want to express instead of simply blowing off steam. Don't give up that advantage by sending off a first-draft e-mail—it may not even express how you really feel, let alone how you'll feel after you've cooled off a bit.

4. ***Keep e-mails private.*** Agree ahead of time with your friends that everyone's e-mails are confidential. E-mail makes it really easy to pass messages along to third parties. But that's often like throwing oil on the flames. Having all those other people involved in *your* fight may be temporarily comforting, but it doesn't settle anything in the long run. Keep your private communication private—you might be surprised at how much more quickly conflicts are resolved when you do.

5. ***When in doubt, don't send!*** E-mail often carries with it a kind of urgency—"Oh, they wrote me, I have to write back right away!" But you're allowed to take your time. Many a hasty e-mailed reply made a fight bigger, when just waiting an hour or so to send a reply might have made the fight smaller.

6. ***Use e-mail to buy yourself some time.*** E-mail can help give your friend time to come to terms with what you said; it's terrific for slowing things down and giving people time to cool off. Writing a friend about something that concerns you can be a terrific way to start a difficult conversation.

Just make sure that you're available to talk when he or she wants to reply. Sending a painful e-mail just before you leave for a two-week vacation with your family means that your poor friend has to sit and stew while you're gone.

7. *Use Netiquette.* Sending messages in all caps indicates you are yelling or emphasizing loudly, which can feel very abrasive to the recipient. Teach your child some of the nuances of e-mail communication, such as using italics for emphasis rather than capital letters.

8. *Acknowledge the good things as well as the bad.* Even if you're mad at your friend, he or she is still someone you care about—or you probably wouldn't be so upset. Remind your friend about the good things in your friendship as well as sharing your concerns. "I know you're a really good friend," "I'm sure we can fix this," "I really care about you even though I'm mad," and "I want to be your friend—but I want us to talk about this," are all good ways to keep a conflict in perspective.

Learning how to make and keep friends and how to be part of a family are two of children's most important developmental tasks. While Cyberworld may require some new skills, your child's basic challenges are the same—and so are yours. If you can help your children learn how to value themselves, respect others, appreciate their loved ones, and work out conflicts—in real time and Cyberworld alike—you'll have taken a huge step toward preparing them for a happy and healthy adulthood.

CHAPTER 11

· · · · · · · · · · · · · · · · · · · · · · · ·

# SEXUALITY AND DATING

Recently, a friend told us a disturbing story about her niece's experience with Internet dating. The niece—we'll call her Toni—had made plans to get together with a good friend, whom we'll call Caitlin. Caitlin had told Toni that some friends of hers would be hanging out with them, including a guy that Caitlin was interested in dating. Both Toni and Caitlin were part of a large circle of high school friends that included both guys and girls, so Toni didn't think anything of it.

The friends and Caitlin picked Toni up at the nearest bus stop in her suburban town and went back to Caitlin's empty house. Toni soon realized that these weren't actually friends of Caitlin's; they were two guys Caitlin had met online, and this was actually their first face-to-face meeting. Toni had assumed that Caitlin already knew these friends, especially the prospective boyfriend—she couldn't imagine that her friend would want to date some guy she hadn't even met. But Caitlin felt that she *did* know her prospective boyfriend, because she'd started an e-mail correspondence with him on MySpace. Having read his profile and written him a few times, she considered him a friend.

All four young people were high school seniors, and the guys hadn't misrepresented themselves in any obvious way—they weren't predators or con artists. But Toni didn't like the way they talked about women, or about people in general. She didn't feel safe with them—and she was shocked that Caitlin did. Stuck without a ride, she had the boys drive her home, and the next day she called Caitlin in a fury.

"Don't you ever put me in that position again!" she told her friend. "I can't believe you'd do anything so reckless—meeting two guys for the first time alone and bringing them back to your house when your mom wasn't there—guys who don't even go to our school? Anything could have happened to you—and anything could have happened to me, too."

We were struck by Toni's story, because Toni herself had such good judgment. She never would have arranged to hang out with strangers in an empty house—she wasn't even interested in online dating. But she'd known Caitlin for years and had never realized what poor judgment her friend had. As soon as she figured out the situation, she asked to be taken home. But she'd put herself in a position where she had to rely on the good faith—and good driving—of two potentially dangerous strangers.

Toni described the whole incident to her mother, who appreciated the steps her daughter had taken to protect herself. But the incident drove home to the whole family—and to us—how Cyberworld has complicated the whole area of teen sexuality and dating. In a pre-Cyberworld era, Caitlin would have had very few occasions to meet those guys from two towns over; her contact would likely have been limited to guys in her own school. Of course, sexual assault can happen anywhere, but classmates would have been far less likely to view Caitlin as some anonymous conquest: they'd expect to see her in school the next day, and they'd know that her parents could very easily track them down.

Even if Caitlin had met guys from further away—say, at a party, dance, or sporting event—her first pre-Cyberworld encounter with them would have been by definition a face-to-face meeting in a public place. She wouldn't have had the chance to build up all sorts of fantasies about them by e-mail—she could have seen them for what they were and made her decisions accordingly.

As it happened, Caitlin didn't like the online guys either and didn't plan to see them again. So in that regard, Toni's sense of her friend's judgment was justified. She'd accurately pegged Caitlin as someone who liked the same kinds of guys she herself liked, which was why she'd been interested in meeting them in the first place. What she hadn't realized was that Caitlin hadn't distinguished between actually knowing these boys and only having an e-mail correspondence with them. She hadn't realized how Cyberworld might affect the way Caitlin described the situation—referring to strangers as friends, saying she'd met someone whom she hadn't ever seen.

"Next time, I'll know some more questions to ask," Toni told her mom. Her mother had the same feeling: Next time, I'll know some more questions to teach my daughter.

Cyberworld has its pros and cons as a place to learn about sexuality and to explore dating relationships. The pros include safety, distance, and the chance to take things slowly as a younger teen builds an online romance with someone he or she has never met—potentially good practice for the real-life relationships that come later. The cons include objectification, unreal expectations, and the many possibilities for deception, self-delusion, and potential danger. As always, you, the parent, need to help your child negotiate this new terrain.

Of course, another element of cyber-sexuality is pornography, which is all too readily available online. The seductive aspect of porn to a teenager—especially a teenage boy—is that it separates sexual satisfaction from the difficult business of actually forming a relationship. Instead, pornography encourages young men to think of women purely in terms of how they look or, more specifically, in terms of how they measure up to some ideal standard of "sexy." Not only is your teenage son unlikely to meet a girl his age who fits that porn-level standard, but the lessons he learns from pornography aren't going to help him build relationships with the girls he does meet.

Teenage girls may be less interested in porn, but, as with Caitlin, they frequently develop romanticized relationships with online correspondents they've never met. Just as your son probably won't meet a real-life porn star at his high school, your daughter won't meet her Prince Charming there either. And in both cases, a pseudo-relationship with a sexual or romantic object has the potential to replace a real-life involvement with an actual person, depriving your child of important developmental knowledge.

Kids who want to explore gay sexuality online face similar challenges. The pornographic or romantic images they're likely to find are so far removed from real-life prospects—especially for high school–age kids—that teenagers can feel intimidated before they've even begun.

Having said that, we must admit: the prospect of your children's first romance being with an online person whom they've never met is not actually so bad, as long as they eventually move on from this idealized stage to a real-life relationship.

Had Caitlin been a dreamy fourteen-year-old engaged in months of correspondence with an online boyfriend, instead of a somewhat experienced eighteen-year-old looking for a real relationship, Cyberworld might have been a terrific context for her first few "dates." While we don't think online romances are a healthy long-term solution for your teens' dating life, they might allow your younger adolescents to practice being in a relationship, while giving you a chance to help them take those first scary steps.

So let's take a closer look at how Cyberworld affects teen dating and sexuality, from romance to relationships to Internet porn. As Toni's mother learned, even a teenager who's not interested in cyber-dating needs to know the rules of the road.

## Dating in Cyberworld

As we observe online dating among both teens and adults, what strikes us most is the way that online dating partakes of all the best and worst of cyber-culture.

On the plus side: You can meet people who share your interests whom you'd never have met in real life—you're not limited to your own school anymore! You can engage in extensive e-mail correspondence that might offer you a chance to exchange more information and express more feelings than might easily take place on a first or second date. You can explore your own changing identity and take risks in a somewhat protected environment. And when your first several encounters with someone are through e-mail, you can get help and support from parents and friends in ways you never could with face-to-face meetings in real time.

On the minus side: It all feels so unreal. It's an anonymous culture that often seems to promise "no consequences"—not necessarily the best environment for beginning an intimate relationship. The consumerist aspect comes into play, too; people create dating profiles as though they were writing advertising copy, and they read other people's dating profiles as though they were ordering a potential mate from a catalogue. There's the illusion that you can choose whom you want based on a set of criteria that you request or read about, as if you were ordering a couch or a new coat. And if you don't like what you've ordered, you can go back to the store and buy something else—the other person's feelings just don't seem as real, because you've never even met.

And yet, as so often happens in Cyberworld, it's hard to keep the boundaries straight between virtual reality and reality itself. Your child *feels* as though she's met someone, as though she's gone through a genuine process of acquaintance, when all she's really done is read and written and looked at some photos.

Think of all the information your child gets on a live first date. Is the date considerate enough to show up on time? How is he dressed? What image is she trying to convey? Does that image match your child's own sense of his or her true identity? Does the date seem comfortable with himself? Is he really into impressing your daughter, or does he seem more real? Is she genuinely interested in your son, or does she seem more interested in his car, his clothes, his rating on the cool meter? When it comes time to choose a movie together, do both kids show respect for each other's opinions and take responsibility for the evening together? Or is she super-bossy, while he's too shy even to make a suggestion? If the date includes hanging out at a pizza place, how does this potential boyfriend treat the waitress? Does this possible girlfriend flirt with other boys? Is she overly critical of others? How does your child's date talk about his or her family? What about past relationships—is he still hung up on an old girlfriend he can't stop talking about? Does she have a long string of terrible boyfriends she can't find a good word for?

These are the kinds of things your child notices in person, maybe without even realizing it. The whole art of dating is figuring out what to look for and how important it is—and that's exactly what your teenager is supposed to be learning, or at least starting to learn. Ideally, he or she is figuring this out in a protected environment, with you there to set some boundaries and, ideally, to offer support and advice.

Now compare that information-rich—if often uncomfortable—real-life date with the process of cyber-meeting. Your child is basing everything on a profile and a photo, so he or she is essentially relying on how photogenic and how good with words someone is—not totally irrelevant qualities, perhaps, but not the most important ones for a future relationship, either. Your child has no idea if someone helped your date write his profile or if he's retouched his photo. He doesn't know if this potential girlfriend means any of the things she says, or if she just thought they made her sound cool—and because he's not in the room with her as she's saying them, he can't really use his gut instinct to find out. As long as teenagers stay online, they're failing to learn the most important thing about dating: how to train your gut instincts to help you make better choices.

Now, let's not go overboard. Often, cyber-dating leads to actual meetings, and it's not so terrible to have some information before you actually meet someone. But even for adults that first cyber-encounter can lead to several layers of fantasy and a false sense of already knowing someone that can distort your judgment (as it did Caitlin's). All that preparation sometimes affects a child's ability to assess who this person *really* is because he's already got such an investment in who he *thinks* they are. And for people who don't photograph well, haven't mastered the art of writing about themselves, and create idiosyncratic profiles, online dating may put them at a disadvantage even more severe than the usual teen judgments about popularity and dateability.

In the illusory world of cyber-culture, it can be especially hard for teens to figure out which qualities matter and how to tell if a potential mate has them. Cyberworld culture reinforces the idea that illusions and appearances are all that matters—you *have* to judge a book by its cover, because the cover is all there is. Worse, the sense of Cyberworld's infinite possibility suggests that there is always someone better out there—someone *perfect* out there. Instead of working with the real-world limits of his or her high school classmates, your child is free to imagine an idealized mate—perhaps based on the pornography he's been viewing or the romanticized movie she saw recently—and then return over and over again to the cyber-pool, always searching for something better.

Having said this, we see a lot of positive aspects to supporting your child's choice to try online dating, if he or she is interested in going that route. After all, an increasing number of adults are meeting people that way, so it's a skill that your child may need to master, as much as the skill of dating itself. For younger teenagers and preteens, the protective distance of online dating can allow them to take things much more slowly, with far more support, than in traditional face-to-face dating. And for quirky kids with unusual interests, or kids who've been doomed to dorkiness or un-dateability at their own high schools, having a wider field to choose from can be a godsend.

So let your child be your guide. If he or she wants to explore online dating, see if you can find ways to offer help and support while setting protective limits and making your values clear. And even if your child never uses the Internet to meet someone, e-mail and TM will likely play a role in any relationship he or she does have, so check out the advice in Chapters 2, 3, and 10 as you help your child negotiate the challenges of integrating cyber-communication into a relationship. Either way, don't forget: Cyberworld has a culture of its own—a culture that your child needs to understand.

## If Your Child Is Cyber-Dating . . .

If your child is posting profiles on a dating site and looking to meet online dates, see if you can offer your help and support. Your child may not be receptive to your involvement, but at least you can let your child know that you understand the basic protocols of cyber-dating. Your involvement may also keep them more honest, while at the same time letting them see that you're interested in what they're doing.

### The Profile

The fundamental unit of cyber-dating is the online profile. Usually it includes one or more photos, a questionnaire for participants to fill out, and some open-ended questions for which people can write anywhere from a few sentences to several paragraphs.

If your child wants guidance, look at some profiles together.

Pretend that you're a person of your child's preferred sex, checking out potential dates. What do these other profiles include? How do these people present themselves? Can your child see any means of presenting his or her special qualities in a way that makes your child seem both regular and unique?

Help your child identify the code that these profiles tend to use—or ask your child to help *you* identify it, and see what he or she comes up with. The basic point, which your child probably doesn't fully understand, is that these profiles are not necessarily truthful and so are *not* to be taken at face value. Depending on how people feel about themselves and whom they want to impress, online daters may present themselves as more or less sexually experienced, athletic, smart, romantic, or confident than they really are. Your child will be mightily tempted to believe every word of these profiles and to feel that he or she is the only one in this Cyberworld who doesn't own a car or who hasn't had several relationships already. Even if your child knows for a fact that a friend has misrepresented himself online, even if she's planning to distort her own profile, the overwhelming tendency—even for adults who know better!—is to believe what you read and to feel intimidated, impressed, or attracted.

We suggest that you ask your child to share with you the names of some other kids they know whose profiles are on one of the social networking sites like MySpace. Together, log onto one of your child's friends blogs or read her friends' profiles; you are bound to see exaggerations or even downright untruths that only people who know them would catch. It's a terrific lesson in how profiles of people your kids *don't* know may also be distorting the truth.

If your children don't want to look at dating sites with you—a perfectly healthy teenage response—find ways to convey this basic truth about online profiles and dating in general. See if you can casually share your own dating experiences with them, letting them know, for example, that guys tend to exaggerate how much sex they've had or that girls often portray their boyfriends as much nicer and more romantic than they really are. Help them see through the facades that are so much a part of teen dating—facades that are even harder to penetrate in Cyberworld.

## First Contact

Once your child has seen a profile of someone he or she likes, the next step is to e-mail that person through the site. Most dating sites discourage direct contact or the sharing of e-mail addresses until a few e-mails have been exchanged in this more protected environment.

Some sites also offer a range of ways to contact someone. On some sites, for example, each participant keeps a list of people in whom he or she is especially interested. If two people end up on each other's lists, the site may contact both of them. It's a less risky way of making contact, but there's no guarantee that someone you like will ever get around to putting you on a list—even though he or she may well respond to a message you send directly.

If your children are interested in meeting people through cybersites, encourage them to put themselves out there, contacting people who seem interesting. Waiting and hoping to be contacted in Cyberworld, a person can easily get lost in the shuffle, especially someone without a super-hot photo or other outstanding profile feature. And in Cyberworld, either guys or girls can make the first move.

That first contact should ideally be short, personal, but not too intimate. It's hard to remember that you don't really know each other yet—but you don't. Suggest that your child imagine what he or she would say to a stranger at a party or to an interesting classmate who sits nearby in assembly. Explain that a first note should sound like that. Suggest that your child choose two or three things that he or she liked about the person's profile to comment on and offer a clear invitation about what to do next. For example:

Dear PartyGirl,

I really liked reading your profile. *X-Men* was one of my favorite movies, too! I liked it when you said you enjoy people but need time to be alone—me, too. And I thought that was a great photo.

You sound like someone I'd like to know! Write back if you'd like to talk more. I bet we have a lot of things in common—can't wait to find out if I'm right!

StantheMan (aka Jimmy)

Usually, the site is set up so that anyone you write to can see your profile. Your child doesn't have to say a lot about himself or herself, because the person who gets the letter will check out the profile.

Often, letters like this may get no response, and the first-time cyber-dater may be crushed. Having seen someone's photo and read his or her profile, your child can easily get the idea that he knows the person and has already begun a relationship. Then, when he gets no answer to his carefully written note—a note that may have cost him a lot of courage and effort—he might feel as though he's been rejected, very personally.

In fact, that's one of the cruelest illusions of Cyberworld. No one knows you yet, so they can't reject you—but still, it feels that way. Hey, for teenagers, it feels that way when a stranger at a party walks away from them—in fact, we know a lot of adults who feel rejected in those circumstances, too. But at least you never found out much about that stranger. When kids read an online profile, they know their potential dates' favorite movies, the cars they drive, the music they listen to, their ideal colleges, and their favorite subjects in school. They feel as though they're already on the road to being friends—maybe more—and then, no answer? You child could end up feeling like the most unattractive person in the universe.

Cyberworld makes it even easier than Real World for a teen or preteen to spend hours obsessing over her shortcomings or to wonder what he should have said differently. If possible, help your child overcome that sense of being rebuffed. Remind him or her that, despite the profile, that other person is still an unknown quantity. Maybe they're not very nice. Maybe they have lots of dates already or even a steady boyfriend or girlfriend and are just trying to build up their egos by trying to get lots of responses to their profile online. (We've spoken with several adults who've confessed to this behavior on adult dating sites, so we know how common it is.) Or maybe the other person actually *didn't* like something in your child's profile, photo, or note. Without more information, it's impossible to draw any conclusions. Help your children break through these cyber-illusions, while also seeing if your child might actually improve his or her presentation and approach.

Suppose the other person does respond and an e-mail correspondence begins? Then your child faces another set of challenges, related to the cyber-illusion of intimacy. Alone in her room, writing to a person who's only a photo and a set of words, it's easy for your child to imagine a deeper relationship than actually exists. She might open up to her cyber-correspondent, confessing intimate secrets, sharing heartfelt dreams, admitting to feelings she's never spoken of before. Her imagination fills in the rest, especially if her correspondent matches her, secret for secret, so that she feels deeply the extent to which both of them are really opening up. Sitting before the computer screen, she feels as though she's overcome all the barriers that have kept her from connecting to everyone else, and that finally she's found her soulmate.

But of course, your child is too young to understand that she's had a good reason for not spilling her secrets to all the guy's she met *in person*. Private information isn't meant to be shared lightly; most of it should be saved for people she can really trust. Boys as well as girls can fall into this kind of secret-telling romantic fantasy, in which a private e-mail correspondence takes on the illusion of real intimacy. As a parent, you may not be able to keep your child from this kind of cyber-romance, but do what you can to give him or her some perspective. Help your child realize, too, that this correspondence can be forwarded and shared with others. Honestly, though, that's less of a danger than that the relationship will simply fizzle out—and that your child may then feel betrayed, abandoned, or heartbroken. That's painful enough when the relationship was a real-life first crush or first love, but emotions can run faster and hotter in Cyberworld, where there are so few reality barriers to slow things down. Do what you can to help your child keep things in proportion—a difficult task for teenagers at best.

---

### Teens Meet in Real Time

According to a March 2006 survey conducted by the National Center for Missing and Exploited Children and Cox Communications, some 14 percent of teens aged thirteen to seventeen have had face-to-face meetings with someone they first encountered online, while one-third of teens said they were considering such a meeting.

---

### Ongoing Contact

Cyberworld has created a new phenomenon in teenage life: the boyfriend or girlfriend whom your teenager has never met except online. Sometimes these relationships involve phone sex or cyber-sex—young people bring themselves to orgasm while speaking on the phone, chatting in chat rooms, or instant messaging. In fact, according to a recently released University and College Sex Survey published by CampusKiss.com, some 87 percent of university students confessed to having virtual sex, using IM, Web cams, and telephones.

We've counseled several high school students and young adults who claim to have boyfriends or girlfriends whom they know only as a digital photo and an e-mail correspondence. In many cases, these young people refuse to go out to real-life social events for fear of neglecting their online mates. If your child seems to be overly preoccupied with an Internet dating partner, we suggest you monitor the situation very carefully. For some children, especially younger adolescents, a pen pal relationship is a terrific transition into more mature kinds of dating, especially if your child is looking for a face-saving way to avoid the dating culture in his or her high school. For other children, an online dating partner is a way to avoid genuine relationships—and these kids may need help reaching out.

How can you tell which group your child belongs to? Go by your gut feeling, and observe your child. If he or she seems happy, grounded, and generally social, maybe the online mate is an appropriate way of negotiating this new dating identity, delaying more intimate relationships until he or she is ready. But if your child seems uneasy around most people, has few friends, and has organized most of his or her social life around the Internet, help your child build friendships and relationships in real life. See our suggestions in Chapters 7, 8, and 10 to help your child overcome his or her isolation.

## A Guide to Handling Online Relationships

Do what you can to help your teenager negotiate the deceptive intimacy of Cyberworld. If your kid comes directly to you for dating advice, terrific. If not, try to open the conversation casually and obliquely, while engaged together in another activity, such as cooking, shopping, or yard work—anything that doesn't look like a deliberate attempt to talk.

One way of imparting this adult wisdom is to tell stories about your own dating experiences or those of people you know. We promise you, your teen is absorbing far more than you realize. Don't expect him or her to thank you for the help—but do expect your perspective to sink in. Here are some points you might try to make with your teen.

**Don't heap too much on a person at one time.** Even someone who really likes you can be scared off by too much intensity—and that intensity can build really quickly with intimate, confessional e-mails and multiple TMs. Don't share too much or barrage your significant other with messages; be selective and take it slow.

**Remember what you really know about the other person.** It's easy to feel as though you're soul mates, but you may know less about each other than your feelings suggest. Would this eloquent letter writer be fun to actually hang out with or would there be long, awkward silences? Is this sensitive e-mailer able to sit down and listen when you talk or would there be constant interruptions and changes of subject? If he were offered the answers to a test he hadn't studied for, would he cheat? If she were told something mean about another person, would she repeat it? Try to remember that there are lots of important things you can't know about another person until you've hung out with them for a while and seen them under pressure. What someone *says* about who they are may not match who they *really* are.

**Accept that there's a risk in any relationship.** Although people have been trying to foolproof relationships for thousands of years, it can't be done. Everyone gets hurt sometimes, and then, well, it just really hurts. However, you can minimize the hurt somewhat by taking things slow and seeing how the relationship progresses; so try to protect yourself if you can, while still remaining open to what the possibilities might be.

## Maintaining a Cyber-Relationship

What if your children do become deeply involved in cyber-relationships? Here are some suggestions that may be helpful to you.

**Introduce the hypothetical possibility that the other person may not be what he or she seems.** "You know, that's funny, my friend Kathy's daughter had a boyfriend she met online. It turns out that the guy wasn't really fourteen, like he said—instead, he was thirty-nine!" "I heard about this one girl, she found this gorgeous photo in a magazine and scanned it onto her computer—she was kind of embarrassed about her braces, so she used someone else's picture." Don't ask your children to choose between their new love and you—they will almost never choose you! (Wouldn't you have done the same at their age?) So don't put them in the position of defending Mr. Maybe-Not-So-Right or Ms. I'm-Not-So-Sure-About-Her. Use a hypothetical example and let your kids draw their own conclusions.

**Help them find nonjudgmental ways to help them become more savvy.** "You know, it's natural that people might fib a bit in these situations . . . you may have even done it . . . so don't be too hard on him if you find out he hasn't been telling the whole truth." "You know, lots of online photos don't exactly look like the person—it's normal to want to make a good impression—so don't think too harshly of her if she doesn't quite look the way you imagine her." Sentences like those might enable your kids to open up to you about their own fears and suspicions, or such talks might send them to their best friends with their doubts and concerns. Either way, you haven't made yourself the enemy, and you've made it much easier for your children to come to you if they do decide they need your help.

**Find out what the correspondence is like.** Encourage your children to share as much as they can. Are they talking about their stamp collections, their interest in politics, or the latest movie they both saw? That's a fairly healthy correspondence and pretty good practice for a future real-life relationship. Or is the guy pressuring your daughter for cyber-sex, sending her inappropriate pictures, or pushing on her boundaries in some other way? Is the girl asking your son inappropriate questions, pressuring him for more involvement, or pushing on *his* boundaries? Help your kids evaluate these relationships for themselves, supporting them in their right to feel safe and comfortable in *any* relationship.

**Find out how often they're corresponding.** Is she getting instant messages from her boyfriend every half hour? Is he constantly getting TMs from his cyber-girlfriend? Are they always on the phone together? Ask your kids, and, if necessary, check the cell phone bill. (You can request detailed billing from most companies.) If you feel the need to limit contact, make it clear to your child that you're not responding to this particular cyber-guy or -girl, who may well be terrific. Rather, you're acting on your own ideas of what a healthy relationship looks like. You should also gauge your child's own sense of things and maybe take some action: "I see you're having a hard time setting limits with this boy, so let me help you. I'm happy to be the bad guy—tell him Mom said you're only allowed to see him twice a day." Or, "I'm getting the feeling that you'd rather not be on the phone with Jenna all the time. Tell her that Dad is cutting you back to thirty minutes a day—that way, you can really enjoy the conversations you do have."

**Make your position clear.** "I'm more comfortable with your first relationship being online where I can help you through it, help you learn how to flirt . . . When you're ready to do this in real life, I'm there for you, too . . . If you have questions about what your person is saying, I promise not to be judgmental, I want you to be able to come to me." Be available but give your children the space to make their own decisions. They will anyway—so you need to create a situation where they can come to you without losing face.

**Offer the support of other adults.** "If you don't want me, your parent, to be involved, can we get someone else to help you? Your aunt or uncle, a teacher, a grad student, a therapist?" It's natural for teenagers to want some space from Mom and Dad when it comes to sex and romance. That doesn't mean they should fly solo the first time out. See if you can help them find someone you both trust to talk them through those first few relationships.

## When Your Child Is Lesbian, Gay, Bisexual, or Transgendered . . .

LGBT kids face special challenges when it comes to dating. They may have trouble identifying other LGBT kids, and they may even be worried about their physical safety if they approach anyone at their school for a date.

For these children, online dating can be a godsend, as it can at least enable them to start relationships with other kids who have clearly identified their potential interest. Ideally, you'll help these children move from online to in-person relationships as well, but they may want to rely on Cyberworld to get started. Don't stop there, however. If at all possible, help them find community events for LGBT children their own age. They need to know that they're part of a larger world in which there are lots of people like them, even if they can't necessarily identify classmates or neighbors who are—or who are comfortable being that way.

Of course, as with any child, make sure your LGBT child knows how to avoid sexual predators. Check out the suggestions we make in Chapter 1 on page 22. Help your child feel comfortable coming to you if he or she runs into trouble. Let your child know that you love him or her and will always be there for support and protection.

## Moving the Relationship into the Real World

Suppose your child is deeply ensconced in an online romance but isn't doing any real-life dating. You may be wondering just how healthy these cyber-romances are and at what point you may need to help your child make the transition from Cyberworld to the real world.

Obviously, this is a very individual decision that will depend on your child's age, temperament, and social situation, as well as on your own values—and on your gut feeling about what's right for your child at any particular time. But here are some general guidelines that might help you think through the situation.

**If your child is fourteen or younger, and his or her main dating activity is online, no problem.** Although kids seem to be dating younger and younger, we ourselves think that it's just fine to wait. Maybe Cyberworld can give your child some breathing room, allowing him or her to have a boyfriend or girlfriend without engaging the pressures of real dating before he or she is ready.

**If your child is an older teen and is dating exclusively via computer—never meeting any of these online romances—find**

**out more about the relationships.** Older teens may not be ready for dating, either. If your child's online correspondence seems to be mainly about platonic topics—books, movies, school activities, and so on—that may be a healthy way to avoid a sexual/romantic relationship that he or she isn't ready for. If your older child has some good real-life friends and satisfying real-life activities, we wouldn't worry about online dating.

But if your older teen's cyber-romance is hyper-romantic—if your child talks about being in love, seems to be idealizing this cyber-partner, and says the two of them have made promises of fidelity—then we think it's time to encourage your child to date in real life. Help your child find ways to socialize with age-appropriate real-life people, including people who may not attend the same high school. Religious, political, ethnic, and special-interest groups may offer your child a wider social circle than his or her classmates, along with opportunities to find a real-life boyfriend or girlfriend. Like Mady's parents, you may need to be the bad guy, limiting the amount of time your child is allowed to spend online with the cyber-boyfriend or -girlfriend, and you may need to help your child assuage his or her guilt over being unfaithful to this cyber-mate.

Alternately, you might consider helping your child to actually meet this cyber-date in real life, especially if he or she lives within a reasonable distance. Find some safe, chaperoned, or public ways that your child can move from cyber-dating to real-life dating, so that he or she can find out whether the e-mail correspondence carries over to a live conversation.

# Protecting Your Child from Internet Porn

Pornography on the Internet has become a kind of running joke on sitcoms and late-night TV, but really, it's no laughing matter. When social worker Jill C. Manning testified in November 2005 before the Senate Judiciary Committee's Subcommittee on the Constitution of Civil Rights and Property Rights, she cited several studies that detailed the effects of repeated exposure to standard, nonviolent, and commonly available pornography, including

1. increased callousness toward women
2. trivialization of rape as a criminal offense
3. distorted perceptions about sexuality
4. increased appetite for more deviant and bizarre types of pornography (escalation and addiction)
5. devaluation of monogamy
6. decreased satisfaction with partner's performance, affection, and physical appearance
7. doubts about the value of marriage
8. decreased desire to have children, and
9. viewing nonmonogamous relationships as normal and natural behavior.

Manning wasn't specifically talking about Internet pornography, which in our opinion has an even more exploitative and addictive quality than the print or DVD variety, and of course, is far more easily available. We've treated a number of adult men and women who see themselves as addicted to some aspect of Internet sex, whether online pornography or late-night encounters with strangers for cyber-sex. An increasing number of couples and families are negatively affected by these activities. If you've ever had trouble pulling away from your computer—even if you're only surfing the Net or checking your e-mail—you know firsthand what that cyber-addictive quality is like. Throw in the sexual satisfaction of pornography, and it's easy to see how people of any age might become compulsive about their viewing.

No doubt about it, Internet pornography is big business. In January 2005, the Nielsen/NetRatings estimated that one in four U.S. Internet users—34 million people—viewed porn sites every month. Child pornography is big business, too: each week, according to the National Society for the Prevention of Cruelty to Children, more than 20,000 images of child pornography are posted online. A Forbes.com columnist estimated that the industry generated close to $4 billion.

A 2007 statistical roundup by Internet Filter Review put the average age of first Internet exposure to pornography at eleven years old. That early viewing may happen accidentally as your child searches for another site or clicks innocently on an enticing "x"—but the largest consumers of Internet porn are twelve to seventeen-year-olds, with some 80 percent of fifteen- to eighteen-year-olds cited as having "multiple hard-core exposure." Perhaps more disturbing is the revelation that 90 percent of eight- to sixteen-year-olds had viewed some pornography online, most while doing their homework. Our sense is that the teenagers are active consumers, while the younger children are accidentally clicking on the wrong links—a particularly likely possibility when you consider that some 26 children's character names are linked to online pornography, including Spongebob Squarepants, Pokemon, Barbie, and Action Man.

Now, having heard all this, how should you handle the whole

question of pornography and your own home computer? Obviously, your own values and judgment will be your primary guide, but here are our suggestions.

**Install the best possible antipornography filters on your home system so your children can't access porn sites, even accidentally.** If the adults in the house want to access online pornography, they can use their passcodes to do so, but your children won't be able to look at cyber-porn at home. (For more on filters, see page 110.) We can't resist sharing one story we heard about an eight- and ten-year old pair of brothers who were surfing the Web in their one precious daily hour of allotted Web time. The boys accidentally clicked onto a porn site, which they had no interest in viewing, but they didn't want their parents to think they'd gone there deliberately. So they went into the computer's history to erase their visit (interesting that they knew how to do that, huh?). To their surprise, several other pornographic sites were in the history, all of them having been visited around 2 a.m. or 3 a.m. the previous night. The boys knew their father often worked late and arrived home after midnight—so now they knew something else about his nightly activities! Their innocence, not to mention his privacy, could have been protected with better filters.

**Either put your children on the honor system for "no porn," or, if you're comfortable with the idea of your children viewing other forms of pornography, put them on the honor system for "no Internet porn"—on your computer or anyone else's.** Why are we suggesting that you steer your children away from Internet pornography in particular? We have several reasons. First, although the First Amendment protects most other forms of pornography, child pornography is illegal. If your child downloads it on your computer—even accidentally—he's putting all the adults in the house at risk of a felony conviction. And in the world of Internet porn, where one link leads easily to another, accidentally accessing a child porn site is not very hard to do.

We can't stress too greatly the potential danger to your child and your family of even a brief, accidental visit to a child pornography site. Child pornography is banned by the same law that forbids transporting a minor across state lines for immoral purposes—the Internet is considered to be such a transport—and so these sites are regularly monitored by the Federal Bureau of Investigation. Yes, it's unlikely that they'll pick up a onetime accidental visit to the wrong site, but it *is* possible, and it's not a risk that anyone in your family needs to take. Remember, one pornographic link leads easily to another, often without the user realizing where he's going, so why put your child in the position of making such a dangerous and consequential mistake?

Second, while Internet images and videos may be similar to what your child could see in magazines and videotapes, there's a third type of Internet pornography that's qualitatively different: live-action sites, where your child can request an actual person to perform various types of acts as he watches. To us, that's a level of desensitization and exploitation that goes far beyond anything that's available at the newsstand or adult bookstore, and it involves your child in a qualitatively different experience than looking at a prepackaged image. Again, with links leading so quickly and easily from one to another, it's very difficult to set clear boundaries on Internet porn. We think it's safer and simpler to ban it all. If you're comfortable with pornography per se, allow your child to view it elsewhere, but not online.

**Whatever boundary you set, have a full and frank discussion of it with your child.** We also suggest that you acknowledge how contradictory and inconsistent your ground rules are likely to be. Preclude your child's charges of hypocrisy by readily admitting that there's a fine line between pornography and, say, the Victoria's Secrets catalogue, the *Sports Illustrated* swimsuit edition, and the many other eroticized images of women in magazines from *Cosmopolitan* to *Popular Mechanics*. In all cases, women's bodies are being offered up in an objectifying and probably exploitative way—you can make the same case about men's bodies in GQ, *Vanity Fair,* bodybuilding magazines, and other nonpornographic images of nearly naked men— and perhaps you're not happy about any of it. But a person has to draw the line somewhere, and you're drawing it here.

If you're a single mother and you've got sons, we urge you to find a male friend of the family who can talk to your boys, since most guys, appropriately, don't want to talk about this with their mothers. If you're the straight parent of a gay or lesbian child, or vice versa, we suggest finding an adult who shares your child's sexuality to have this conversation. In all cases, what you want to convey is a positive idea about sex and a supportive view of your child's sexual feelings, even as you share your values and rules concerning pornography.

We ourselves consider pornography of all types to be exploitative of the models and performers and believe it creates exploitative and degrading attitudes toward sex among its viewers. So our personal recommendation would be to let kids look at erotic photographs and art, but not at pornography per se. You may draw the line quite differently, but wherever you draw it, you need to be clear with your child about why you feel strongly and how your values are driving your choices.

Why is this important? Because, as with so much of Cyber-world, your children pretty much have access to anything that's out there, so you're going to be relying on the honor system. Yes, install your filters and make your rules—you wouldn't be good parents if you didn't. But acknowledge that your children can always access a computer somewhere. If they are bound and determined to look at Internet pornography, they will find a way to do it. Your best defense is not to monitor their every move—you simply won't be able to—but rather to help them internalize their own version of your values, just as you want them to do with cigarettes, alcohol, and drugs.

To this end, we have one final suggestion, which we realize may not be for every parent, but which may work for some. Before you institute your final ban on Internet pornography, you might consider giving your child a modified tour of it. Say to your child something like the following:

> Look, I know that there's a huge part of our culture that thinks porn is just fine—and it's certainly available at the click of a button. I personally don't think anyone your age [or anyone at all] should view it, and I'm going to tell you why. [And share your reasons.]
>
> But I want you to know what I'm keeping you from, so that you'll understand my reasoning. I want you to see some of what's out there, so that you can see why I don't want you viewing it on a regular basis.

Then, if you show your child some porn sites, explain why you have a problem with them. If you find the pornography models erotic or attractive, acknowledge that as well, and explain why, even so, you think it's a bad idea to look at them. Encourage your children to wonder about the humanity of the women or men who are asked to pose and help them see past the pornographic imagery to imagine the actual lives and feelings that are exploited in order to produce this product. (If you've already helped them develop a sense of empathy and compassion, they should at least get your point, even if they can't help being more preoccupied with the models' sex than with their humanity.) Help them understand the difference between a real-life sexual relationship and the kind of fantasy sex that pornography promotes, in which people become objects and bodies become consumer items. (Again, this is the kind of discussion that a same-sex parent should have with a child and that a gay adult should have with a gay child. Otherwise, your child may think it's sexuality itself that's being criticized, rather than a particular way that sexuality is being exploited.)

Think for a moment about what happens if you don't have an open conversation about pornography, with or without the visuals. Your son, in particular, is almost certainly going to have chances to view print, video, or Internet porn with his friends—pornography is such a big part of teen male culture that unless your son is completely isolated, he's going to be exposed to it. If your son is gay, he may be even more interested in pornography, which he may see as his opportunity to find out more about a sexuality that's so rarely portrayed anywhere else. One way or another, your son will almost certainly be viewing pornography, with or without you. If you want him to understand your objections, you'll need to tell him exactly what you think and why, because it's very unlikely that he'll be having this kind of conversation with his friends. You may also need to be clear about what kinds of sexual images and information he *can* find that you consider a healthy alternative.

Now, having said all of this, let us add one more contradictory note: if you discover that your child has been viewing pornography in any form, please don't overreact! Whatever your own feelings about pornography, your child's interest in it could well be a healthy expression of his or her sexuality. If you react too strongly, you'll only distance yourself from your child and make it more difficult for him or her to approach you with questions or concerns. And strong overreactions can foster extreme interest or a sense of rebelliousness.

Cyberworld is a confusing, contradictory, and potentially dangerous place, for adults as well as children. But it also offers a thrilling set of opportunities and is an almost magical doorway to new worlds, new people, new ideas. One of your greatest challenges as a parent may well be guiding your child through Cyberworld, but we think you'll discover that the effort is well worth the reward.

# ACKNOWLEDGMENTS

We are indebted to our agent, Jeff Kleinman, our editors Patricia Medved and Rebecca Cole, and the marketing staff at Broadway Books. Thanks also to Bob Sullivan, our tireless and generous consultant at MSNBC. You are all the best!

We want to acknowledge the stellar work of Henry McMaster and the South Carolina Attorney General's office. The SCAG's Internet Crimes Against Children Task Force, including Special Agent Cynthia McCants, has done excellent work, and our children are safer for it.

We applaud *Dateline NBC's Internet Predator* series in conjunction with their work with the staff of Perverted Justice. It has really highlighted the problem of persons who prey on underage children and given parents a lot to think about.

We also want to recognize Darkness to Light (http://www .darkness2light.org/), an organization dedicated to keeping children safe from childhood sexual abuse, whose tireless efforts to prevent abuse were an inspiration to us.

Special thanks to Paul F. ("Pete") Wellborn III, of Wellborn and Wallace, for his help with legal approaches to cyberbullying.

Special thanks also go to Steve Grossman (www.stevegross man.com) and Ched Davis (http://www.web-friend.com/) for their generosity with content on their Web sites.

To Claudia, Kaylan, and Keegan Hufham. Thanks for your input on short notice. To Emma Walker, thank you for your help as well. And thanks to Laura Kranz, consultant extraordinaire.

To our families, friends, and clients—thanks for your support.

And course, to Rachel Kranz, whose collaboration and insights were invaluable in the writing of this book. We can't thank you enough!

# REFERENCES

## Chapter 2

1. Jay M. Pomerantz, M.D., "Behavioral Health Matters: ADHD More Prevalent or Better Recognized," http://www.medscape.com/viewarticle/511173, posted September 6, 2005, citing D. S. Mandell, W. W. Thompson, E. S. Weintraub, et al., "Trends in the diagnosis rates for autism and ADHD at hospital discharge in the context of other psychiatric diagnoses," *Psychiatr Serv.* (2005), 56–62.

2. Claudia Wallis, "The Multitasking Generation," *Time* 167, 13, 51–54.

## Chapter 3

1. Fight Crime: Invest in Kids, press release, August 17, 2006.

## Chapter 4

1. Patricia Williams, "The 600 Faces of Eve," *The Nation* 283, 4 (July 31/August 7, 2006), 8.

## Chapter 11

1. Jill C. Manning, M.S., "The Impact of Internet Pornography on Marriage and the Family: A Review of the Research," Testimony, Hearing on Pornogra-

phy's Impact on Marriage and the Family, Subcommittee on the Constitution of Civil Rights and Property Rights, Committee on Judiciary, U.S. Senate, November 10, 2005, citing R. E. Drake, "Potential Health Hazards of Pornography Consumption as Viewed by Psychiatric Nurses," *Archives of Psychiatric Nursing* 8, 2 (1994), 101–6; D. Zillman, and J. Bryant, "Pornography, Sexual Callousness and the Trivialization of Rape," *Journal of Communication* 32, 4 (1982); 10–21; D. Zillman, and J. Bryant, "Effects of Massive Exposure to Pornography," in N. M. Malamuth and E. Donnerstein, eds., *Pornography and Sexual Aggression* (Orlando, FL: Academic, 1984), (115–38). D. Zillman, and J. Bryant, "Effects of Prolonged Consumption of Pornography on Family Values," *Journal of Family Issues* 9, 4 (December 1988), 518–44.

2. Marc Hansen, "There's No Debate: Porn Is Very Big Business," *Des Moines Register*, January 19, 2005, 7A.

3. Jerry Ropelato, "Internet Pornography Statistics," *Internet Filter Review*, http://internet-filter-review.toptenreviews.com/internet-pornography-statistics.html. Viewed on January 11, 2007.

# GLOSSARY

**acronym.** Abbreviation of a phrase, taken from the initial letter of each word; for example, "LOL" for "laugh out loud" (see also the listing of the most common acronyms, page 355).

**block/blocking.** Prevent computer access to a particular Web page or type of Web page; for example, you might attempt to block access to all online gambling or pornography sites.

**blog.** Short for Web log; an online journal.

**blogger.** Writer of a blog.

**blog hosts.** Those who create and maintain Web sites that feature blogs.

**Chat.** Online communication in real time, accomplished by keyboarding your responses to other chatters.

**Chat rooms.** Online sites where people chat to one another in real time.

**Cut and Paste.** Electronic transfer of text, images, or other online information from one electronic space to another; for example, a child doing homework might cut and paste information from a Web site directly into his or her notes or even into a school report.

**cyber-bullying.** The use of electronic information and communication devices—including e-mail, instant messaging, text messaging, blogs, cell phones, pagers, and Web sites—to harass others.

**cyber-sex.** Electronic sexual encounters in which participants send each other sexually explicit messages; participants often pretend they are having actual sexual intercourse; the goal is often to achieve sexual climax.

**cyber-space.** The electronic medium of computer networks, in which online communication takes place.

**Cyberworld.** A virtual world of electronic communication via computers, cell phones, Web cams, and other electronic devices.

**domain name.** The main part of a Web site or e-mail address that identifies the unique aspect of the site or address; for example, in our own Web site, www.cybersisters.biz, "cybersisters" is our domain name.

**DSM-IV-TR.** *Diagnostic and Statistical Manual*, 4th ed., Text Revision, the latest published edition of the volume used to diagnose and treat the comprehensive range of emotional and cognitive disorders; often needed for school referrals and insurance reimbursements. The fifth edition, *DSM V*, is due to be published in 2011.

**ee.** Electronic emission; includes e-mail, instant messaging, text messaging, and other electronic communications.

**e-mail.** Electronic mail.

**emoticons.** A sequence of ordinary printable characters intended to represent a human facial expression and convey an emotion (see page 359 for listing).

**ergonomics.** The science of making work environments as compatible, productive, and healthy as possible for human workers; the goal is to maximize productivity by reducing operator fatigue and discomfort, creating the most efficient use of energy, and reducing the possibility of work-related disorders, such as repetitive strain injury (RSI), that might otherwise result from long hours at the keyboard.

**filter/filtering software.** A program that blocks objectionable words used in e-mails and other applications; filters can also be set to block sites that contain certain keywords, such as "gambling," "sex," or a wide variety of sexually explicit terms.

**forum.** A Web site focusing on the discussion of particular topics.

**geek.** A person fascinated with or expert in obscure or very specific areas of knowledge, usually electronic or virtual in nature; formerly an insult but now often used admiringly.

**hyperlink.** An electronic coding in the body of a document that can take you to another site, if clicked; an article on Shakespeare, for example, might include a hyperlink for the Globe Theatre that would take users to a Web site with additional information on the Globe. Hyperlinks appear as language within a regular text but in a different color, sometimes underlined; for example: "William Shakespeare often presented his plays at the Globe Theatre though after it burned down he had to find another venue."

**IM.** Instant messaging; a way for participants to send each other electronic messages instantly in real time without having to go through an e-mail program.

**ISP.** Internet service provider; the company that provides you with access to the Internet, such as AT&T, America Online (AOL), Earthlink, Microsoft Network (MSN), or Optimum.

**keylogging.** The process of registering every keystroke that a user types; keylogging software allows its owner to view and record Web searches, chats, e-mail, and passwords entered on his or her computer.

**leet speak.** Short for "elite speak"; a specialized form of electronic communication that uses words and letters to form a secret, coded language; for example, "leet" might be written as "l33t."

**link.** Short for *hyperlink*.

**Listserv.** Program for communicating by e-mail with people who have subscribed to the list; typically, Listservs are organized around a specific topic, such as special-needs children. They may also be set up for members of an organization or for people who wish to receive regular information from an organization. Listserv subscribers can usually e-mail everyone else on the list, with the permission of the Listserv moderator.

**moderator.** A person or small group of people who manage a Listserv or newsgroup. Members of the Listserv or newsgroup send e-mails to the moderators, who then determine which messages can be seen by everyone on the list.

**monitoring.** Oversight of Web sites visited on your computer.

**MySpace.** MySpace.com, frequently known as MySpace, is a free Web-based service that allows individuals to meet and develop relationships online. Members register for permission to post user profiles, photos, and blogs. They can e-mail one another through the site and participate in forums.

**Net.** Short for *Internet*.

**Netiquette.** The unwritten rules of etiquette used on the Internet; for example, messages in all capitals are perceived as shouting.

**newsgroup.** A discussion group conducted by e-mail in

which messages are submitted by many users on a particular subject.

**pop-up.** Advertisements that pop up without the user's request, intruding visually and sometimes with sounds upon the viewing of a Web site, so that the user has to click on something to make the pop-up go away.

**plagiarism.** The false presentation of someone else's writing as one's own; illegal in the case of copyrighted work, and generally considered a major offense by most schools, colleges, and universities.

**pro-ana.** A social movement promoting a view of anorexia nervosa as a lifestyle choice rather than a disorder; many pro-ana Web sites portray flattering photographs of anorectics and give advice on how to pursue extreme weight loss while hiding it from one's parents.

**profile.** Description that each person using instant messaging, chat rooms, or social network sites such as MySpace formulate to describe themselves; profiles are often partly or wholly false, even with regard to basic information such as age and gender.

**snail mail.** Regular mail sent through the U.S. Postal Service; in contrast to the much faster *e-mail*.

**social network sites.** Web sites on which users register themselves in order to meet new people, rendezvous with friends and acquaintances, find dating partners, or invite others to social events such as a party or movie opening.

**surfing.** Clicking from one Web site to another, either with the intention of searching for something in particular or simply enjoying the wealth of information on the World Wide Web.

**TM.** Text messaging; a brief message sent via cell phone that appears as written text on the phone itself; given the difficulty of typing and reading text messages, TMs often include abbreviations and acronyms.

**tracking software.** Programs used to monitor the Web sites visited on a particular computer.

**Web cam.** Short for "Web camera"; a real-time video camera whose images can be accessed using the World Wide Web, instant messaging, or a PC video calling application.

**Web log.** See *blog*.

**Web site.** A collection of Web pages common to a particular domain name on the Internet.

**Word.** Short for "Microsoft Word"; a popular word-processing program.

**WordPerfect.** Popular word-processing program.

**World Wide Web.** Defined by Web inventor Tim Berners-Lee, it is "the universe of network-accessible information, an embodiment of human knowledge."

**Xbox.** Microsoft's first independent venture into the video game console arena.

**YouTube.** Web site that allows users to view and share video clips.

# 100 ACRONYMS AND ABBREVIATIONS YOU MIGHT NEED TO KNOW

The following shortcuts are used for text messaging, instant messaging, and e-mail. They change all the time and new ones are constantly being added, but this list should give you at least some idea of how your cyber-kids are communicating.

| | |
|---|---|
| 121 | one to one |
| 2nite | tonight |
| 20 | location |
| AEAP | as early as possible |
| ALAP | as late as possible |
| ASL | age, sex, location |
| B4 | before |
| B4N | bye for now |
| BBS | be back soon |
| BEG | big evil grin |
| BIBO | beer in, beer out |
| BTW | by the way |
| BMGWL | busting my gut with laughter |
| BOHICA | bend over, here it comes again |
| CID | crying in disgrace |

| | |
|---|---|
| C-P | sleepy |
| CRBT | crying real big tears |
| CRS | can't remember s**t |
| CSG | chuckle snicker and grin |
| CUL8TR | see you later |
| CUOL | see you online |
| CUZ | because |
| DDSOS | different day, same old s**t |
| DSTR8 | damn straight |
| DWPKOTL | deep wet passionate kisses on the lips |
| EMA | e-mail address |
| EMFBI | excuse me for butting in |
| EG | evil grin |
| F2F | face-to-face |
| FMTYEWTK | far more than you ever wanted to know |
| FUD | fear, uncertainty, and doubt |
| GMBO | giggling my butt off |
| GYPO | get your pants off |
| HHIS | hanging head in shame |
| HUB | head up butt |
| IC | I see |
| IHA | I hate acronyms |
| ILU | I love you |
| IPN | I'm posting naked |
| IWALU | I will always love you |
| IWSN | I want sex now |
| J/C | just checking |
| K4U | kiss for you |
| KPC | keeping parents clueless |
| LMIRL | let's meet in real life |
| LUWAMH | love you with all my heart |

| | |
|---|---|
| LY4E | love you forever |
| MILF | mother I'd like to f*** |
| MUSM | miss you so much |
| N-A-Y-L | not in a while |
| NALOPKT | not a lot of people know that |
| NAZ | name, address, zip |
| NIFOC | nude in front of computer |
| NP | nosy parents |
| NSTLC | needs some tender loving care |
| NVNG | nothing ventured, nothing gained |
| OLL | on line love |
| OL | old lady |
| OM | old man |
| OTH | off the hook |
| P911 | my parents are coming! |
| PA | parent alert |
| PAL | parents are listening |
| PEBCAK | problem exists between chair and keyboard |
| PITA | pain in the ass |
| PLZ | please |
| PM | private message |
| POS | parent over shoulder |
| POTS | plain old telephone service |
| QLS | reply |
| QT | cutie |
| ROFL | roll on floor laughing |
| ROFLMYAO | roll on floor laughing my ass off |
| RUMOF | are you male or female |
| RYU | roll your own |
| S^ | what's up |
| SHID | slaps head in disgust |

| | |
|---|---|
| SII | seriously impaired imagination |
| SMEM | send me an e-mail |
| SMIM | send me an instant message |
| SNERT | snot-nosed egotistical teenager |
| SOMY? | sick of me yet? |
| STR8 | straight |
| SUYF | shut up you fool |
| TDTM | talk dirty to me |
| TPS | that's pretty stupid |
| TPTB | the powers that be |
| TAW | teachers are watching |
| TILII | tell it like it is |
| TMI | too much information |
| TOM | tomorrow |
| TOY | thinking of you |
| ^URS | up yours |
| US | you suck |
| UV | unpleasant visual |
| VBG | very big grin |
| WTGP? | want to go private? |
| WYRN? | what's your real name? |
| WTH | what the heck (or substitute an F for the H) |
| YBS | you'll be sorry |
| *YS* | you stinker |

# EMOTICONS

Symbols are also an important part of electronic communication, so here are some of the most commonly used. As do acronyms and abbreviations, these continue to evolve, but this list should at least give you some idea of what your cyber-kid is writing.

| | |
|---|---|
| :-), *s*, *S*, ‹s› | smile |
| :o) | smiles (w/nose) |
| :-))))))) | lots of smiles |
| *g*, ‹g› | grin |
| ;-), *w*, ‹w› | wink |
| *g* | giggles |
| :-( | sad |
| :,-(, ;'-( | to cry |
| 8-) | wears glasses |
| #8-) | nerd, or or person with glasses and crew cut |
| :-o | talking, or surprised |
| ‹:-\| | curious |
| :-x | keeping mouth shut (note "x" for mouth) |
| >:-\|\| | mad / angry |
| :-/ | perplexed, confused |

| | |
|---|---|
| ;~) | being cute |
| ;-P | sticking tongue out |
| P | sticking tongue out |
| =:-O | scared |
| ;-)~ | sexy tongue, or drunk |
| :-x | I'm keeping my mouth shut |
| :-ƺ | embarrassed |
| :-\| | bored or no opinion |
| :-> | grin/mischievous |
| >:-( | angry |
| \~/ | glass with a drink (usually liquor) |
| :-O | shouting, or shocked |
| ;-)~~~~~~ | giving someone the raspberry |
| ^5 | high five |
| ~~\*-8-o | bad hair day |
| :*) | drinking every night |
| :%)% | has acne |
| :-# | has braces |
| :-x | kiss |
| X-( | mad |
| :-(O) | yelling |
| 3-] | pet dog |

# RESOURCES

## Books

Aftab, Parry. *The Parent's Guide to Protecting Your Children in Cyberspace* (McGraw-Hill, 2000). Focuses on how to keep your child safe on the Internet; does a great job of outlining the dangers and offers great tips on rules for Internet behaviors and more. The attorney-author regularly speaks on cyber-law, cyber-crime, and Internet safety and privacy issues.

Caldwell, J. Paul. *Anxiety Disorders: Everything You Need to Know* (Firefly Books, 2005). Has a great chapter on anxiety in children and adolescents, with overviews and checklists on a variety of anxiety disorders that occur in childhood.

Carnes, P., D. L. Delmonico, and E. Griffin. *In the Shadows of the Net: Breaking Free of Compulsive Online Sexual Behavior* (Hazelden, 2001). Educates you about Internet porn addiction helps you to understand the syndrome and recognize the signs.

DesMaisons, Kathleen. *Potatoes Not Prozac* (Simon & Schuster, 1999). Great nutritional book; discusses effects of different foods on mood.

Eliot, Lise. *What's Going On in There? How the Brain and Mind Develop in the First Five Years of Life* (Bantam, 2000). An especially useful book for the parents of young children who want a sense of how to help their infants and toddlers grow and learn.

Erickson, Erik H. *Childhood and Society* (Norton, 1955). Only one of the fine books of Erik Erickson that details the developmental stages, but one that is particularly accessible and easy to read.

Evans, D. L., and L. W. Andrews. *If Your Child Has Depression or Bipolar Disor-der* (Oxford University Press, 2005). A guide to getting effective help for adolescents with serious mood disorders; has sections on psychiatric med-ications and current treatments.

Ferber, Richard. *Solve Your Child's Sleep Problems* (Simon & Schuster, 2006). Gives hands-on advice on how to help your child deal with sleep disrup-tion, sleep schedule abnormalities, and the like.

Gianetti, Charlene C., and Margaret Sagarese. *Cliques. Eight Steps to Help Your Child Survive the Social Jungle* (Broadway, 2001). Concrete advice on how to support your middle-school boy or girl in coping with bullying, cliques, and social networks.

Kurcinka, Mary Sheedy. *Sleepless in America: Is Your Child Misbehaving or Miss-ing Sleep?* (HarperCollins, 2006). Offers approaches to managing chal-lenging behaviors and helps you recognize whether your child's behavior problems stem from sleep problems rather than other factors.

Kutscher, M. L., T. Attwood, and R. R. Wolff. *Kids in the Syndrome Mix of ADHD, LD, Asperger's, Tourette's, Bipolar, and More!: The One Stop Guide for Parents, Teachers, and other Professionals* (Jessica Kingsley Publishers, 2005). Highly recommended book which outlines current information on causes, symptoms, interactions with other conditions, and treatment for a variety of disorders that occur in childhood. Compensatory techniques/ strategies are offered.

Levine, John R., Margaret Levine Young, and Carol Baroudi. *The Internet for Dummies*, 10th ed. (Wiley, 2005). If you're a technophobe, this is the book for you! It's especially helpful in teaching you how to do online re-search.

Okie, Susan. *Fed Up! Winning the War against Childhood Obesity* (Joseph Henry Press, 2005). Written by a family physician, this book offers tips on healthy eating and lifestyle; practical suggestions on teaching children how to eat for life; and how to find help for your overweight child.

Pollack, William, S., Ph.D., with Todd Shuster. *Real Boys' Voices* (Penguin, 5th ed., 2001). The influential author of *Real Boys* collected firsthand ac-counts from boys about the difficulties of growing up male, including the threat of being bullied, and the many temptations to bully.

Polly, Jean Armour. *Net-Mom's Internet Kids and Family Yellow Pages* (McGraw-

Hill, 2002). Fabulous overview on various Web sites and Internet sources for children of all ages and interests.

Richardson, J., and M. Schuster. *Everything You Never Wanted Your Kids to Know about Sex (But Were Afraid They'd Ask)* (Crown, 2003). Good resource on parenting techniques and childhood sexuality. Includes a section on parenting your sexually active child.

Roberts, Walter B., Jr. *Bullying from Both Sides: Strategic Interventions for Working with Bullies* (Sage, 2005). An even-handed look at bullying among boys that focuses on helping both the bullies and the bullied.

*The Rough Guide to Internet 12* (Rough Guides, 2006). An excellent beginners' guide to the Internet, which will help even the most technologically ignorant person get up to speed.

Sicile-Kira, Chantal. *Adolescents on the Autism Spectrum: A Parent's Guide to the Cognitive, Social, Physical, and Transition Needs of Teenagers with Austistic Spectrum Disorders* (Berkley Publishing Group, 2006). Offers parents strategies for helping their autistic adolescents of various ability levels, focusing on how to prepare them for adulthood. Great section on transition planning for life after high school.

Simmons, Rachel. *Odd Girl Out* (Harcourt, 2003). A journalist looks at bullying among girls and discovers a disturbing amount of aggression and violence. The basis for the Lifetime TV movie of the same name. (See "Movies," below.)

Vanderlip, Susie. *52 Ways to Protect your Teen: Guiding Teens to Good Choices and Success* (Intuitive Wisdom Publications, 2005). Offers tips on improving relationships with parents and peers, as well as insights into the how and why of teen thinking and suggestions for how to prepare children of all ages for peer pressures and tough decisions.

Walsh, T. W., and V. L. Cameron. *If Your Child Has an Eating Disorder: An Essential Resource for Parents* (Oxford University Press, 2005). Provides tips on understanding eatings disorders, navigating the health care system, and looking at current treatment issues, along with practical advice on handling day-to-day life after diagnosis is made. Has a fabulous resource section as well.

Wiseman, Rosalind. *Queen Bees and Wannabes: Helping your Daughter Survive Cliques, Gossip, Boyfriends, and other Realities of Adolescence* (Three Rivers

Press, 2002). Gives you insights into the world of girls' friendships, with a special focus on bullying, offering many helpful tips on how to help your daughter navigate the competition and cliquishness of girlhood.

## Web-based Resources

### BLOGS

*http://www.livejournal.com/* and *http://www.sixapart.com/typepad/*. Web sites that host blogs with some costs attached; they also include topic-oriented groups and social networking options.

*www.blogger.com/start.* Web site for free Web log hosting; walks you through how to create a blog.

### BULLYING

*www.bullying.org.* Provides educational information about preventing bullying and a speakers list for presentations to groups, communities, schools, conferences, and the like.

*www.bullypolice.org.* Highly recommended site that advocates for bullied children and promotes anti-bullying legislation; rates the various states' anti-bullying laws; tracks where anti-bullying law action is taking place; and lists various support groups. Offers practical advice on how you can get involved.

*www.cyberbullying.org.* Award-winning Web site that gives you examples of what cyber-bullying looks like and the many forms it can take. Download their thirteen-page document, which gives information on how to report cyber-bullying along with step-by-step instructions on how to copy headers and forward them to the appropriate authority using all types of programs; tips on how to report to major ISPs; and instructions for copying screenshots of offensive content for reporting purposes. Great resource lists and information on how to access support groups as well.

## CHAT LINGO

*www.netlingo.com.* A great Web site and resource for translating acronyms (but not leet speak); updated regularly.

*www.stevegrossman.com/jargon.htm.* Informative Web site that includes translations of acronyms and emoticons; hosted by our friend Steve Grossman; highly recommended.

*www.city-net.com.* Web site hosted by our friend, Ched Davis, which has a chat slang page and emoticon translations.

*www.learnleetspeak.com.* Web site that offers information and history on leet speak, as well as a leet speak translator.

*www.microsoft.com/athome/security/children/leetspeak.mspx.* Article "Leetspeak: A Parent's Primer to Computer Slang," also includes translation of common leet speak words.

*www.teenangels.org.* Web site that offers a chat translator to decipher acronyms (but not emoticons or leet speak).

*www.urbandictionary.com.* Another great source for leet speak and computer slang terms.

## CHAT ROOMS

*www.ICQ.com.* Not a recommended Web site for your children. Parents, however, may want to see what this racy social network site is all about. It has a variety of topic-oriented groups that may surprise you; you may want to visit a chat room to get the full flavor.

*www.perverted-justice.com.* To read actual chats between predators and adults posing as children, check out this Web site. You'll get up close and personal with predators—not for the easily offended and *not* for your children—but it's a terrific resource for you. Recently spotlighted on Dateline NBC *To Catch a Predator* series for their invaluable work.

## CRIME

*www.cybercrime.gov/reporting.htm.* Walks you through how to report computer-related crime; includes various types of crimes and the best agency to contact.

*www.CyberTipline.com* or 1–800–THE–LOST (843–5678) to report missing or exploited children, including instances of child pornography.
*You should also report any child pornography or other Internet-related crime to your local or state law enforcement agency or your local FBI office.*

## DEPRESSION

*http://www.mayoclinic.com/health/depression-and-exercise/MH00043.* Article "Depression and Anxiety: Exercise Eases Symptoms," extols the virtues of exercise in relation to depression and anxiety and gives you realistic tips and goals from the esteemed Mayo Clinic.

*www.jasonfoundation.com.* Web site offering free educational curriculums and training programs about teen suicide for students, educators/youth workers, and parents.

## EATING DISORDERS

*www.anred.com.* Web site for Anorexia Nervosa and Related Eating Disorders, Inc., a nonprofit organization that provides information about all types of food and weight disorders; lots of great self-help tips and information about recovery and prevention.

*www.bluedragonfly.org.* A popular pro-ana (pro-anorexia) Web site—not recommended for your children, but we include it here to give you an idea of what's on the Web. The site gives tips on how to avoid detection, lose more weight, and the like.

## E-MAIL ACCOUNTS

*www.hotmail.com* and *www.yahoo.com.* Free e-mail accounts are available at these sites, and kids regularly access these services.

## ERGONOMICS

*www.wristband.com.* Web site with ordering information on wristbands/wristwands for kids whose wrists get stiff from repetitive keyboarding.

## FRAUD

*www.snopes.com.* A Web site dedicated to exposing frauds, rumors, hoaxes, and urban legends. If you get an e-mail or read something on a Web site that seems questionable, Snopes is a great first stop on your search to finding out whether it's true.

## GAMBLING

*www.teenage-gambling-addiction.org.* Web site providing a wealth of information and resources such as local stop gambling telephone numbers, helpful stop gambling Web sites, and practical exercises for teenagers with addictions to learn about self-esteem, trust, and the like.

## LEGISLATION AND LOBBYING

*www.ftc.gov/ogc/coppa1.htm.* Children's Online Privacy Protection Act of 1998.

*www.missingkids.com.* Web site for National Center for Missing and Exploited Children, national leaders in preventing crime against children; this site has a wealth of information, including legal resources for child-sexual-exploitation cases and ways you can get involved in lobbying on a national level for legislation to protect children.

## LIGHTBOXES AND OTHER LIGHTING OPTIONS

*www.lightforhealth.com.* Web site with information on full-spectrum lighting and products, including bulbs and light boxes.

*www.naturallighting.com.* Web site with information on light boxes, lightbulbs, floor lamps, and overhead lighting, all using full-spectrum light.

## MENTAL HEALTH AND FINDING PROFESSIONAL HELP

*http://www.aacap.org.* Web site for American Academy of Child and Adolescent Psychiatrists. Great information and links, includes Child and Adolescent Psychiatrist Finder.

*www.naswdc.org.* Web site for National Association of Social Workers, includes a link to Find a Therapist.

*www.apa.org.* Web site for American Psychological Association, includes a link to Find a Psychologist.

*www.1-800-therapist.com.* Web site dedicated to helping people find the right therapist for their specific needs.

*www.counseling.org.* Web site for American Counseling Association; includes a section on how to find a counselor in your area.

## MOVIES

*We highly recommend you view some of these movies with your children as a way to begin conversations on Cyberworld.*

*The Ant Bully*. Directed by John A. Davis, 2006, Warner Brothers. Cartoon portraying a boy who is bullied taking out his rage on a colony of ants in his backyard—until he finds himself shrunken to their size and dealing with them head-on.

*A Cinderella Story.* Directed by Mark Rosman, 2004, Warner Brothers. Shows you responsible—and typically extensive—use of cell phone/text messaging; the plot revolves around a teen couple who know each other only through their texts, unaware of each other's real-life identities.

*Cyber Seduction: His Secret Life.* Directed by Tom McLoughlin, 2005, Lifetime, www.lmn.tv. The story of a teenage boy who gets addicted to pornography.

*Defending Our Kids: The Julie Posey Story.* Directed by Joanna Kerns, 2003, Lifetime, www.lmn.tv. Tracks the real-life actions taken by Julie Posey, a mother angered by a pedophile propositioning her daughter online; she goes online herself to pose as a lonely teenager in order to expose sexual predators.

*Every Mother's Worst Fear.* Directed by Bill L. Norton, 1998, Lifetime, www.lmn.tv. Naïve teen gets kidnapped by man she meets online.

*Hoot.* Directed by Wil Shriner, 2006, New Line Cinema. Great movie about a boy whose family moves often and how he has to adjust to new surroundings and make new friends. Bullying also depicted. Based on book of the same name by Carl Hiaasen.

*How to Eat Fried Worms.* Directed by Bob Dolman, 2006, New Line Cinema. Entertaining (but possibly hard to stomach!) movie showing a boy who triumphs over a school bully. Based on book of the same name by Thomas Rockwell.

*Mean Girls.* Directed by Tina Fey, 2004, Paramount. Although this movie doesn't deal with cyber-issues per se, it's a real bird's-eye view of bullying. Adapted from the excellent *Queen Bees and Wannabes* by Rosalind Wiseman.

*A Moment of Truth Movie: A Secret Between Friends.* Directed by James A. Contner, 1996, Lifetime, www.lmn.tv. This movie is about two teenage girls, one bulimic and one anorexic; shows all the classic eating-disorder signs to watch for.

*My Daughter's Secret Life.* Directed by John Fawcett, 2001, Lifetime, www.lmn.tv. This movie is about an honor-roll student who gets into trouble gambling on the Internet and goes on to higher stakes.

*Odd Girl Out.* Directed by Tom McLoughlin, 2004, Lifetime, www.lmn.tv. An excellent portrayal of cyber-bullying based on Rachel Simmons's book of the same name. This movie is particularly useful for showing how girls who don't want to bully get caught up in pressure from the head bully.

*The Pact: A Love Story.* Directed by Peter Werner, III, 2002, Lifetime, www.lmn.tv. A story of teens who enter into a pact to commit suicide based on Jodi Picoult book of the same name.

*Painful Secrets.* Directed by Norma Bailey, 2000, Lifetime, www.lmn.tv. Spotlights the problem of adolescent girls committing self-mutilation; really helps you understand the various reasons for cutting.

*She's Too Young.* Directed by Tom McLoughlin, 2004, Lifetime, www.lmn.tv. Portrays teens who are sexually active as early as age fourteen, often in response to peer pressure.

## NETIQUETTE

*http://www.netmanners.com.* Fabulous Web site with all you will ever need to know about being polite on the Net. Includes a pledge to quit sending humorous forwards. For information about the stories sent in those forwards see: http://www.snopes.com.

## ONLINE ENCYCLOPEDIA

*www.wikipedia.com.* This free site is updated collaboratively by any viewer who wants to improve the entries, so the advantages are that it's generally up-to-date and accurate; the possibility exists, though, that it may be inaccurate. For basic cyber-information, you're probably on sure ground; for anything else, cross-check all the information elsewhere.

## PARENTING ADVICE/RESOURCES

*www.talkwithkids.org.* Web site offering tips on talking to your kids about tough issues.

*www.goaskalice.columbia.edu.* Web site that gives health information; great feature (especially for kids) includes "Ask Alice," which lets your child anonymously ask questions about relationships, sexuality, sexual and emotional health, fitness, nutrition, alcohol and other drugs, and/or, general health. Dependable Columbia University site.

## PLAGIARISM

*www.plagiarism.org.* Web site where teachers and parents can enter phrases from term papers to see if the papers have been plagiarized.

*www.turnitin.com.* Web site that can instantly identify papers containing unoriginal material; a powerful deterrent to stop student plagiarism before it starts.

## SAFETY

*www.cyberpatrol.com.* Web site for Cyberpatrol, a tracking/monitoring software program; especially useful features include time-management features, the ability to control program downloads, privacy protection, the blocking of harmful sites and images, and monitoring logs.

*www.enough.org.* Donna Rice Hughe's Web site dedicated to protecting children and families from the Internet dangers of pornography and sexual predators.

*www.familyguidebook.com.* Site created by Parry Aftab, including "Ask Parry," a section where you can ask questions of this renowned expert on child safety and the Internet; under Site Contents/Quick Guide, you can choose "Parent's Guide to the Internet Book" to download her entire book, *The Parent's Guide to Protecting your Children in Cyberspace,* which focuses on how to keep your child safe on the Internet.

*www.fbi.gov/publications/pguide/pguidee.htm.* FBI's Guide to Internet Safety for Parents.

*www.mapsexoffenders.com.* Nationwide sex offender mapping; shows where predators say they live in relation to your home.

*www.netnanny.com.* Web site for Netnanny 5.5, a tracking/monitoring software program (now owned by ContentWatch); especially useful features include time management (Internet time restrictions and time allowance), the bility to monitor/record chats and to block sites or chats of your choosing, and remote management.

*www.netsmartz.org.* Web site aimed at kids five to seventeen; uses interactive games to teach about dangers on the Internet.

*www.teenangels.org.* Law-enforcement-trained teens helping each other stay safe online.

*www.wiredcops.org.* Web site staffed by specially trained volunteers who patrol the Internet looking for child pornography, child molesters, and cyber-stalkers.

*www.wiredsafety.org.* Web site for the largest online safety, education, and help group in the world, with more than 9,000 volunteers worldwide, headed by Parry Aftab, international cyberspace privacy and security lawyer and children's advocate. Parry is the author of *The Parent's Guide to Protecting Your Children in Cyberspace* (McGraw-Hill). In addition to education and information, the group provides help for victims of cyber-crime and harassment and they assist law enforcement worldwide on preventing and investigating cyber-crime.

*www.wiredwithwisdom.org.* Web Wise Kids teaches children and their caregivers strategies for safe Internet use, including methods of detecting and deterring online predators. Their game **Missing** is an interactive, multimedia computer game designed to show, rather than tell, kids about predators who use the Internet to target and groom children and lure them away from home.

## SEXUALITY/SEXUAL ORIENTATION

*www.waf.org.* Website for We Are Family, whose mission is to encourage straight, gay, lesbian, bisexual, transgendered, and questioning members of our community to value one another through education. It has a wealth of information and links to other educational resources.

*www.goaskalice.columbia.edu.* Web site that gives health information; great feature (especially for kids) includes "Ask Alice," which lets your child anonymously ask questions about relationships, sexuality, sexual and emotional health, fitness, nutrition, alcohol and other drugs, and/or, general health. Dependable Columbia University site.

## SHOPPING

*www.paypal.com.* Web site where you can set up an account for online shopping or bill paying.

## SLEEP DISORDERS

*http://www.nhlbi.nih.gov/health/prof/sleep/index.htm#youth.* Web site offering information about current research with a special section on sleep disorders and youth.

*http://www.nlm.nih.gov/medlineplus/sleepdisorders.html.* Another information site that also includes information on children and sleep.

## STATISTICS AND STUDIES

*http://www.apa.org/releases/media_violence.html.* Article "Childhood Explosure to Media Violence Predicts Young Adult Aggressive Behavior," on American Psychological Association Web site; a longitudinal study about children and viewing violent television.

*http://www.haltabuse.org.* WHOA is a volunteer organization that exists to fight online harassment through education of the general public, law enforcement personnel, and empowerment of victims. Also has great cyberstalking statistics.

*http://www.pewinternet.org/PPF/r/152/report_display.asp.* Article "Reports: Family, Friend & Community," taken from the Pew Institute Web site. The Pew Internet and American Life Project produces reports that explore the impact of the Internet on families, communities, work and home, daily life, education, health care, and civic and political life. The project aims to be an authoritative source on the evolution of the Internet through collection of data and analysis of real-world developments as they affect the virtual world.

*http://www.surgeongeneral.gov/library/mentalhealth/chapter3/sec5.html.* Article "Depression and Suicide in Children and Adolescents" offers excellent prevalence statistics.

## TIMERS

*www.corel.com.* Web site for Corel, where you can purchase computer software; a timer program is automatically included with their WordPerfect programs.

*www.microsoft.com.* Web site for Microsoft; either search for "alarm clock" or go directly to http://msdn.microsoft.com/coding4fun/inthebox/SysTrayAl Clock/default.aspx or to http://www.microsoft.com/downloads/details.aspx? familyid=508EC8F2-386F-4BBA-A70C-A756205B2510&displaylang=en and follow instructions to download your free alarm clock from Microsoft.

## WEB SITES FOR CHILDREN AND TEENS

*www.Americaslibrary.kids.us.* Web site for children and young teens with games and activities from the Library of Congress, with such divisions as Meet Famous Americans, Jump Back in Time, Explore the Capitol, and America at Play. The site stresses that it uses primary sources to provide fun, interactive games that makes history come alive for young people.

*www.americangirl.com.* A range of activities for girls who like the popular American Girl dolls. Although a lot of the site is commercial—focused on shopping for the dolls and related products—it also includes games, travel information, and articles about a wide range of topics.

*www.apple.com/itunes.* A commercial site sponsored by the makers of the iPod, with information on downloading music and electronic games.

*www.crayola.com.* This site, sponsored by the makers of Crayola crayons, offers chances to buy Crayola products as well as arts and crafts projects, card-making, and other fun with colors.

*www.disney.go.com.* The official Web site of the Disney company offers the latest information on Disney movies, games, and other products, as well as contests, travel information, and articles of interest to children and young teens.

*www.enchantedlearning.com.* A subscription site ($20 per year as of this writing) that offers games and interactive fun, kid-friendly dictionaries in a number of languages, and a range of articles and information about topics that kids will like—everything from butterflies to volcanoes.

*http://kids.discovery.com.* The portion of Discovery Channel's Web site that's devoted to kids, offering games, articles, puzzles, videos, and information about programs on the Discovery Channel.

*www.kids-space.org.* Operated by Kids' Space Foundation, a nonprofit international group dedicated to helping children "explore and communicate using new technology." There are places for children to view and display art and music, and also great opportunities to make friends and find pen pals from around the world.

*www.netmom.com.* A site operated by author, librarian, and mother Jean Armour Polly, dedicated to finding safe Web sites for children. The site offers games, reviews of other sites, and suggested Web sites, as well as other resources for parents looking to help their children safely explore the Internet.

*www.Nickjr.kids.us.* The site of Nickolodeon, offering children chances to play along with their favorite characters, including Dora the Explorer and Blue of Blue's Clues.

*www.PBSKids.kids.us.* A children's site maintained by the Public Broadcasting Service, offering games and information for children aged three and older.

*www.timeforkids.com/TFK.* *Time* magazine's site, with news geared to children.

*www.worldkids.net.* A site run by the World Kids Network, a nonprofit charitable group dedicated to connecting children around the world through the Internet, and to making creative technological possibilities available to kids. If your child wants to meet other kids around the world, this is a terrific site to visit.

# INDEX

BARBARA MELTON, M.Ed., is a licensed professional counselor (LPC) and supervisor in private practice; she regularly works with families with challenging kids, conducts workshops, and lectures on a variety of topics. Her practice is in Charleston, South Carolina. SUSAN SHANKLE, MSW, LISW-CP, is a licensed clinical social worker who focuses on the treatment of adolescents experiencing difficulty due to modern technology. She lives in Mount Pleasant, South Carolina. Both authors have been featured in MSNBC.com articles addressing adolescents, parenting challenges, and technology.